I0014092

INVENTING DIGITAL TELEVISION

The Inside Story of a Technology Revolution

INVENTING DIGITAL TELEVISION

The Inside Story of a Technology Revolution

Martin L. Bell

The London Press

First published in Great Britain 2007
by
The London Press Ltd.

Copyright © 2006 Martin L. Bell

The right of Martin L. Bell to be identified as the author of this work has been
asserted by him in accordance with the Copyright, Designs and Patents Act 1988.

All rights reserved. No part of this book may be reproduced, stored in or
introduced into a retrieval system, or transmitted, in any form, or by any means
(electronic, mechanical, photocopying, recording or otherwise) without the prior
written permission of the publisher.

ISBN 978-1-905006-21-2

A C.I.P reference is available from the British Library

Cover illustration shows
the television transmitting station at Sudbury, Suffolk.
Photograph by the author

Acknowledgements

Official histories will tell it one way. The individuals who helped to make history will tell it differently. Apart from anything else, a story based on personal accounts will have an immediacy and a human dimension that more formal works usually lack, and sometimes individuals will be more candid about what actually went on. With that in mind, I chose to base this book largely on interviews supplemented by my own reading of a selection of primary and secondary sources. Most of those that I interviewed are engineers, and all were closely involved with the development of digital television broadcasting. The story that follows to a great extent reflects their perspective.

My thanks go to Dr. Ian Childs, Richard Cooper, Barry Cox, Chris Daubney, Ian Dixon, Gordon Drury, Dr. S.R. (Bob) Ely, Norman Green, Chris Hibbert, David Johnston, Phil Laven, Peter Marshall, Arthur Mason, OBE, Henry Price, Dr. Vassilis Seferedis, Michael Starks, Professor Ulrich Reimers, George Waters, Ed Wilson and David Wood, all of whom gave generously of their time to be interviewed for this book. I have made extensive use of extracts from their responses in the narrative. Others preferred to speak to me off the record, and I am grateful also to them for their insights.

But for each of these people there were ten or twenty more who made material - sometimes crucial - contributions to the creation and application of the technology, Some of their names crop up in the narrative. Many more appear as the authors of technical papers which in the course of researching this book I have consulted and drawn from. These papers are principally those published over the years in the quarterly *EBU Technical Review*, given at the International Broadcasting Convention and published as part of the *IEE Conference Publications* series, given at the now defunct Montreux Symposium, or published by BBC Research and Development. Read as a chronological sequence, they offer a vivid narrative of the evolution of the thinking behind the technology and its development, first hand accounts written by those who had the ideas and did the work. Many of these papers are highly technical, but they have been a valuable resource and I pay tribute to their authors. A list of those which I have found particularly useful can be found in the Bibliography, together with other published works - from books to periodicals - which I have also consulted.

Many who were interviewed for this book readily agreed to read the chapters in which extracts attributed to them were included, and I am grateful to them for their helpful comments. When I began to research this book, my old mentor from the days of the BBC's Digital Broadcasting Project, Bob Ely, offered me much encouragement. Both he and Gordon Drury, another distinguished engineer, read the whole manuscript and contributed much in the way of advice and correction to my rather inadequate grasp of technical detail, and suggested additional material. I gladly record my particular gratitude to them both. My thanks also go to Lesley Watson who gave generously of her time to read the manuscript and comment on it. I must also record my gratitude to my wife Penny who undertook the onerous task of proof-reading, and who gave me constant support and encouragement throughout the project. Any errors or omissions that remain are solely my responsibility.

CONTENTS

For all the engineers, remarked and unremarked,
who achieved these things.

INTRODUCTION

It all started very slowly, and a long time ago. It took time to find its feet and longer before it got into its stride. And it could have no real value until it entered the world of commercial reality. The discovery and development of digital technologies for broadcasting followed the exponential curve so familiar to mathematicians. After a lengthy gestation, the actual digital television revolution took place during the last fifteen years of the twentieth century, as a variety of enabling factors all appeared simultaneously.

In Europe and America in the late 1980s four trends were becoming apparent. The consumers of broadcast television - the viewers - with rising disposable incomes wanted more television channels to choose from, and many were prepared to pay to get them. There were potential new entrants circling around the industry, entrepreneurs willing to provide for the market's need. Some of these entrepreneurs came up with technologies which disrupted the established order of things: one of them, satellite television - particularly pay TV - was crucial. Thirdly, governments were keen to see the development of new technologies, particularly if they could be home-grown, in the hope of establishing an industrial lead in the international market. Some favoured deregulation of existing communications industries and the injection of greater competition and consumer choice. In particular, governments could see that the introduction of terrestrially broadcast digital television might in the longer term free spectrum which could profitably be sold at auction to more new entrants. And the incumbent broadcasters - in Britain the BBC, the other analogue terrestrial broadcasters ITV and Channels Four and Five, and the bold and successful newcomer, the satellite pay-TV operator BSkyB, together with some of their equivalents in other European countries - saw the emerging new broadcasting technology as an opportunity, and were prepared to put resources into making it happen.

Then there was the state of technological development itself. At the beginning of the 1990s, much of the understanding and most of the technologies needed to create new digital television broadcasting systems were in place. Manufacturers of microchips had been making great strides in improving the ability of their products to handle greater and greater masses of data, to manipulate, to process, and to do so faster and cheaper, so opening the way for innovative applications. By 1990, these advances had reached a tipping point from which the dream of digital television could begin to turn into a reality.

Great progress had been made in the previous decade on three key technologies. First, much improved techniques of digital compression were becoming available, built partly on the increasing processing power of microchips, promising the imminent delivery of a technology to reduce the vast quantities of data that form a television picture to the more manageable amounts which could practically be broadcast. Second, a revolutionary new modulation system had been demonstrated which might allow a host of new digitally broadcast television channels to share a nation's airwaves already filled to capacity with analogue broadcasting. And new techniques in frequency planning gave a much improved set of tools to predict in theory how a broadcast radio wave would behave when it left its transmitting antenna, where it could then be received, and what its weak remnants would do to interfere with other broadcasts at distances well beyond the intended coverage area.

In the window of technical, economic and political opportunity that suddenly opened, a crucial consensus was found between the engineering representatives of a multitude of technology users and providers which made it possible to draw up specifications so that a truly international system could be standardised. It is this story of the development of digital television technology that dominates the pages which follow.

Part one, *Before the Revolution*, charts the formative years of the analogue television technology that became so successful. The engineer's quest for pictures of higher and higher quality led inevitably to the goal of high definition, yet the technology and the markets were not there to sustain such an advance, and the quest led instead to a new and largely still analogue television system for satellite broadcasting called MAC - an advance certainly, but not a sufficient step forward.

Part two, *The Building Blocks*, deals with the development of the technologies involved in digital television - for many years after introduction used only within the broadcaster's studio. Later, as it was realised that both the technology and the market were close to the point where digital broadcasting would make engineering and business sense, it was again the quest for high definition that drove research engineers on in an international effort to create a family of digital television standards. And again, what came out of the work wasn't high definition, but a system that would make more efficient use of the scarce spectrum available for broadcasting, yet permit many more channels of 'standard definition' with improved technical quality.

While the first half of the book has a partly international canvas, the second half of the book concentrates much more on what was happening in Britain. I make no apology for such parochialism, or for writing almost exclusively about the terrestrial platform: Britain was first to deploy the new technology in a terrestrial public service, and did so rapidly and on a large scale. The successful introduction of an infant technology within the complexities of a horizontal market was a very considerable achievement. The pioneering work that was done - and the mistakes that were made - proved valuable to those elsewhere in Europe and further afield when their time came to begin terrestrial broadcasting.

Part three, *Britain's Digital Adventure*, is largely given over to tracing in some detail the engineering story of the creation of Britain's digital terrestrial service - a world first in a number of important respects. Here too is the story of how Britain, anxious for an early start to digital broadcasting, formed new industry alliances at home, but for a time found itself in a minority of one in the international forum, the DVB, as the final detail of the technical specification was argued over.

The final part, *Triumph and Tribulation,* takes the story of Britain's move into digital television broadcasting through the public launch, and the woes that beset the ill-fated ONdigital, to the relaunch and rejuvenation of the terrestrial platform that followed from the launch of its successor, Freeview. The final chapter covers in brief the similarly rocky progress of the early launches in Europe.

Technologies, and indeed the industries like broadcasting which make use of them, do not exist in a vacuum: they are part of the social and political fabric of a nation. So here can be found also the inevitable digressions which bear on the political and the business aspects of broadcasting. But treatment of these aspects is there to place the main thread of the engineering story in necessary perspective and cannot claim to be exhaustive.

Neither does technology stand still. As the book is being completed, the switching off of all analogue services and a move to all-digital television broadcasting is about to begin in Britain and in many of the countries of Europe. High definition, that long sought-after quantum leap in picture quality, is now being introduced. Newer technologies - the delivery of tele-vision to computers and mobile handheld devices, for example - continue to appear. It is too early to judge the long-term success of most of them, and examination of these things will have to await the work of a future historian.

The migration from analogue to digital-based technology which is now taking place is rendering broadcast television fit for purpose in the twenty-first century, capable of doing more better, and placing it firmly as an important part of a family of related technologies which we broadly term new media. The process by which the present-day digital television technology was conceived, created and standardised took time, involved specialist knowledge and inventiveness of a high order, and saw a hitherto unprecedented scale of co-operation between engineers from many nations. It was one of the great engineering achievements of the twentieth century's closing years.

But it was an essentially evolutionary process, and so this story of how digital television came to be must begin with the technology it was eventually to usurp: analogue.

Part One

Before the Revolution

1
Analogue and Digital

Even now, a decade or so after digital television became a household term, engineers who know what they are talking about do not rubbish analogue television. The first technology that television used had served the broadcasters, the manufacturing and retail industries, and most importantly the viewers who consumed its products - the receivers and the programmes - well for over 60 years.

At the outset, it was a state of the art technology delivering black and white pictures. But over the years, having morphed into the analogue PAL colour system, it came to be seen by engineers as a simple, straightforward and reliable technology - an old friend, as it were, whose foibles were understood and tolerated, whose shortcomings could be mitigated with loving care, and which wouldn't - in the end - let you down. In the words of some of those engineers:

> Beautifully built for what it was intended for ...

> Forgiving ... you knew where you were with PAL.

> It just went on getting better.

Like a favourite aunt, the wrinkles didn't begin to show until well into middle age:

> Well in the late 70s nobody thought what other format is there to use other than the standard meat and drink of the industry which was PAL. Everything was done in PAL, even production. People realised later, of course, that it was limiting ...

By the time that digital technology seriously challenged its pre-eminence, analogue had for many years delivered television pictures of a remarkably high quality to homes all over the world using a range of closely related variant systems. In Britain, analogue television brought us the richness of public service broadcasting through the formative years of the fifties and sixties. It survived and flourished in the years of expansion into commercial television. In the eighties it was the technology of choice for the early manifestations of the new multi-channel world of cable and satellite distribution. Analogue television technology survived the changing business environment better than some of the businesses themselves.

This all-conquering technology was developed in the early 1930s by a small team at the EMI company at Hayes in Middlesex[1]. The principles of design - and many of the details - survive to this day. It was a remarkable achievement. But engineers are never fully satisfied: they are always looking for ways to improve things. In analogue television, improving it meant using a growing engineering knowledge to refine the performance of cameras and the other bits of electronics that link the studio to the receiver at home, and it involved adding colour. It also involved the most obvious means of improving the sharpness and fidelity of the picture: adding more lines.

A television picture is made up of a number of lines of light drawn on the TV screen: the more lines, the more detailed the picture. But the early designers faced the difficulty that as the number of lines chosen went up, so too did the amount of information the system had to deal with. Early on, the electronic circuits to handle large amounts of information were difficult and expensive to construct. Nor was it a straightforward task to build a camera to capture detailed pictures or to build a display that would reproduce them in a receiver. So progress was slow. John Logie Baird's lumbering but pioneering mechanical system of the 1920s and 1930s began by using 30 lines, later rising to 180, and finally to 240. A German system used at the Berlin Olympic Games in the summer of 1936 also used 180 lines. The all-electronic system devised by the EMI company used 405 lines, and it was that system which was adopted by the fledgling BBC Television Service from 1936 until the outbreak of the Second World War.

The difference between pictures composed of 240 lines and 180 lines is not very marked. But 405 lines, according to a contemporary source, represented a real advance. When the service was launched, on 2 November 1936, it was billed as 'the world's first regular public service of high definition television programmes.' Today, we would regard 'high definition' as describing something altogether more impressive: in 1936, it meant 'our pictures are better than anybody else's.' By the outbreak of the war in September 1939, when the television broadcasts from Alexandra Place in London were abruptly shut down, the pictures were still better than anybody else's.

But experts understood that the pre-war system, while good, could in time be improved further. The tiny TV screens of the 1930s would become larger with time and as the technologies used to build them improved and

---

[1] A very similar system was quite independently developed in America by the Radio Corporation of America at almost the same time.

as prices became affordable there would come a demand for better pictures. Despite the imperatives of the war, many areas of British public life were enlivened with committees of the great and good who were tasked with the worthy business of planning for a better post-war society. In many fields - education, health, town and country planning, and others - opinions were canvassed, expert advice sought, evidence sorted, deliberations took place, and recommendations were presented to government. The future of television broadcasting was no exception.

The Television Committee, which advised the government of the day on such matters, met for the first time in October 1943 and looked particularly at what line standard should to be used when TV resumed after the war. With remarkable foresight, it considered that there was a need to develop a new technical system with a much higher picture definition - of the order of 1,000 lines. The Committee judged that the pre-war system would take a year to restart, that it gave good results, and that its potential had not yet been fully exploited. A new system, however desirable, would be five to seven years away, and such a long wait would be likely to retard commercial development and lead to dispersal of skilled teams from the pre-war service. Unstated, of course, was the understanding that Britain was broke, and had better make the most of what it already had, at least for the time being.

The report was published in March 1945, and approved by the government in October. It recommended that the pre-war system should be restarted as soon as possible after the end of the war, using 405 lines, and that the service should be extended to other population centres outside London. It also recommended that vigorous research work on a radically improved system of television should begin as soon as staff could be made available, that picture definition should eventually be of the order of 1,000 lines, and that colour television should be developed.

In the 1950s many other countries in Europe launched television services. For a time, a confusing mix of line standards was in use, often reflecting national decisions made before the war. France, confusingly, ran two systems side by side, one of 441 lines, and another using 819 lines. This naturally made the exchange of programme content between countries a technical nightmare, and led to the development of a crude 'standards converter' which was pressed into use in 1953 for the relays to France, Holland and Belgium of live television coverage of the Coronation. The quality of the converted pictures was dire, although live pictures of any description from another country seemed at the time little short of miraculous. The need for a pan-European standard was obvious. Not only would it ease programme exchange, which with the formation of the Eurovision partnership of broadcasters, was beginning to expand, but it would also offer manufacturers the potential for a single design that could be sold all over western Europe.

In 1950, that universal system had been settled on. The International Radio Consultative Committee - known by the abbreviation of its French title as CCIR[2] - decided on the use of 625 lines. One advantage of this system was that it was close to the American 525 line system in many of its technical characteristics. Although with fewer lines, the American system used 30 pictures a second, while the European system used 25. This meant that the rate at which the picture lines were sent in each system was almost the same. This made it possible for a greater commonality in the component parts of much television equipment used on either side of the Atlantic.

The European system's standardisation came too late for 625 lines to be adopted in Britain when the television service resumed operation in 1946. In any case, manufacturing industry and government agencies were more disposed to support their existing national standards and to seek to spread their use elsewhere. Both the British and the French at different times tried and failed to get their respective systems adopted in what was then occupied Germany. But over the next decade the logic of using a common system prevailed, and as most of the countries of western Europe, and some in the East, launched television services, all adopted the new CCIR 625-line standard.

In France the old services were quickly replaced with a new one using 625-lines. In the UK, however, 405-line services were well established and were now available throughout much of the country. A second service, ITV, had launched in 1955 also using the 405-line standard. Nearly six million homes owned a TV set, and the numbers were growing fast. Migration to the higher standard was always going to be more difficult.[3]

Bound up with the question of whether and how to adopt 625-lines were many issues surrounding the future of television in Britain. The BBC had ambitions for a second service of its own, and the general consensus was that the future meant more channels (after all, even in the early sixties, New York City had seven or eight). Naturally the task of sifting through the possibilities and the desirables fell to a group of the great and good. The 1960 Pilkington Committee on the Future of Broadcasting concluded that the existing 405-line system would not be adequate for the future. It recommended the adoption of the 625-line system to be transmitted in new frequency bands[4] and the introduction of colour. The government agreed.

---

[2] Comité Consultatif International des Radio Communications
[3] As it turned out, the 405 line system remained in use until 1984
[4] Existing BBC and ITV networks broadcast in VHF (very high frequency), the former in Band I (41-68 MHz), the latter in Band III (174-216 MHz). The new 625-line services were to use UHF (ultra high frequency) in Bands IV and V (470-582 MHz and 614-854 MHz respectively) where there would be room for a total of four services with nationwide coverage.

The BBC was given the green light to plan for a BBC-2 in colour and on 625-lines and, to follow its launch, BBC-1 and ITV would start duplicating their 405-line services in 625-lines and in colour.

But what of that 1943 recommendation to go to 1,000 lines? Already by the early 1960s this sort of quality was now being referred to as 'high definition', but serious development work by broadcasters or manufacturers was not happening. A very few high definition systems were being developed for specialist industrial, medical or defence uses, but there seems to have been no incentive on the part of broadcasters or manufacturers to go beyond what would soon be termed 'standard definition' 625-lines. For the consumer, who buys a television set to watch pro grammes, the coming of 625-lines and colour promised a viewing experience of a quality unimaginable twenty years earlier. Something even better was neither sought after nor could have been afforded.

Colour was the next major advance in the quest for better television pictures. The BBC's research department started to experiment with an early system immediately after the end of the Second World War. In America, meanwhile, the National Television Systems Committee (NTSC) had developed a much more sophisticated approach which was agreed for US use in 1953. By 1954, the BBC had adapted it to the British 405-line system and begun to examine its potential. The great advantage of the NTSC system lay in its ability to be 'compatible' with existing black and white (or monochrome) television receivers. In the NTSC system, a 'luminance' signal conveys information about the brightness of parts of a picture which is all a monochrome TV set needs to show a good monochrome picture. Colour receivers use also a second 'chrominance' signal to add a good reproduction of the colours in the original picture. The chrominance signal is simply ignored in a monochrome receiver, which shows a perfectly good black and white version of the colour picture being transmitted. This compatibility meant that colour could be introduced to an existing service without rendering existing monochrome television sets obsolete. Yet much more development work and many years were to pass before the introduction finally came.

The NTSC system was a magnificent technical achievement, the product of unprecedented co-operation between competing American manufacturers. But it had one major drawback, as American broadcast engineers rapidly discovered. Television signals have to be sent along landlines or microwave links over considerable distances: from outside broadcast location to studio, or between studio centres in different cities, from studio centre to transmitting station, and of course over the air from transmitting station to the viewer's aerial. During these journeys NTSC had the bad habit of changing colour (unkindly, some wag christened NTSC "Never The Same Colour") because it suffered from the effects of differential phase distortion in transmission and reception and needed constant resetting. Indeed American TV sets had an additional knob on the front for that purpose: besides the brightness, contrast and colour (intensity) controls now familiar to European viewers, a hue control was added which allowed the discerning viewer to restore flesh tones to a more natural colour from the blue or green they sometimes appeared.

In the early 1960s, as European manufacturers and broadcasters began to think seriously about introducing colour television, researchers began to wonder if NTSC's vulnerability to phase distortion could be cured. Solutions eventually emerged: all of them retained the same basic principle adopted in NTSC of using a high-frequency subcarrier above the video band to carry colour information but changed the way that the colour information (the two 'colour difference' signals) modulated the subcarrier. The eminent French engineer Henri de France came up with a modified form of NTSC which was termed SECAM[5]. This transmitted the colour difference signals using frequency rather than amplitude and phase modulation. Frequency modulation is inherently immune to differential phase distortion and hence SECAM avoided the hue errors to which NTSC was prone. However, frequency modulation could convey only one of the two colour difference signals on each picture line: one colour difference signal was sent on one line and the second with the following line. A memory store in the receiver then delayed the first until the second had been received, and recombined them. With other minor modifications[6] SECAM was a distinct improvement on NTSC albeit with reduced vertical colour resolution.

Shortly after the invention of SECAM, Dr Walter Bruch of the German Telefunken company took things a stage further. His system, termed PAL[7], maintained transmission of both colour difference signals on each line via amplitude and phase modulation (as in NTSC), but reversed the phase of one of the two colour difference signals on alternate lines (hence the name Phase Alternation Line). In the receiver each of the two colour difference signals is averaged over two lines by using a delay of a duration equal to one line period. Using this phase alternation line technique in combination with the delay-line decoder largely mitigated the effects of phase distortion and, at the expense of slightly greater complexity and cost in the receivers, overcame certain limitations of SECAM.[8]

---

[5] Séquentiel Couleur à Mémoire; developed by Compaignie Francaise de Télévision
[6] the SECAM colour subcarrier was frequency modulated, rather than amplitude and phase modulated as in NTSC
[7] Phase Alternation Line
[8] notably that SECAM signals could not be added or mixed. Countries that used SECAM had to use PAL in the studio.and convert to SECAM for transmission.

With three contending systems on its plate, the European Broadcasting Union's working group on colour television met in London to try to agree on the choice of a common system. The group's membership was limited by agreement to representatives of those countries who were actively engaged in colour television research. So engineers from the UK, Holland, Germany, France, Switzerland and Italy began a series of meetings and visits to laboratories, witnessing demonstrations and weighing up the arguments.

Full agreement in the end proved impossible. Of course, it was fairly easy to agree not to use NTSC: both SECAM and PAL were better, and in any case, NTSC was American. But deciding unanimously between SECAM and PAL proved impossible, as national pride asserted itself. There was hope of an agreement when the Plenary Assembly of the CCIR met in Oslo in 1966, but that hope was not fulfilled. The Assembly had to content itself with agreeing on specifications of each of the three systems. In the end, France decided to go with its own system, SECAM, to be joined later by many Francophone countries together with Russia and the Eastern Bloc, as well as Greece and Saudi Arabia. The rest of Europe, including the UK, opted for PAL, followed by the Commonwealth countries including much of the non-French influenced countries of Africa, some other Middle Eastern countries, together with - intriguingly - Yugoslavia (demonstrating, no doubt, as this communist country did from time to time, its immunity to the Moscow line). The exceptions were in the United States, where the NTSC 525-line system was entrenched, and which was used in countries within the American sphere of influence, notably Canada, Mexico, parts of South America, and in Japan, Taiwan and South Korea

Meanwhile the BBC was putting a vast amount of research and development effort into colour. It had first transmitted NTSC on 405-lines in the VHF band in 1955, and in the following year had equipped a small studio at Alexandra Palace with colour cameras to originate material for more test transmissions. In 1957, the same system was being transmitted in UHF. By 1962, the test transmission were using the 625-line standard (and being shown publicly at the Earl's Court Radio Show). In 1965, the BBC dropped the NTSC system and began testing PAL. Finally, in early 1966, after much lobbying and demonstrating of the BBC colour pictures to Members of Parliament and other influential figures, the Postmaster-General gave the BBC the go-ahead. With the outside broadcast coverage of Wimbledon in July 1967, BBC-2 began Europe's first regular colour transmissions.

Colour was an immediate hit with the public. The spectacle was just so much better than the silvery black and white pictures. Colour was a must-have. For many, however, the cost of a colour TV set was beyond their means. And the early sets were big, ugly, usually gave garishly unrealistic colour, and a few had a disconcerting habit of bursting into flames. But within a very few years, colour rendition improved greatly, and the sets became affordable, particularly through the rental market, for which the coming of colour was a commercial opportunity readily grasped.

The programme-makers, producers and engineers, designers and lighting directors, quickly grasped the challenges of working in colour. The approach at the BBC was to introduce colour simultaneously in all programme genres, from the obvious light entertainment spectacular or costume drama to children's programmes, discussion programmes and news. This was in sharp contrast to the American practice, which was to use scarce colour production studios exclusively for peak-time spectaculars, or for westerns shot on film. Potential pitfalls were anticipated: in BBC production studios, the picture monitor showing the mixed output from all the cameras was placed alongside a black and white monitor showing the same picture. This was to ensure that what made a good colour picture also looked good in monochrome: designers quickly learned to avoid using two contrasting colours which appeared on monochrome pictures as similar, un-contrasting, shades of grey. Lighting directors learned to exploit the greater subtlety of colour in a scene, avoiding the temptation of garishness. A newly developed camera tube - the plumbicon - allowed a reduction in size of colour cameras as well as giving very much better colour resolution. One of the early 'hits' of the new BBC-2 colour service was *Pot Black,* outside broadcast coverage of snooker, a sport hitherto unknown on television.

As television production techniques became more sophisticated, producers and directors looked for new ways of manipulating the picture. How could they 'inlay' the picture from one camera into the picture of another? How could they create other methods of transition between shots besides the basic grammar of cuts, mixes and wipes? Could there not be a better way of putting text on the screen - for programme titles and other information - than printing on to a piece of card and sticking it in front of a camera? Engineers strove to oblige, producing new pieces of equipment which did for a while, but were themselves limited in scope: as fast as new kit came along, producers and directors wanted more.

For their part, the engineers were beginning to bump up against the inherent limitations of an all-analogue system. Their very professionalism equipped them with a hyper-sensitivity to the technical quality of the television picture and sound. They were acutely aware that doing *anything* with the signals introduced a quality loss. Pictures were recorded on tape, editing them involved a copying process, and with each 'dub' the quality was reduced a little bit: the signal was sent over long-distance circuits: from outside broadcast to the studio centre; from the originating studio to the transmitter. To reach the Kirk o'Shotts transmitter which served central

Scotland, the picture signal had to travel over 400 miles from London by a series of microwave links: each 'hop' covered sixty or seventy miles or so, and at each repeater the by now slightly weakened signal had to be amplified before being sent on its way. "By the time it got to its destination," said one engineer, "It looked like it."

By the early 70s, in the research laboratories of the broadcasters, at some manufacturers, and elsewhere in the industry - most notably at the research base of what was then the General Post Office, who were already using digital transmission systems for telephony - engineers were asking themselves if the digital techniques being adopted in the computer world could help. The development of digital technology had two fundamental building blocks: the concept of turning information into strings of 0s and 1s; and the invention of the transistor, which proved to be the ideal device for manipulating the stream of digital 'bits'.

In the late 1930s Alec Reeves, a British research engineer, invented Pulse Code Modulation - now the standard method of encoding signals in many modern communications systems. He was one of a number of researchers whose theoretical work in the 1930s and 1940s laid the foundations of modern information technology.

Another was Claude Shannon who in 1940, while working for his masters degree at the Massachusetts Institute of Technology, published a paper entitled *A Symbolic Analysis of Relay and Switching Circuit*: this showed how the Boolean logical symbols, 'yes', 'no', 'and', 'or', etc, could be treated in an electronic signal as a series of on or off switches. Later, in 1948, he published a second *paper A Mathematical Theory of Communication*, which provided the mathematical foundations for modern digital communication systems in which all messages - voice, pictures or other information – are represented as strings of binary digits.

Until the late 1940s, this growing body of theoretical understanding was running far ahead of the practical means of using it. The device which would enable these basic concepts of information technology to be put into practice was the transistor.

The transistor revolutionised the way electronic circuits were made to function. Hitherto, all electronic circuits relied on thermionic valves - or vacuum tubes - to function. A valve was effectively a glass bottle inside which were intricate arrangements of metal coils, plates and gauzes, all in a high vacuum, with electrical connections passing through the glass envelope. A heated coil of wire in the centre of the valve emitted electrons, which were then attracted or repelled, accelerated or decelerated by the application of voltages to the other metal objects inside. They were commonly used as amplifiers, but found uses in circuits for other purposes, like oscillators (used for generating a sound or radio wave) or rectifiers (to convert alternating current to direct current). Television camera tubes and cathode-ray tube screens were similar in construction. By the 1950s, valves were highly reliable and ubiquitous devices, and had undergone a certain degree of miniaturisation: radio and television sets contained a dozen or more of them, but they tended to use considerable amounts of electricity, sometimes at voltages well above 240 volts. And they got hot, wore out, and needed frequent replacement.

The transistor was born in November 1947 when researchers at the Bell Telephone laboratories in America discovered that adding an impurity to a small lump of silicon or germanium would produce a device which could operate like a valve. The choice of impurity could introduce either surplus electrons (a negative charge) or a deficiency of electrons (a positive charge).which could be made to flow between an input and an output under the control of an applied voltage - just as happens in a thermionic valve. But the transistor was tiny by comparison: just a centimetre long, compared with the seven or more centimetres of a typical valve. Transistors required no heating element and they operated at much lower voltages, six or nine volts instead of a typical valve's 240, and so consumed very much less power and consequently gave off very much less heat. By the 1950s transistors were beginning to enter general use, allowing miniaturisation of everything from early electronic computers, to portable radios - the 'trannic' which brought joy and misery in almost equal amounts to holiday venues.

Miniaturisation and economy of power consumption in electronic devices brought commercial benefits, and by the late 1950s transistors had been widely adopted by manufacturers of professional and consumer electronics. So great were the benefits, that the search was on for something even better. But it was not easy to make a transistor much smaller and for an assembly line worker still to be able to solder its connecting wires to the other components on the electronic circuit board.

The invention of the integrated circuit is credited to two individuals, who hit upon the same notion independently at about the same time towards the end of the 1950s: Jack Kilby at Texas Instruments, and Robert Noyce at Fairchild Semiconductor. Both realised that a whole circuit could be made out of silicon - the wires, the coils, capacitors and resistors as well as the actual transistors could all be incorporated in a single 'chip'. These new 'integrated circuits' - or 'microchips' - were quickly developed for commercial use, and enabled the trends of reduction in size and power consumption of electronic devices to continue. The complexity of these circuits-on-a-chip increased rapidly. By 1965, the co-founder of Intel, Gordon Moore, made the now famous prediction that the number of transistors on a silicon chip would continue to double every year. Modified in 1975 to read 'double every two years', 'Moore's Law', as it is now known, has proved remarkably accurate over the years. As manufacturing technologies improve, and as volume production of microchips increase, costs rise less quickly, so that each new generation delivers much improved performance at around the same price.

This rapid progress was helped by the discovery that chips could be grown in thin films, instead of sliced out of a lump of crystal. Impurities were introduced by bombarding the crystal film with atoms in a very high vacuum using a process known as molecular beam epitaxy or MBE. (The machinery involved was extremely expensive, and at the UK chip-maker Mullard, MBE was known as "mega bucks expenditure"). Lithographic techniques were used to 'print' on to the chip surface the layout of the transistors (or 'gates' as they were beginning to be called), connectors and other components. This was microscopic precision engineering of an advanced kind: the silicon film of the microchip over time became very thin and very small, and manufacture took place in thoroughly sterile and clean conditions. By 1966, chips had moved from small-scale integration (fewer than 100 devices on a chip) to medium scale (up to 1,000 devices): three years later large scale integration permitted up to 10,000 devices and by 1975 the term very large scale integration (VLSI) was in use to describe microchips with over 10,000 devices. By 2002, chips could accommodate millions of them, each less than two *millionths* of a millimetre in size, and chip-maker Intel was predicting that by 2010 it will be putting 10 billion transistors on to a single chip..

And as techniques of micro-engineering improved, and as the size of each gate became smaller, the distance between them could also be reduced. With less distance to travel, the electrons took less time to travel from gate to gate - a small incremental acceleration in a single journey from one gate to another, perhaps, but multiplied hundreds of thousands of times it meant that the speed with which a chip operated improved enormously. Such powerful integrated circuits allowed engineers to think in terms of sophisticated electronic circuitry at affordable cost and able to conduct complex processing of digitally-encoded data.

Researchers understood that great advances could be made if the processes involved in television studios could be undertaken digitally. A stream of digits is much more easily manipulated than an analogue signal, and as microchips became more powerful, it became possible to envisage devices which could do much more complex processing at a price which was still affordable. Using complex arrays of transistors on a chip, engineers developed ways of making the microprocessor undertake the mathematical functions of multiplication and division, of trigonometry and calculus. This opened up a whole range of possibilities in many applications which would lead eventually to the ability to handle the complex mathematics required for advanced digital compression.

In the mid-1960s, many potential digital techniques were being examined. In a BBC Research Department Report written in 1967[9] the authors discussed the potential benefits in using digital methods for a number of television uses, including standards conversion, magnetic (tape) recording, and programme distribution. They wrote that they had been unable to discover any such work going on anywhere else, but noted the probable reasons: while microchips were developing apace, they were still too slow and too expensive to use for processing or storage of the large amounts of data that would result from digitising television pictures. They had to be content with recommending that their organisation should think seriously about looking into developments in this field against the day when the capabilities of microchips improved and their price came down.

That day came sooner than expected.

---

[9] *Digital Methods in Television.* G.D. Monteath and V.G. Devereux, BBC Research Report no T-127

2
Digital Stirrings

Throughout the two decades of the 1970s and 1980s, broadcasting engineers steadily accumulated an understanding of digital techniques and how they could be applied. As the demand for processes which could enhance programme production grew, more and more innovative solutions depended on using some form of digital processing. The designers were constrained by the progress being made in semiconductor technology, on which they grew increasingly to depend for the manipulation and storage of television picture information. Building an experimental device that worked could usually be done: the constraint was the cost of building production versions at affordable costs. If the costs were expected to be prohibitive, the concept usually stayed on paper. There were incentives which mitigated this constraint: the digital devices which, by the middle of the 1980s, were proliferating, were confined to professional equipment used in the studio, or for point-to-point transmission between studios. In professional equipment cost and benefit are traded, and the benefits on offer were either having something that could not be done in an analogue domain, or improved quality, or both. By the end of 1980s digital devices were in use at so many stages in programme production that an all-digital means of interconnecting them was sought, devised and standardised. The way to an all digital studio was open.

"The sound always comes first, because it's easier." The words of a veteran research engineer. Digital sound for distribution indeed came first: by 1972 the BBC was using an early Pulse Code Modulation system to carry programme feeds to FM radio transmitters. Not quite digital broadcasting, but it is certainly true that the television-consuming public were using one 'digital' service long before the word itself entered everyday use. In 1974, teletext was introduced in the UK.[10] This used a few of the vacant lines at

---

[10] The BBC branded it 'CEEFAX', the IBA and the ITV companies preferred 'ORACLE'.

the top of the analogue television picture for a simple digital code which carried the information to make up a series of 'pages' of text. The teletext information pages became immensely popular with television viewers, and became the first truly 'interactive' feature of a television service.

In another 'first', the BBC introduced, in 1984, the terrestrial transmission of stereo sound with television from Crystal Palace using the digital system later known as NICAM 728. Behind the scenes, an earlier system known as 'sound-in-syncs' had been devised by engineers which piggy-backed a digital audio signal on to an analogue television waveform. A digital 'burst' was placed in the quiescent periods at the end of each line which otherwise carried only a single synchronising pulse. In that way, the picture and sound could share the same circuit: no longer would the feeds back to the studio from an outside broadcast location have to travel by quite separate routes.

All the time, research engineers were grasping the opportunities to develop television equipment which could do new things, or existing things better, by employing digital techniques, and their understanding of how to use digital storage and processing to do hitherto impossible things was growing. The immediate priorities included the development of better recording techniques - in which quality was not lost every time a copy was made, designing devices which could manipulate in new ways television pictures in the production of programmes (special effects), and enabling the lossless and more cost-efficient transmission of television signals over long-distance circuits.

The first challenge was to find the best way of turning the analogue PAL signal into a stream of digits. Here, the broadcast industry discovered that the Post Office was ahead of them. The Post Office at the time was a public authority whose remit extended well beyond the Royal Mail. It operated the national telephone system and had a statutory monopoly to operate all long-distance 'trunk' circuits, which included the copper wires of the telephone system, as well as the newer co-axial cables and microwave links, and later the new international satellite links, all of which could carry bulk quantities of any information in electronic form. Both the BBC and the Independent Broadcasting Authority, therefore, used Post Office circuits for contribution and distribution of television pictures and sound, and both had developed a close working relationship with their opposite numbers - particularly the research and development people from the BBC labs at Kingswood Warren in Surrey, and IBA labs at Brompton Road in Knightsbridge (later at Crawley Court near Winchester), and the Post Office research labs, first at Dollis Hill in north London and later at Martlesham Heath, near Ipswich. In the labs of the professional equipment manufacturers, too, interest in digital was stirring. Gordon Drury worked at GEC, which made equipment for the Post Office:

When I graduated in the late sixties I went to the research labs at GEC in Wembley. There was a media lab next to the lab I worked in, so I was working on digital transmission for telecoms, and these guys had been working on television but it was winding down because the company wasn't that interested in consumer products any more. We were building analogue-to-digital converters for wideband telephony - comparable in bandwidth with video: our intent was transmitting television by digital means for GEC to build equipment to sell to the Post Office.

British Telecom - by now separated from the Post Office (it was to be privatised in 1988) - had recognised very early on the benefits to be gained by converting its telephone exchanges to digital operation, as Drury discovered:

The driving force for BT and their sister companies around the world - the public service telephone companies - were that the costs of transmission are relatively small compared to the cost of switching. Now digital switching made telecom maintenance costs and reliability so much better. I went to BT after GEC in '72, and did my stint for a few weeks in a telephone exchange in Brighton, and you walked in at any time in the 24 hours and there were lights blazing, people walking about, and this horrendous noise because of these relays clacking as people dialled phone calls. You go to the same place now - it's not a big building any more, it's very small, it's air conditioned because there's computers in it, it's locked. There's nobody in it and it's driven by software. It's the switching and routeing of signals that matters. So that was driving BT.

The broadcasters, too, recognised that if a television picture could be converted successfully to digital form, quality would be much better when sent over BT's long-distance circuits. The discussions about how to do it began. Gordon Drury remembers the gist of the discussions, with the broadcasters saying to BT:

We'll continue to offer you PAL because we can't foresee any other format - and you code it. So BT would say OK we'll code it and we'll choose how. And the broadcasters said, hang on a minute, we'll choose how if you don't mind, because this PAL thing's rather delicate: we've discovered in our researches unless you do it right funny things happen. Now we knew that in the lab at GEC in 1967 - I remember doing the experiments. So we were aware of it in the telecom area as well.

By the mid-sixties, the broadcasting labs were working on analogue-to-digital and digital-to-analogue converters for use in a number of applications.

The basis of turning an analogue signal into a digital stream of 'bits' is the same whether it is sound (audio) or picture (video), and similar for the very high amount of information carried in a television picture, or relatively low amount which is required for the small and coarse picture that a picturephone might use[11]. An analogue signal is a continuous wave which at any point in time represents the brightness (and the colour information) in the succession of lines that make up the picture. In a television studio, this analogue video signal uses exactly one volt to represent white, 0.3 volt to represent black, with the intermediate values representing varying shades of grey.

Digital coding uses a technique known as Pulse Code Modulation which samples this voltage at intervals, assigning a numerical value to each sample and rendering this value as a binary number (which is a sequence of 1s and 0s). So that a picture reconstituted in a receiver from this digital stream can be indistinguishable from the original analogue picture, the frequency of the sampling must be sufficiently high, and the steps between the numerical values used in each sample must be sufficiently small. But sample too often, and choose too many value 'steps' and you end up with far too much data to transmit economically; sample too little and use too few value 'steps' and the picture will lose its fidelity. And there are a couple of other factors which means you can't arbitrarily choose any values for the frequency at which you sample.

The first is a thing called the Nyquist Theorem[12] which says that when an analogue waveform is turned into digits, frequencies above half the sampling frequency must be excluded.[13] If this is not done 'aliasing' (i.e. folding back of the higher frequencies into the lower frequency bands) makes it impossible to correctly reconstruct the original signal. The second is the presence of the colour sub-carrier in the PAL (or NTSC) original: early experiments showed that unless the sampling frequency was three or four times that of the subcarrier frequency[14], and accurately locked to it, the results were less than presentable even with the application of filtering and other remedial measures.

So the numbers began to emerge. The PAL colour subcarrier frequency is approximately 4.43 MHz, which for best results required a higher sampling frequency of three times that, i.e.13.29 MHz, or preferably four times, 17.72 MHz. Each sample value was described using 8-bit codes, which gives an overall bandwidth for digitally coded PAL of 8 x 17.72 MHz, which is 141.76 MHz - call it 140 MHz in round numbers. At which point the discussions between the broadcasters - who were developing the coders, and BT - who owned and operated the long distance circuits, hit a

---

[11] 'Picturephone' was the name of a system of analogue video phone launched by Bell in the USA in the 1960s. It never took off: it was expensive and well before its time.

[12] Harry Nyquist, 1889-1976, Swedish-born telecommunications engineer who retired from the Bell Telephone Laboratories (US) in 1954

[13] by lowpass filtering the input to the analogue to digital converter.

[14] The colour subcarrier is at the centre of the frequencies comprising the transmitted colour information – hence sampling at twice colour subcarrier results in the frequencies which were above the subcarrier being aliased into those below; the shortcomings of such 'Sub-Nyquist Sampling' can, however, to some extent be mitigated by the use of sophisticated 'comb filters'

problem. BT's circuits had been designed to use multiples of 64 kbit/s, which was based on their own basic sampling frequency of 8 MHz (at 8 bits). So the established BT long-distance circuits came in pre-determined flavours: 64 kbit/s; 8,448 kbit/s; 34.368 Mbit/s (referred to as 34 Mbit/s); and 139.264 Mbit/s (referred to as 140 Mbit/s). As Gordon Drury re-members, because the broadcasters were using a different basic sampling frequency dictated by the vagaries of the PAL television system, supplying a suitable digital version to BT was not entirely straightforward ...

> ... particularly when you had to match them to a hierarchy whose numbers are determined for telephony reasons and not for television. I remember a long discussion with BT and others in the CCIR about, well, why couldn't they have chosen more convenient numbers and of course they said, "We were here first, and anyway, your numbers are not convenient for telephony, and that's where the money's made." Because of the telephony dominance in their networks BT charges for TV transmission were based on the number of displaced telephone channels.

Nevertheless, with careful housekeeping, the digital PAL signal could be squeezed into BT's highest available bandwidth, and by 1975, BBC Research in collaboration with BT had succeeded in transmitting digital PAL over BT's Guildford to Portsmouth coaxial cable link.[15]

A major challenge for research engineers was finding a practical way to store a television picture. Magnetic recording on tape was widely used, of course, for moving picture sequences or whole programmes. What was needed was a device to store one line, or one field, or a handful of frames of a picture, as part of a process for manipulation. Analogue methods did exist - one involved a series of quartz blocks through which a television signal passed in the form of an ultrasonic beam. The device was heavy, bulky and expensive. Gradually, semiconductor storage became available, and as the costs fell and capacity rose, the most intractible barrier to the widespread introduction of digital process for picture manipulation was removed.

Digital storage enabled great improvements to be made in the equipment in use for the tricky challenge of converting pictures between US and European standards. Field rates[16] in the world's television systems were linked to the frequency of the alternating current in the mains supply. Early on, some annoying picture disturbances on domestic TV sets could be avoided if the same frequency for the picture repetition rate and the mains electricity supply was adopted. In North America and Japan, the

---

[15] The IBA also participated in similar tests on this system.

[16] Analogue television picture scanning used an 'interlaced' system, whereby each frame (complete picture) was made up of two 'fields'. The first field consisting of all the odd scanning lines, the second of all the even lines.

mains was at 60 Hz; in Europe it was 50 Hz, so television systems on separate continents developed with different parameters. Very early converters developed in the 1950s had used the primitive technique of a camera working on one standard pointed at a TV screen showing a picture in the other standard. The results were passable, but there was obvious room for improvement. Field store standards converters worked by storing three fields from the incoming NTSC picture for long enough for it to be 'read' at the other standard, PAL[17]. Analogue versions of these converters first developed by the BBC entered use in 1967 using quartz blocks to store the fields. These award-winning designs reduced the quality loss of conversion to acceptable limits for news and events coverage live from another continent, where the miracle of instantaneous images from the other side of the world still went remarked in the public mind. But for the other staples of the television schedule, entertainment and drama, the quality loss was too great. Many popular American shows which were bought by UK broadcasters - *Sergeant Bilko*, *The High Chapperal*, and any number of sitcoms like *I Love Lucy*, were shot on 35mm film and required no conversion. But others, like the 1960s series of *The Perry Como Show* shown on BBC 1, or *Rowan and Martin's Laugh-in* on BBC-2 in the 1970s, were recorded on videotape and the standards conversion that was necessary introduced a loss of picture quality - no worse than that suffered by the news and events coverage, but more noticeable in the context of entertainment.

For the early converters, the designers had considered using digital technology but concluded that the cost of the digital storage required would be too high. By the early 70s, although those costs were still high, they had reduced enough to consider developing a digital version. The IBA's Research Department was the first to tackle the challenge. Chris Daubney, later himself in charge of R&D at the IBA remembers:

> The IBA at the time when Howard Steele was Director of Engineering - very forthright D of E, very advanced thinker - he employed some very bright people. One was a chap called John Baldwin, the man who invented the original digital standards converter - DICE[18]

A successful digital standards converter would address to a large extent the picture quality shortcomings of existing devices. As it happened, Howard Steele had a pressing need for something better.

At Associated TeleVision, which held the ITV Midlands franchise, the entrepreneur Lew Grade (later Lord Grade) wanted to emulate the Americans by carving out an US market for some of the programmes his company was making for the ITV network. But for programmes supplied on videotape - which was Grade's original approach - the Americans

---

[17] conversion in the opposite direction, from PAL to NTSC, was of course equally possible.
[18] DICE: Digital Intercontinental Conversion Equipment

insisted that they should be supplied at their 525/60 standard. Amongst the IBA's regulatory obligations was that of policing the technical standards of the ITV companies output The technical shortcomings of existing analogue converters worried the IBA's Director of Engineering, Howard Steele. Norman Green was co-ordinating engineer at the ITV Companies Association, and remembers how the first digital standards converter, DICE, came to be built:

> Lew Grade was making programmes for sale to North America and what he did - for the first ones - was to record them in 525 lines 60 fields and then convert them to 625/50 for UK and European consumption via a Fernsh optical converter. The converter was a clever one that converted the luminance and the chrominance signals separately. The IBA said that the 625 line quality was not good enough. and the consequence of all this was Howard built DICE to go from 525/60 to 625/50 first, so that Lew could get his programmes converted almost transparently. The converter was installed at ITN so that all the ITV network 525 line programme material, primarily news and sport, could be converted. Then, when the IBA had made the reversible converter, 625 to 525 and 525 to 625, Howard insisted that Lew Grade's programmes were made in 625 and standards converted to 525. The design and success of this converter allowed the IBA to progress into other areas of digital video.

The DICE converter was first used for 525/60 to 625/50 conversion in 1972 and for the reverse direction in 1975: BBC Research followed with their version - ACE, which used different digital techniques - in 1979.

The IBA's work on the DICE converter provoked a brief turf war between the IBA and the companies. Norman Green found himself in the middle of it:

> It was typical ITV. The IBA, which was now under the technical leadership of Tom Robson, wanted to take over all the R&D concerned with engineering in ITV. The programme companies thought that would be the thin end of the wedge and it would end up with the IBA specifying the equipment they would have to buy and install in their studio centres. There was a big consultation in the Royal Garden Hotel which Lady Plowden[19] attended where the two sides put forward their proposals. And ... ITV won the day. That night when we'd finished, Bill Brown of Scottish Television (then chairman of the ITCA) came up to me and said, "Now we must work out how we can put together a system that they can approve." And so we came to a situation whereby we had three laboratories, one in London at Thames, one at Granada in Manchester, and one at Scottish Television in Glasgow. The engineers were paid for centrally by all the companies, and I supervised them. By breaking it up, which we really didn't want to do, it would be more difficult for the IBA to gain control and put it on a green field site somewhere. And our great argument was these labs were in the studio centres so they worked with the people who used the systems

---

[19] Lady Plowden was chairman of the Independent Broadcasting Authority from 1975 to 1980

Ed Wilson, who worked on digital coding at the IBA, remembers that the turf war between the IBA and the ITV companies operated in both directions:

> We covered the whole gamut of the work in what was called the Experimental and Development Department. I was told that it wasn't allowed to call it a Research and Development Department because it was paid for by the ITV companies who said, "We don't want you doing any research. You can do some experiments and you can develop things, but you're not doing any blue sky research."

A decade or so later, and despite this terminological nicety, it was these same IBA researchers who would make a major contribution to the development of digital broadcasting.

Throughout the 70s, with improving knowledge of how best to design analogue-to-digital converters, and with such devices now becoming available on microchips, digital techniques were applied to many parts of the television production chain. High on the list of priorities was to devise a means of digital recording. By now, the analogue videotape recorder was ubiquitous, and more and more programmes had come to rely on editing, rather than simply to record a complete programme 'as live'. But editing involved re-recording the desired sections on a second machine, and in doing so, there was a perceptible loss of quality. Repeating the process, by going to third and fourth generation versions, caused serious quality loss: so much so that it was usually only contemplated in special circumstances. If recordings could be made using digits, then the quality loss over repeated generations would be very greatly reduced: effectively, a copy would be a 'clone' of the original.

The first demonstration of an experimental digital television recorder, which was devised by BBC Research Department, took place in 1974 at the International Broadcasting Convention at the Grosvenor House in London. It was a brute of a machine, based on the large tape recorders being used for data storage in mainframe computers. It used a 1 inch tape running at 120 inches per second with 42 parallel recording tracks. Working near the upper limit of the available technology, it could handle digital PAL recordings only by reducing the sampling to twice the frequency of the colour subcarrier[20]. Its purpose was purely experimental, to provide a test-bed and to gain experience. But it worked well and was a ground-breaking achievement.

After the IBA's research team had finished their work on the DICE standards converter, they too turned to the challenge of studio and network

---

[20] The visibility of in-band alias components produced by the sub-sampling was reduced by comb-filtering the signal both before and after the sampling process.

systems design, and particularly digital videotape recording, but with a different approach. They took an analogue 1 inch helical scan machine currently in production by a German company and modified it to record digits, again as a laboratory tool to investigate possibilities and to gain understanding. It was demonstrated at an industry symposium at Montreux in June 1977, by which time a number of major videotape recorder manufacturers were also building experimental models. With this growing body of experience, the EBU Technical Committee decided to poll its members views in order to form a consensus view of what the needs and expectations of users would be. But it took the appearance of an international standard for digital video coding before the first commercial digital videotape recorder could be produced, and that would not be until 1981.

As the EBU working groups gathered views from around the world about the requirements for digital video recording it became clear that the two imperatives - of a pan-European agreement and a high quality, future-proofed solution - could not be satisfied using digitised composite PAL. PAL, and the other analogue systems, SECAM and NTSC, took the basic picture information of luminance signal (Y) and the two colour difference signals (U and V), and combined them together, but each system did it differently. SECAM, in particular, was very difficult to digitise. A component system would keep the luminance and each of the two colour difference signals entirely separate - and unsullied - throughout. Gordon Drury remembers the thinking:

> The EBU had a strong focussing role in this. Some older members of the EBU at the time of the early 70s were thinking, we remember the colour - let's not have that again, let's have a uniform standard in Europe, none of this SECAM nonsense and all these variants of PAL. When we go to digital we must have one standard. So we have to go back one stage - go away from composite and go back to components. This is about '77, '78. There was a meeting at the EBU Technical Committee in Venice in April 1977 at which there were demonstrations of various working digital studio systems. And the decision was made: we can't have a European standard - a single standard - which was composite. It's going to have to be component.

And that meant starting with one of the most central processes in the production chain: recording. Some early digital devices had had to use component signals extracted from PAL, including the early experimental digital videotape recorders. Some of the other innovations of the time, which included storage of still pictures, electronic character generators, graphics design workstations, and particularly the growing range of special effects devices which allowed the programme-maker to manipulate pictures with ever-increasing sophistication - all required picture information in component form. By the early 80s, many individual processes in the production chain were digital - and increasingly digital component - but which interconnected using PAL. Each device therefore incorporated an analogue-to-digital converter at the input, and a digital-to-analogue converter at the output. In the course of its life, and before it even left the studio en route to the transmitter, a television picture might undergo a dozen double conversions, and at each conversion, there was the inevitable loss of quality. The EBU's support for a component future made an immediate impact, as Gordon Drury remembers:

> From IBC (International Broadcasting Convention) 1978 on - if you look at IBC papers you will see an awful lot on component - what are the implications, why should we do it, what are the problems, how are we going to overcome them. What happens if you come from PAL to component, fiddle a bit, go back to PAL for one reason or another, and (repeat the process) ... the cascading problem becomes serious .... PAL wasn't designed for going in and out of; it was designed for coding once in the studio and decoding once in the receiver at home and that was it. .....

Around the same time, Norman Green at the ITCA was experimenting with an all-digital studio:

> The idea was that we would put together the building blocks of a digital studio. So the digital component vision mixer was designed by John Wood at ITN, but because he was too busy we got Mike Cox Electronics to build the design and the development of it was undertaken by Brian Pethers. One of my laboratories up in Scottish Television specialised in doing all the routeing - component routeing - and they built the matrices. The laboratory in Granada Television did all the test signals generation equipment. During this time the engineer who designed the ITN vision mixer had become the technical director of Aston Electronics and he modified an Aston character generator to give out digital components. The equipment was installed as part of Thames Television's Teddington studio 1 complex. Here you had the three vision control/lighting, production, and sound control rooms side by side, and there was fourth production control room which was completely digital with two digital videotape recorders. The first programme completely made digitally and then transmitted by a broadcaster was a Fourth Year English Course schools programme entitled *Mr Magus is Waiting for You* in 1986. This programme had sequences of matting that could only be done digitally.

Other organisations were working on all-digital studios, with important pioneering work taking place at the laboratories of CCETT in Rennes, France and at CBC in Canada. The logic of the situation pointed to some digital interconnection standard which would preserve the picture in digital form from creation through the many stages of manipulation. The early digital studio work used a variety of interconnection protocols which at the same time were being discussed and developed within the EBU and other international bodies. The process took nearly three years: Gordon Drury was part of the discussions:

> When the Americans and the Japanese realised that Europe was going the way it was, they could see the value of getting away from NTSC - because its got similar problems if not worse problems (than PAL). There wasn't a great deal of argument about component versus composite; the problem was the numbers. What are we going to do about the 625/50 - 525/60 thing? And there was a lot of argy-bargy about the numbers and I remember in January of 1981 at Crawley Court there was an EBU summit of technical people with the intent to try and resolve this numbers issue. The following month, February, was the SMPTE[21] meeting which was the right meeting for the Americans to ratify whatever they wanted to do. So the cusp of this decision was the early part - the first two months - of 1981. And fortunately after a lot of demos and skulduggery, argument and counter argument and so on, we came up with a compromise.

The crucial aspect of this agreement was that it would be a world standard, but which included subsets for the European 50 Hz system and the 60 Hz system in use in Japan and America. But the choice of coding parameters - the 'numbers' as Drury puts it - was made so that a single piece of equipment could be specified and manufactured which, at the flick of a switch, would operate equally well at 625/50 or 525/60.

The key to devising a coding system suitable for both standards was a shift away from luminance sampling at a frequency locked to that of the colour subcarrier, which gave, at four times the subcarrier frequency, values of approximately 17.73 MHz for PAL and 14.32 for NTSC. These values had no common factors which might allow for development of a single system. There was, however, an alternative approach, which was to sample at a frequency locked instead to the line frequency[22]. Most engineers doubted that this would yield any benefit until an engineer working for the American broadcaster NBC, Stanley Baron, noted a mathematical curiosity. There was a simple arithmetic relationship between the line frequencies of PAL and NTSC, which were 15.625 kHz and 15.735 kHz respectively. Multiples of both frequencies were also multiples of a common factor, 2.25 MHz - 143 times the NTSC line rate, 144 times the PAL line rate - which pointed to a workable common luminance sampling frequency of 13.5 MHz.

At a series of meetings during 1980, both the EBU and the SMPTE studied the detail of a 13.5 MHz system, and compared it with two other contending systems which employed 12 MHz and 14.318 MHz luminance

---

[21] The Society of Motion Picture and Television Engineers.

[22] This produces a static orthogonal sampling grid in which samples on the current line fall directly beneath those on previous lines and fields and exactly overlay samples on the previous picture. This orthogonal sampling structure has many advantages for signal processing. The sampling is not only locked in frequency but also in phase which means that if the same signal is sampled by different devices the resulting samples will be identical.

sampling. In January 1981 the EBU met and saw demonstrations of candidate systems and in February 1981 the SMPTE, jointly with the EBU, also conducted demonstrations. They proved the viability of 13.5 MHz sampling.

Finally, the desired industry standard emerged later in 1981 as CCIR Recommendation 601. It laid down that in both the 625/50 system and in the 525/60 system the brightness of the picture (the luminance component) would be sampled 720 times in each active picture line, and each colour difference signal 360 times in each active line period.[23] Each sample was allocated an 8-bit value, allowing 256 values for luminance and rather fewer for colour difference signals. This all results in a datastream of 270 Mbit/sec, a considerable size, and while easy to handle inside a building such as a television studio, is expensive in circuit capacity when sent over landlines, microwave links or satellite links. And it is a very high bandwidth for recording on videotape. Nevertheless, by 1987 the D1 digital component recorder had been developed by Sony in Japan. But they were very expensive, and broadcasters baulked at the cost of adopting them wholesale only to find that in an analogue infrastructure they remained a digital 'island'. They were adopted for specialised uses, where very high quality and the ability to copy pictures many times was important. For day-to-day broadcasting use there was a push subsequently to generate the D2 and D3 formats which were digital composite. They were designed as interim solutions, to be used as a direct substitute for analogue recorders in existing installations.

The new standard came in two interconnect flavours, serial and parallel. In the simpler version, parallel digital interconnection used multiple cable connections, consisting of eight circuits to carry digital picture information, plus two more for 'housekeeping' purposes. The serial digital interconnection provided the same signals but multiplexed - combined together - so that they could be carried by a single cable or optical fibre.[24] Serial digital could then travel down the existing coaxial cable routes which analogue installations commonly used, avoiding the need for massive amounts of re-cabling in studio centres. The problem was that creating

---

[23] With Rec 601 sampling there are 864 luminance and 432 chrominance samples per line (including the line blanking) in 625/50 systems; for 525/60 systems there are 858 luminance and 429 chrominance samples per line (including the line blanking); the number of samples in active line period (720 for luminance and 360 for each chrominance signal is, however, the same for both systems: this commonality was of considerable importance in the later development of MPEG compression standards and related chips.

[24] In the early 1980s, a serial interface for Rec. 601 signals was recommended by the EBU. This interface used a bit-rate of 243 Mbit/sec. However, it did not support ten-bit precision signals, and there were some difficulties in producing reliable, cost effective, integrated circuits. A few years later an improved serial interface was developed and was standardized as SMPTE 259M and EBU Tech. 3267. This has a bit-rate of 270Mbit/sec for digital component signals (including the digitised audio signals).

serial digital required an additional - and at that time rather expensive - chip to do the multiplexing of the components, Y, U and V.. But it was clearly the way to go. At the ITCA's experimental studio at Teddington, Norman Green's team had engineered the installation

> In the first instance it was all parallel, but it took a great deal of circuitry to go from YUV to Rec 601 and back again, so we decided to design a single chip that could do both processes. But it would be expensive in terms of our budget, so I persuaded Aston and I think it was Acorn that all three of us all put in money to have a company design the chip for us. It was a great success and I'm told that the company that made the chip only took it out of production a couple of years ago - it's amazing how long it had lasted.

The agreement of a digital interface standard gave a benchmark for the future. Manufacturers now had the confidence to design and market more and more digital devices for studio use, but the wholesale conversion of studio centres to digital component could not be undertaken overnight: it was going to take years. As the equipment became available from the manufacturers and as the costs began to come down, it became possible to contemplate constructing all-new, all digital, installations.

Chris Daubney was Chief Engineer at Channel Four just at this point: the company was beginning to outgrow its first London premises in Charlotte Street and had earmarked a site at Horseferry Road in Victoria on which it planned to build a new headquarters. Daubney realised the attractions of making it all-digital - if the costs made sense.

> We were utterly determined - and luck was on our side for all sorts of reasons - to actually build it all-digital if we could do it. Digital component. Digital audio was going to be easy that was guaranteed, but what we did with the video, that was the difficult bit, because by then digital component equipment for 601 was coming in but it was still very expensive. We were on a fixed budget. In the end, because of the delays in actually buying the Horseferry Road site and building the centre we lost a year of the original timescale. And prices in that year while we were treading water, prices were coming down, and in the end we managed to build what we wanted which was fundamentally Europe's first main digital centre.

If anything, the digital 'islands' in an analogue installation were becoming more common and their size and complexity was increasing. In these newer installations, the production of a programme in the case of the ITCA's studio, or the playout of a network service, as in the new Channel Four building, everything was digital. But elsewhere smaller digital 'islands' became more numerous, each undertaking a specific function digitally in the midst of an analogue environment. At which point there arose the concept of a half-way house - of using analogue component to bridge the gaps between the increasing number of digital 'islands'. Gordon Drury again:

> There was a period of about three or four or five years in which lots of work was done on this very question: how do we get there? How do we get away from analogue PAL to component digital? Once you've got some digital you can start to send some digital component, but not everywhere. But you don't want to go back to composite, do you, so (use) analogue components. You could use analogue plant to carry analogue component signals which were seen to be a stepping stone. I wrote papers on the subject at the time - this was the early eighties.

Analogue component caught on. Sony produced a new recording format - a professional extension of its ill-fated Betamax domestic VCR format - called Betacam SP, which recorded picture information in analogue component form. Beta SP very quickly became the industry standard format for the new production technology of ENG - electronic news-gathering. It used a camera small and light enough to go on a person's shoulder and which carried an integral cassette recorder: in many ways the direct electronic equivalent of the ubiquitous 16mm film camera. In another important digital development, the cameras dispensed with the electronic tubes, and for imaging now used a new generation of photo-sensitive chips - charge coupled devices, or CCDs, in which the brightness and colour content of a scene was 'read out' pixel by pixel.

People were now thinking of components all the way to the home. But there were two obstacles: first, the digital component bit-rates of 240 - 270 Mbit/s were very high: all right inside a building but uneconomical for long distance transmission. Some means of compressing them to manageable sizes had yet to be devised although some early work was looking promising. The second obstacle was that there was no over air broadcast transmission format available which would carry the components. In due course the interim analogue transmission format of MAC would appear, but a fully digital component system was still unexplored territory. In the early eighties, digital television to the home still seemed a long way off.

Meanwhile the commercial business of television was about to undergo a transformation: governments would seek to expand the consumer choice and introduce competition for the established broadcasters, and private sector entrepreneurs - who would later fundamentally change the technology and business of television - would take their first steps towards a new means of delivering television to the consumer that would challenge the settled state of European broadcasting, and change it for ever.

3
MAC: The Technology that Failed

After the successful introduction of colour television the remaining principal consumer aspiration, for more channels, began to exercise policy-makers minds. The issue had been partially addressed with the introduction of a third network, BBC-2, in 1964, and the frequency plan allowed for a future fourth national channel. But the industry - and government - knew that three or four channels were not always going to be enough to satisfy a public appetite for greater choice which was slowly beginning to grow.

Long before 1955, when ITV started in the UK, finally breaking the BBC's single channel monopoly, big American cities had three network stations and one or more local independents. The US philosophy of broadcasting was that it was commercial. The regulator, the Federal Communications Commission (FCC), was keen to see competition between companies big and small who thought they could make a business out of broadcasting. In Europe, things were different. The authorities sought to regulate use of the airwaves to prevent the commercial free-for-all that characterised American broadcasting. The BBC, which was founded as a Company in 1922, had become a Corporation in 1927. It was granted a Royal Charter, which guaranteed it a status independent of government, but with a clear public service remit, which it later applied just as assiduously to television as it did to radio. Even the advertising-funded ITV was created to be bound by certain public service obligations, licensed and regulated by the Independent Television Authority[25], itself a creation of government.

As television services began in the countries of Western Europe in the 1950s, the British model was followed to a greater or lesser extent, often by creating a principal BBC-like broadcaster with a strict public service remit, and usually financed, partly or wholly like the BBC, by a licence fee. Later, as additional commercial services were allowed, these too were regulated and licensed by the state. The model also spread to many countries of the British Commonwealth: Australia's ABC and South Africa's SABC are examples: even in Canada, usually constrained to follow US practice, a Canadian Broadcasting Corporation was created.

There were other differences between American and European practice. In America, television stations broadcast in discrete 'markets', usually restricted to a major city or conurbation, leaving many remote areas with no coverage. A television transmitter would be built somewhere central, usually on top of one of the highest buildings in downtown. The three national networks, CBS, ABC and NBC, were allowed each to own only a handful of these stations. To get their programmes into additional 'markets' in other cities, they made affiliation agreements with local independents. Competition was intense, and technical quality sometimes suffered. In Europe, by contrast, broadcasting was primarily a public service, and administered as such, with great care given to engineering best practice. The broadcasters remit was to cover as much of the country as was financially viable, and to strive over time to reach universal coverage. For that reason, high power transmitters were sited on high ground, often far outside any one city or conurbation, in order to serve as much of the population as possible.

One important consequence of this European practice was that transmitter coverage areas soon began to overlap. In anticipation of this, the planning of their frequency allocations and sites was done carefully to avoid any interference between them. In practice this meant that adjacent transmitters needed to use different radio frequency channels for their transmissions, and the nearest station which used the same frequencies had to be a great distance away - over a hundred miles for a high power site. The planning of television channels was and is an international process under the auspices of the International Telecommunications Union. The ITU Stockholm plan of 1961 allocated all the countries of Western Europe TV channels and power levels for a given number of services. Thus in the UK, and in many other countries, the allocation provided for a total of four services using the UHF band. But that more or less used up all the spectrum available for television broadcasting. Once a country had

---

[25] With the addition of responsibility for commercial radio, the regulatory body was renamed the Independent Broadcasting Authority in 1972. !990 it became the Independent Television Commission and, since 2004, Ofcom - The Office of Communications

launched all of its services - as the UK had done when Channel Four opened in November 1982, that was theoretically it.

But there were a number of commercial interests which looked for other ways of providing more channels. They saw no prospect of making money out of television broadcasting while the spectrum for broadcasting remained limited, full, and tightly regulated by governments in the interests of public policy. Looking once again across the Atlantic, they saw the beginnings of growth in cable television. People there were signing up to an increasing attractive alternative to over-the-air television. By paying a monthly subscription to their local cable company they received their TV programmes over a cable that ran down their street (and sometimes was strung up over their houses or apartment blocks). Not only did they get all the local over-air stations by cable, they were supplied with a growing choice of additional programmes, and the whole offering came without the problems of over-the-air reception, which in downtown areas as well as in the far-flung suburbs, could sometimes be problematic. And the ability of the cable companies to provide additional channels became much easier when the programme providers began to use satellites to distribute content to cable head-ends in real time.

By the mid 1970s, communications satellites had been around for ten years, ever since Intelsat's Early Bird entered service in 1965. In geostationary orbit, they appeared to stay fixed in the sky, enabling signals to be relayed by them to receivers beyond the earth's curvature. They quickly gained commercial viability for telephone and telex traffic, and broadcasters had occasionally used them for the point-to-point relay of major events between continents, despite their early expense. Their growing availability and reducing costs led entrepreneurs to lease carriage for delivery of channel content to cable head-ends across the United States. Two pioneering companies began the trend, Home Box Office and Cable News Network. HBO leased space on an RCA domestic satellite - Satcom I - for distribution of movies, and the cable pay services which it supplied created a new market for the rights owners in the Hollywood studios. And Ted Turner, who ran a TV station in Atlanta, Georgia, created another broadcasting revolution by establishing a 24-hour news channel for cable systems - Cable News Network. More suppliers followed, and by 1985 Manhattan, for example, had 35 cable channels.

In Britain, simple cable systems did exist relaying the four analogue terrestrial channels on coaxial cable. But coverage was patchy and the incumbent operators unwilling to expand. Yet fibre optics was coming, promising an increase in capacity - of establishing 'broadband' services.

Together with the reducing costs of satellite-to-cable delivery, this opened up possibilities of multi-channel television in Britain.

In the early 1980s, the government, encouraged by the 1977 Annan Report on the Future of Broadcasting, was keen to see deregulation of the telecoms industry, which principally meant breaking BT's monopoly on providing telephone services and encouraging a new breed of cable company. The resulting Cable and Broadcasting Act came into law in 1984 and established the Cable Authority, which like its existing counterpart in television, the IBA, was there to licence and regulate cable franchises. The new Authority carved up the UK into a large number of franchise areas and by 1991 had licensed 124 of them. The first to begin services was Swindon Cable, in September 1984, and the last, Great Yarmouth and Lowestoft, became operational in 1997.

The cable companies faced the enormous expense of installing an all-new infrastructure, particularly since it involved digging up the roads and the pavements in front of their customers' houses. Progress was not rapid, but by 1997 45 per cent of the population was 'passed' by cable, although of those only a third, 3.5 million, homes had it, and only 2.5 million of them for TV. But the government's intentions had borne fruit: there was now competition in the provision of television services, between the established terrestrial broadcasters and now from the cable companies and from satellite television.

Talk of a new way of delivering television programmes to the home by using satellites began in the mid 1970s. Now that communications satellites that had been exchanging programmes between broadcasters for over a decade, engineers knew that with further advances in the technology it would be possible to envisage a future in which satellites delivered their signals directly to individual small dishes on people's homes. This was termed Direct Broadcasting by Satellite, or DBS. Engineers knew that it was only a matter of time before such satellites were developed and the service they could broadcast would be commercially viable.

Anticipating these developments, the World Administrative Radio Conference met in 1977 to draw up assignment plans for satellite broadcasting using channels in the 12 GHz band. The final plan was known as WARC77 and in it the UK was allocated five DBS high-power channels.[26] At roughly the same time the potential of satellite broadcasting was discussed in a comprehensive way at a symposium organised in May 1977 by the EBU and the European Space Agency. Charles Curran (then the BBC's Director-General and also President of the EBU) came away convinced that the

---

[26] The plan was largely the brainchild of Prof Henri Mertens of the EBU in Brussels and Geoff Phillips of the BBC Research Department, who developed the computer software, and led the meeting to the magic number of five channels for each country.

practical potential of satellite broadcasting had been demonstrated, and that only the political issues remained to be decided.[27] Gordon Drury, by now with the IBA's research arm, recalls:

> The 1977 European frequency plan allocated the countries of Europe orbital positions and frequencies in the bands allocated for the purpose without there being a real plan to do anything at the time, it was simply an engineering exercise with its own momentum which says if we're goi ng to do it, this is how. And it was based on PAL. The studies of PAL in the 70s had shown it was an obsolete format, so we in the IBA said - more or less - why are we building a new broadcasting platform called satellite on an obsolete video format? Surely we should be looking ahead? It's too early to look at digital in '77 but it's coming one day. We need something in the interim which will be cheaper and simpler, because the cost of chips - this is where silicon comes into it, in 1982 - it's got to go into a home receiver: we can't see how that can be done economically. We need something simpler. Surely that's going to be analogue, isn't it?

But not analogue systems like PAL or SECAM. The big idea was to deliver television pictures over the air to the home in analogue component form. There was another factor that influenced the thinking: the consensus at that time had it that PAL was inherently unsuitable for satellite broadcasting. The transmitting power of a satellite transponder would have to be very much less than any terrestrial transmitter: the size of the satellite was limited by the cost and power of the rocket booster that would place it in orbit, and power consumption would be limited by the size and efficiency of its solar panels. So satellites would need to forego the amplitude modulation (AM) of terrestrial UHF transmissions, and instead broadcast using frequency modulation (FM). FM allowed a trade-off to be made between bandwidth and noise performance – by increasing the modulation index[28] the FM signal could be made less susceptible to the noise inherent in weak signals at the expense of increased bandwidth. In satellite broadcasting, power rather than spectrum is at a premium and wideband FM had therefore been specified for Direct Broadcasting Satellite use under the WARC 77 plan. Gordon Drury:

> That was another reason for PAL not being used: its not just obsolete, it just doesn't actually perform well in a noisy [wideband] FM channel. That was one of the drivers for us - the satellite thing. The story continues into the eighties - we're in about 1980-82 here - we're realising 601 is coming, we're realising there's some interface problems which will need an analogue only format, so we have this double driver. And we thought, oh this

---

[27] Source: *A Seamless Robe: Broadcasting Philosophy and Practice*. Charles Curran; Collins 1979

[28] In FM signals the modulation index is a measure of the change in the carrier frequency in response to an input (modulating) signal: the larger the index the greater the frequency deviation and thus the greater the bandwidth.

works a treat doesn't it? We've got a means to get it to the home, and we've got an analogue means of getting it from where programmes are made using existing hardware. So we can do satellite broadcasting whenever you want.

In practical terms it was generally understood that DBS would require the viewer to buy or rent an adapter box to receive and decode the new DBS channels, plugging it in to their existing TV set. So using a new and improved technology to go into the box seemed an opportunity not to be missed. The new market for DBS, when it came, could be promoted with the promise of much improved picture and sound quality. So Gordon Drury and his colleagues at the IBA research labs, led by Keith Lucas and Mike Windram, began to work on a new analogue component transmission standard intended for satellite broadcasting which they called MAC - Multiplexed Analogue Component.

MAC used a system of time division multiplexing to send the two colour 'difference' signals sequentially, using delays to 'squash up' each picture line's signal so that the luminance signal and one of the two colour difference signals could be sent one after the other in the same time as a single 'composite' line of picture. In successive lines, first one and the other colour difference signal was transmitted. In the receiver, the signals were un-squashed, and the first delayed to match the timing of the second and to match the corresponding luminance signal. After the receiver had performed the simple arithmetic, the reconstituted colour primaries were free of the troublesome patterns of earlier systems and picture quality improved[29].

The first thing the IBA researchers had to do was to see if there was an economical method of delaying and reading out the signals. They approached Plessey Semiconductors at Swindon, who were specialists in analogue integrated circuits, who told them that analogue delays could be made available (digital storage and read-out was still bulky and expensive).

The ambition was that MAC would provide the facility for multi-channel sound. The Scandinavians wanted a system in which one service with separate language channels could serve the whole region. But Ed Wilson, who worked in the IBA team on the sound system for MAC, recalls there was a snag:

> The sound quality of the traditional PAL signal was at risk when you put it into a satellite channel because you frequency modulate the PAL signal instead of amplitude modulating it like on terrestrial TV. With FM more noise is added to the higher frequencies in the received signal than in the lower ones. Since the sound is at the top end of the signal bandwidth it suffers from higher noise

---

[29] Unfortunately, the limited improvement in picture quality could not be appreciated on the domestic receivers of the day.

levels. If you wanted subsequently to add several extra sound carriers because you want multilingual sound for European coverage, you would be adding them just at the point where the effect of noise gets worse and worse. Ultimately depending on the reception conditions it would be one of these sound signals which would be the first thing to fail - you'd end up having TV pictures but no sound, and that's not viewer-friendly! So using digital audio for robustness was becoming a good idea, but digital video for delivery to the home was still well away from the timescale we could foresee.

BBC researchers meanwhile had approached the problem of an improved system for satellite broadcasting in a more conventional way, by seeking to improve the existing PAL system. Extended PAL was their preferred solution. It modified the spectrum of the transmitted PAL signal in a way which avoided the chrominance signal overlaying the luminance. This could cause so-called 'cross' effects, one of which - cross colour -was very common: the fashion at the time for wearing Harris Tweed clothing with a prominent check pattern could result in a picture in which the check shimmered with a rainbow of colours, because the detail resulted in a luminance frequency close to that of the chrominance carrier frequency.

Extended PAL split the luminance signal in two, shifting the higher frequency components up the spectrum to leave a hole where the colour information could stay separate, and also to leave room for digital sound and other data if necessary. It would have been compatible with existing PAL receivers, which would ignore the higher frequency components, while a new Extended PAL receiver would display the higher resolution, artefact-free, pictures. The disadvantage of the system was that it needed a much higher bandwidth for transmission, over 10 MHz. This would not have been a problem for a satellite transponder, but would have prevented the signal being carried by the conventional 8 MHz bandwidth of European cable systems.

The original decision that the UK should use a MAC standard for DBS was taken by a government committee set up under the chairmanship of Sir Anthony Part. During their deliberations, the committee visited the BBC Research Department at Kingswood Warren, to see comparative demonstration of MAC, PAL, and the BBC's contending system Extended PAL. Ian Childs was an expert on telecine and camera imaging, and knew a thing or two about the technical quality of television pictures:

> And I remember these vividly because I was the guy who was pushing the buttons for the demo. So, effectively, I was the final quality control element before the pictures were shown to the committee - if I wasn't happy that they were what the committee were being told they were then I had been instructed not to switch them through. So when people were saying "This is PAL, this is extended PAL, this is MAC", I had to be able to distinguish the differences between them - and to be confident in that distinction. But the

committee came to the conclusion that they couldn't see the difference, in picture quality terms. However they judged the business arguments for MAC were better than they were for PAL, which I could never understand.

There were other advantages to the MAC system, which at the time seemed to ensure that it was future-proof: it had an inherent flexibility which meant that it could easily be configured to carry television pictures in widescreen, and it held out the promise of development towards a system of high definition which would be compatible with standard definition.

Forty years on from the prescient findings of the 1943 Television Advisory Committee in Britain, the CCIR had agreed that any future standard for European high definition would be 1250 lines - twice that of standard definition, and that high definition pictures would be widescreen. Cinema films had moved to wider picture formats in the 1950s: the results were more pleasing to the eye and gave a greater sense of realism. Analogue television systems all over the world had always used a screen shape in the ratio of 4 (wide) to 3 (high), which was also the shape of the ubiquitous Academy format of a standard 35 millimetre cinema film. The new widescreen format would use a height to width ratio of 16 to 9, close to many of the new, wider, cinema formats (although not as wide as the popular CinemaScope format, which was nearer 21:9.)

While the BBC was equivocal about the use of MAC, the receiver industry and the IBA researchers who had first dreamed up the idea were lobbying very hard for its adoption. After the decision was made, in 1982, the BBC's Research Department moved to develop their own system of digital sound for MAC, then worked jointly with the IBA team to develop a comprehensive technical specification, and threw their weight behind a UK effort to get the system adopted as the European standard. And, as on many times in the past, exposure of a new technology to scrutiny, discussion and revision in the bid for consensus within the European industry resulted in argument, disagreement, and finally the compromise of having to agree to a number of variants to suit national preferences.

The variant of MAC[30] that the UK took to the discussions was C-MAC, which offered full broadcast-quality analogue component vision signal and

---

[30] The MAC family of systems comprised:

A-MAC: separate sound and vision carriers, both analogue FM modulated. Never used in service.

B-MAC: time-multiplexing of sound and picture (with multi-level sound coding) at baseband: composite analogue vision and digital sound signal conveyed via analogue FM modulation of the carrier. An encrypted form was used in North America by Scientific Atlanta and in Australia, Hong Kong and some parts of Europe. It continued in use until the mid 1990s.

up to eight digitally encoded broadcast quality sound channels. While the concept of analogue component for satellite broadcasting in general, and MAC as a proposed solution, initially met with general interest, various constituencies came up with detailed criticisms and counter-proposals. The receiver industry, looking at C-MAC in detail, pointed out that it used a method of multiplexing[31] which would be expensive to implement, particularly because receiver chips would need to be more complex: and receiver costs would be crucial to any new system's financial viability. Instead, they proposed a variant, called D-MAC, which was simpler although not quite so robust when it came to transmission. The French and Germans pointed out that C-MAC was impossible to use on cable networks and D-MAC used rather more bandwidth than could be accommodated in most cable systems, and cable distribution to the home was growing strongly in some European countries. So they proposed another variant, D2-MAC - very similar to D-MAC, but with half the number of audio channels and a consequent reduction in bandwidth.

Fierce arguments broke out between the proponents of each MAC variant, much reminiscent of the PAL vs SECAM debates of the early sixties, in that technical matters were mixed up with the ownership of patents and national pride, mildly tempered by actual needs. The Swedish Broadcasting Corporation, for example, fought hard to protect C-MAC against D-MAC. With no requirement in Scandinavia to allow for cable distribution, the extra bandwidth capable of carrying additional sound channels over satellite to a pan-Scandinavian audience was important. For the French and Germans, and others elsewhere in Europe, the reverse was true. The differences were not easily reconciled.

C-MAC: time-multiplexing of sound and picture at radio-frequency; vision conveyed via analogue FM modulation of the carrier; sound carried via 2-4 PSK digital modulation of the carrier It was the preferred option for DBS satellite applications, and was selected for UK use but replaced by D-MAC before public broadcasts began..

D-MAC: time-multiplexing of sound and picture at baseband; composite analogue vision and digital sound conveyed via modulation of the carrier; sound carried as duo-binary coding. It was the preferred option for cable (using VSB-AM rather than FM modulation), and was used by BSB in the UK

D2-MAC: same as D-MAC but with 4 instead of 8 sound channels (and therefore half the bit-rate for the digitised sound-signals). Used in Europe other than in the UK.

E-MAC: enhanced vision parameters (e.g. 16:9). Never used in service.

HD-MAC: high definition version of D2-MAC using 1250 lines. Developed under the Eureka95 project see later).

Versions of the C, D and D2-MAC systems were specified by the EBU and known as the 'MAC-packet family of systems'.

In 1983 Ed Wilson and two young colleagues had taken virtually all the IBA's MAC equipment across to the CCETT labs in Rennes where it was married to the French sound system, and from there they moved their equipment to the EBU headquarters in Geneva.

> Then another fourteen or so IBA engineers arrived including Chris Daubney - he was the 'producer' of the show we then put on at the EBU. So in this building where I'm sitting now - it was only four years old in those days and we were worried about risking the slightest damage - we set about building a structure to support all the cabling (using 700 feet of 1 inch square 'Dexion' tubing (if I remember correctly), and turned meeting Room B into a television studio. Just outside in the foyer we had twelve subjective testing booths, with sound proofing and special reference lighting. They were delivered in a pleasant shade of pink by Television Suisse-Romande but subsequently repainted in battleship grey by the IBA team! We had groups of people coming through doing tests on the material we were providing from the studio and broadcasting through racks of equipment to simulate a satellite channel. And we settled on the MAC standard - although there was plenty of argument going on in the meeting rooms as you can imagine.

Finally, after much discussion and prevarication, a unanimous agreement again proved elusive. The EBU Technical Committee, meeting in Seville, Spain, in 1985 reached a final compromise. It was drafted by David Wood. The EBU would recommend both D-MAC and D2-MAC, the choice being dependent on which variant best suited to the environment it was to be used in. In practice this meant D-MAC was used by UK DBS while for much of the rest of Europe it was D2-MAC.

The BBC was granted two DBS channels and planned a satellite head-quarters next to the new Broadcasting House to be built in Newcastle. But the sums didn't add up. DBS was going to be very expensive, and the BBC began to have doubts. The BBC Handbook for the year expressed their reservations in the most diplomatic terms: DBS was certainly the future, it said, but the BBC's involvement in it "should not be at the expense of the licence-fee payer or to the detriment of any of the existing programme services." Undaunted, in May 1984, the Home Secretary proposed a joint project with three channels, run by a 'Club of 21' made up of the BBC, many of the ITV companies together with a number of companies active in the independent programme making sector of the industry. That project, too, ran into difficulties.

In June 1985 came the collapse of Club of 21 amidst recriminations and lawsuits. The Home Office had one more shot in the locker: it proposed that the introduction and early consolidation of DBS in the UK should be placed in the highly commercial hands of risk capital. So it turned to the Independent Broadcasting Authority and asked it to review the prospects for commercial DBS.

The IBA, besides possessing the highly respected engineering research base that developed the MAC system for DBS, and which operated half the nation's television transmitters, was primarily the independent television regulator. The IBA moved rapidly to raise interest in the project, and invited applications to run three channels. Finally, in December 1986, the licence was granted to a consortium made up of Virgin, Pearson and two ITV companies, Granada and Anglia. They called themselves British Satellite Broadcasting - BSB for short.

The company set about its preparations. It ordered a pair of satellites, and receivers from a number of manufacturers, but in a decision that was to prove mistaken, decided to order the chips separately in an exclusive deal with Intermetall, the German subsidiary of the American company ITT. BSB's marketing people lit upon the idea of a different kind of receiving aerial - the 'squarial' - which it was sure would captivate the public imagination. Conventional satellite dishes are parabolic reflectors which focus the received radio waves to a point at which is placed the single receiving aerial. By contrast, the squarial was a 'phased array' made up of a very large number of tiny aerials each half the wavelength of the desired signal and linked to a means of combining all the outputs. Neither squarial nor chip was available as products when the orders were placed: both were complex technical innovations which required considerable development work on them before they could be mass-produced. BSB underestimated the time it would take to complete the development work satisfactorily, and as 1988 turned to 1989, the delays were beginning to mount and the launch was beginning to slip. Eventually the service of five channels went on air in April 1990.[32] But by then BSB was no longer first in the field with a new generation of satellite-delivered television. Rupert Murdoch's Sky TV had launched a four channel service for the UK in 1989 and had already gained the first mover advantage.

Sky began life as a single general interest cable channel for mainland Europe back in 1982, delivered to the cable companies' head-ends by a high powered communications satellite. When in 1988 Astra launched the first of its medium powered satellites, Astra 1a, Rupert Murdoch's News Corporation had already booked space on it for television broadcasting. The engineers advising the Murdoch company reckoned the satellite power levels and receiving dish dimensions stipulated in the WARC77 plan were

---

[32] There was a 'soft launch' to cable homes only the previous month, partly because the receiver boxes were very slow to arrive in any quantity.

ultra-conservative, and could be reduced.

By using the tried and tested PAL technology they could make use of satellites which operated at much lower power than those intended for DBS. This would have a number of benefits: the satellites would be cheaper because Sky would need to pay only for 'carriage' of its channels and not buy the satellite (and the launcher) outright; the receivers would be cheaper and, using the PAL system, more readily made available in the market; and above all, broadcasts from medium-power communications satellites like Astra were not regulated by national governments.

This last was key to Sky's strategy: it would not need an IBA licence, or a licence from anybody else, come to that. It could make its own programming decisions without having to make promises about quality considerations, either of content or of technical performance.

In retrospect, the reaction from the technical experts in places like the IBA and in BBC Research was perhaps over-cautious, or quite possibly purist, born of a culture of excellence. Experts in the mainstream of British broadcast engineering were confident that a medium powered satellite could not deliver sufficient power to a small household satellite receiving dish[33] to ensure that a decent picture could be maintained if it rained. But Sky's engineers had done their sums correctly: the Astra 1 satellite pictures were sufficiently stable to satisfy consumer confidence.

Sky TV's choice of a technical standard was a bold move which undermined the commercial prospects of BSB, but which was to have another longer term effect. BSB didn't last through its first year. Its programming was largely home-grown and expensive and it threw money at premises, marketing and advertising. It made much of the claim that MAC produced better quality pictures than analogue terrestrial, but in practice it was very difficult to tell the difference: to feed the picture to the television set, the BSB box's final technical process was to recode the pristine MAC component signals as PAL, reintroducing all the short-comings that the new system was meant to eliminate. Few TV sets in those days had a SCART socket, which would have allowed a feed of component signals from the box: a later generation of TV sets would have remedied this folly, but time had run out. BSB and Sky began merger talks.

Sky had built a small but successful market but was facing cash-flow difficulties. BSB, on the other hand, still had cash, but had little market success. A merger was viewed widely - in the industry and by the City - as logical and inevitable. But at the negotiations, Sky played the poker game rather better than BSB. Not many months after the merger of the two rivals in November 1990 - to form British Sky Broadcasting (BSkyB) - the Marco

---

[33] The size of the dish was and is limited by planning regulations: in most of the UK dishes larger than 80cm diameter require planning permission.

Polo satellites, the squarials and the MAC system became redundant in the United Kingdom. It began to look less like a merger than a full-blown take-over by Sky.

After the merger BSkyB's subscriber base grew slowly but surely, the growth fuelled by astute and aggressive marketing, by signing up UK rights for premium programming - sport and movies, and by technology that worked first time. Perhaps the writing was on the wall for MAC at that point. The Marco Polo satellites were sold to the Scandinavian consortium whose MAC services continued for a number of years, as did some in Germany. A further variant, B-MAC, survived for longer: it was used with success both for broadcasting and for point-to-point communications North America, Australia, Hong Kong and some parts of Europe. David Wood of the EBU, like many others, had hoped that MAC would provide, for the first time, a truly pan-European system:

> Our central idea in the EBU was that MAC would be the unique system of satellite broadcasting for Europe, and the European Commission shared that dream – that's why they made the first MAC Directive. We could bury the wasteful PAL and SECAM divisions of the past in a united Europe with one single satellite standard. In fact, it turned out that MAC wasn't going to be the single system in Europe, it was actually going to be a third system, and the diversity was not going to get better, it was going to get worse. When it was clear that there would be PAL services on satellite, we could not discourage SECAM, and MAC was actually going to make the situation worse - there'd be more standards than there were before. I was personally heartbroken – maybe it was the nativity of youth. Yes, the MAC system was very good technically, though it wasn't dramatically better than PAL, but it would have been a single system throughout Europe. So you could buy a set in the UK and use it in France or anywhere - that was the dream and that was the real potential value of MAC – uniting Europe. Alas, it couldn't be done - the business economics got in the way.

But the dream of component pictures all the way to the home did not wither as the MAC 'interim' standard did. There were many reasons why eng-ineers were confident that it would come one day. Two factors in particular bolstered their conviction: the first was that techniques of digital man-ipulation were coming on by leaps and bounds, aided by the ability to construct bigger, faster and more powerful chipsets; the second was the appearance on the horizon of a Japanese system of analogue high definition which had all sorts of implications for Europe.

4
High Definition

Throughout these years and despite the advances in technology which had taken place, very little attention had been given to high definition - the ambition, voiced by the Television Advisory Committee in 1944, for a system with 1,000 lines or more. One exception had been a project, undertaken in 1949 by the EMI Research Laboratories, to make two television cameras that were capable of operating on 1001, 615 and 405 lines in order to study the picture quality obtained and to investigate the technical problems of higher line rates. But after these experiments no further work was undertaken: and no systematic development of high-definition, outside specialist uses for industry, had taken place because there was a widespread perception that there was no commercial rationale for it: no 'business case' as the jargon now unhappily puts it.

This view had a number of irrefutable justifications, the most important of which was that high definition needed large screens before the enhancement of an increased number of lines became really noticeable to the viewer. The conventional technology which went into the manufacture of cathode ray tubes, the picture display device of all television sets in those days, had more or less reached its inherent limits. Tubes with screen sizes larger than about 32" could not be manufactured economically, and in any case homes in Britain (and in the rest of Europe) had relatively small rooms. No householder, however avid a television consumer, wanted an enormous set which would dominate their living room (and very possibly collapse through the floorboards because of its weight). Screen sizes of 27" were by far the most popular for big living room sets. So if there was no point in having a small high definition screen, and if nobody could make a big high-definition-capable TV, and nobody had room for it, then there was simply no business to be had, even if the broadcasting technology existed - which it didn't.

Which is why at this juncture an announcement by the Japanese public service broadcaster NHK[34] that they had developed a high definition television system, and intended to start public services in due course, sent shockwaves throughout the European broadcasting industry.

The Japanese high definition system was the product of a concerted effort by NHK which began in 1968 with the goal of developing a viable HDTV system that could be used for satellite distribution to the home. It was made up of two elements, a studio production standard called Hi-Vision, and an analogue transmission system called MUSE[35]

For the studio standard - for signals generated in studio equipment, and used in the broadcast chain between camera and transmitter, and intended for international programme exchange - NHK roughly doubled the number of lines used in the NTSC system (which Japan had inherited from the US), raising the definition from 525 lines to 1125 lines, and retaining the 60 Hz field repetition rate. It produced widescreen pictures, originally in the aspect ration 5:3 (15:9) but later modified to the slightly wider and by then internationally agreed format of 16:9. For the transmission system, the available bandwidth of satellite transponders was then 8.15 MHz, by a long way insufficient for broadcasting the pure analogue high definition signal produced by Hi-Vision. So to squeeze it into this restricted spectrum NHK developed a way of reducing the required bandwidth by a factor of four. It used an analogue means of subsampling blocks within each picture, treating still areas and areas containing movement differently.

MUSE gave very good pictures for its time, but its performance in handling busy, detailed and rapidly changing pictures left something to be desired. Nevertheless, after some minor modifications, NHK launched its service but it never became a massmarket success, and by the time of its eventual closure, in the mid-1990s as Japan embraced a fully digital television strategy, only a few hundreds of thousands of receivers had been bought. But Japan had been first in the field, their system had worked technically. In the mid-1980s it was advocating Hi-Vision as a new world production standard. In 1989, the American National Standards Institute adopted 1125/60 as its HDTV production standard. Alarm bells rang in Europe, and administrators and researchers in Europe began to reorder their priorities in response. David Wood, Head of New Technology at the European Broadcasting Union, remembers the general perception in Europe that ..

---

[34] NHK is constituted very much like the BBC, with a public service remit and funded by a licence fee. It has a commendable history of technological innovation from a world-class research department.
[35] MUSE: Multiple sub-Nyquist Sampling Encoding - which describes one of the bandwidth reduction techniques used.

> ... there was a threat that we were going to lose out to Japan in terms of the receivers and the equipment, the Americans were going to make all our programmes; it seemed there would be nothing left for Europe to do in the HD world except sit at home and watch.

Europeans liked to think of themselves as technology innovators, ahead of the world game, masters of the elegant solution and cost-effective in their engineering implementation. But by the turn of the 1980s, the European broadcasting industry, like motor cars, shipbuilding, and a host of others, was seeing an increasing encroachment on their bailiwick by newcomers from the Pacific Rim, notably Japan. Many of the great UK manufacturing names in the broadcast industry had by then either given up the ghost and folded completely, or were struggling to survive and looking for mergers abroad to stay in business. The original companies which built the BBC's 1936 405-line service, Marconi and EMI, together with others, had gone, or had merged with a competitor in mainland Europe, or were abandoning the broadcast equipment sector completely in favour of the rather safer UK government electronics defence contracts. British broadcasters were now buying their television cameras from Japanese manufacturers like Hitachi, Ikegami and Sony. On mainland Europe the Dutch electronics giant Philips survived and eventually prospered, as did the French manufacturer Thomson. A similar revolution took place in the consumer market place: people no longer bought television sets from Cossor, KB, or McMichael, because Sony, Hitachi and others had cornered the market. In many sectors, European manufacturers were on the defensive, and the European Commission and many national governments were at a loss to stem the haemorrhaging of manufacturing know-how.

As the implications of a Japanese 1125/60 high definition production standard set in, there came the realisation that another industry might become completely dependent on off-shore technology and, worse, Europe would not own any patent rights to it. For the first time, European manufacturers, broadcasters and government agencies began to think about just what would be required from a home-grown high definition system, and about creating a joint programme to develop one.

Their thinking started not with a production standard, but with broadcasting. A prime consideration was that a high definition system for Europe should be compatible with existing receivers. That meant retaining the 50 Hz field repetition rate used by PAL and SECAM, while doubling the number of lines from 625 to 1250. This would make standards conversion in either direction between high definition and standard definition less troublesome. And Europe saw that an evolution of the existing MAC standard, developing a high definition variant, was the way forward. But the Japanese system did not deliver quality high enough to fully exploit the capabilities expected of HD-MAC. These two factors alone were enough for Europe to prefer a home-grown and more sophisticated alternative.

Behind the scenes there were other considerations. Equipment manufacturers - and that includes, crucially, the domestic receiver manufacturers - pay royalties to the holders of patents of any technology included in the product: the sums are small - pence rather than pounds for each unit - but significant if there is volume production, and in a pan-European market for television sets running at tens of millions of sets every year, the total sums involved are considerable. The European Commission, and the governments of European nations generally, much preferred home grown technology for economic reasons: money circulating within Europe is much preferable to money going outside it. So the health of our electronic industry and the wider issues of its contribution to Europe's economic well-being were seen to be at stake. And of course there was the national pride of European countries inside and outside an increasingly confident European Community. There was no alternative: the Europeans between them must develop their own home-grown candidate for a new world high definition system and put it up for international barter.

When the CCIR Plenary Assembly met in Dubrovnik in 1986 to try to decide on a world HDTV studio standard, the European tactic was an emphatic rejection of the Japanese system, and to argue for a postponement of any decision for the time being. After that, and perhaps a little belatedly, work began in earnest to develop a European alternative candidate system. Not all, however, were convinced of the wisdom of this response: one of the sceptics was David Wood, Head of New Technology at the European Broadcasting Union:

> There were different opinions. There were those who believed that an HD extension of MAC was where Europe wanted to go, and they argued for industrial reasons to create know-how to compete with the Japanese. There was certainly an argument there, but it wasn't the view that we had in the EBU Technical Department. Our view was that the time wasn't right for high definition because the receivers were going to be too large and too expensive. Formally, we in the EBU Technical Department didn't become members of the HD-MAC project, though we followed the project and evaluated the system. I know a lot of very fine people did and they did some great work, but that's the way it was. our view was that it would be better to wait until digital technology was available before going to high definition.

The decade of the 1980s saw the emergence of pan-European research and development programmes, encouraged and in many cases funded by the European Commission. Two of these programmes played particular roles in the development of HD-MAC. These programmes were vast in scope, encompassing many technologies and applications from space research to health and safety. The programmes were EUREKA and RACE and both supported within them a whole range of research projects.

The RACE programme was created and funded by the EC and ran from 1985 to 1995. It was a pre-competitive R & D framework concerned with identifying key technologies, investigating the associated systems engineering and pursuing specifications largely in the broad field of digital applications in communications (and later would host some of the key projects in the development of an all-digital television system). EUREKA, also launched in 1985, was set up by an intergovernmental conference as a framework for technical co-operation between businesses and research institutes. As such it was concerned with 'near market' projects covering many areas of advanced technology. In EUREKA, the national governments, rather than the Commission, supplied funds directly to the companies in their own countries who were participating. This was the vehicle chosen to develop Europe's HDTV system, and the project - Eureka95 - was the largest in its field.

The Eureka95 project to develop HD-MAC involved more than 20 European countries, led by the consumer giants Philips, Thomson and Bosch. Although the prime movers of this development work in Europe were, besides the manufacturers, some of the public service broadcasters (including the BBC) and their national regulatory bodies, satellite rather than terrestrial transmission at the time seemed the only viable delivery mechanism. Researchers looked for ways of incorporating new digital technologies into the design of the system. Ian Childs, of BBC Research, was a contributor to the project:

> One of the ideas the BBC had put into the project quite early on was the use of hybrid technology: we thought at that stage that compression wasn't good enough to allow us to transmit 100% digital. What we would do would be to transmit an analogue compressed signal, but with some digital control information which would allow us to decode the analogue compression more reliably. That was "digitally assisted television" - DATV - and we'd put that into Eureka 95 in about 1986 or so. We still had an ambition to do 100% digital, but we just didn't think we could.

Digitally Assisted Television (DATV) used an early form of an idea which would later be used in the MPEG-2 video compression standard. The differences between one television picture and the next in sequence are often mainly in the movement present, so the content of a picture can be reconstructed from the previous picture plus some information about the movements in the scene between the first and the second. DATV, like, most analogue high definition systems then being investigated, sampled each picture at a rate well below what was necessary to reproduce all the detail. But DATV did so twice in different ways. One method was used to sample areas without movement, and another was used to sample areas with movement. Each sampling method was optimised for its particular purpose. In the transmitted signal, an analogue part carried the values of the appropriate samples and a digital signal told the receiver which reconstruction process should be used for each area of the picture.

The use of specific information about movement - motion vectors - was later taken up by other laboratories who were working on a fully digital compression system. Although the DATV concept was not adopted, the engineers who had devised the system at least had the satisfaction of knowing that they had, in Ian Childs words, "Helped to move the argument on a bit."

Rapidly, the parameters of the new HDTV system were defined and agreed: production and programme exchange would use 1250 lines at 50 fields in the 16:9 widescreen format, intended for broadcasting using HD-MAC[36]. The Eureka95 project planned a series of demonstrations of the new system, and set up the EUREKA HDTV Chain Group, which included the BBC, the IBA and the ITCA as members. With Norman Green of the ITCA as its chairman, the group was responsible for all the demonstrations that followed over the next few years.

But before there could be demonstrations, programmes made in high definition were required. And before the programmes could be made, the necessary technical equipment had to be put together. As there were no 'off the shelf' 1250 line HDTV outside broadcast units the BBC and ITCA went off and engineered their own. Both vehicles had two BTS cameras and newly developed videotape machines capable of high definition recording. The ITV vehicle used three analogue HDTV videotape recorders specially built by Bosch Fernsh. The BBC vehicle contained the innovative 'Quadriga' multiplex of four standard Sony D1 digital component video-tape recorders in which each machine recorded a quarter of the HDTV picture and on playback multiplexed them together to form the complete 1250 line picture. Completion of the multiplexer ran late, and only became available days before the first demonstration: the BBC's first two high definition shoots had to be completed without the director or the engineers being able to see a full high definition playback.

These two vehicles undertook the bulk of the EUREKA recordings between 1988 and 1992. The first significant demonstration took place at the International Broadcasting Convention in Brighton in September 1988, and included HDTV digital recordings made by the BBC at Wimbledon, the Cup Final and the Proms. Ian Childs was part of the team doing the demonstrations:

> ... and we were showing pictures which, frankly, were disappointing. They were disappointing largely because of the quality of the displays we were

---

[36] There was an aspiration for an 'ultimate' HDTV production standard: 1250 lines /50 Hz /16:9 aspect ratio but using non-interlaced 1:1 progressive scanning. There still is, but until very recently has been judged too ambitious a goal.

showing them on. It was frustrating for me [because] HD-MAC was nearly there: it hadn't quite got there in terms of my ambitions for quality, but it was close. It was a noticeable step up from 625-line television, but being hopelessly undersold by the poor quality of the displays.

Over the next five years or so, great efforts were made to showcase HD-MAC. Demonstrations of high definition programmes were mounted at a conference in Montreux and at the IFA consumer electronics show in Berlin in 1989 where a fully equipped HDTV studio was used and seven broadcasters co-operated to make and show a series of full length programmes which included sport, light entertainment, drama and documentary. In July 1990, the Vision 1250 group was formed, using HDTV outside broadcast units provided by Thomson and Bosch, and with generous financial backing from the Commission, which funded maintenance, training and promotional activities. Vision 1250's main showcase for HD-MAC was coverage of the Albertville Winter Olympics in 1991, producing thirteen hours of HD programmes each day. While the HD pictures were impressive, there were less satisfactory results, as Bob Ely - also of BBC Research - recalls:

When HD-MAC signals were shown on D2-MAC receivers - a major selling point of the 'compatible' system - there were serious artefacts which were spotted and commented upon by journalists. This was widely seen as the first nail in the coffin of the ailing HD-MAC system.

The official budget of the HDTV project initially amounted to ECU730 million, but already by 1992 the project was reported to have cost over ECU2 billion. More than half had come from the European taxpayer, much to the disapproval of some governments, notably the free-market leaning UK government, which looked askance at what it saw as unwarranted intervention in the market.

Emboldened by the success of the Eureka95 project, the European Commission judged (incorrectly, as it turned out) that all-digital television systems were a long way off, that analogue HD-MAC broadcasting by satellite in Europe was just around the corner and made a key move which in retrospect many viewed as rash and premature: it started to lay down the law.

Between 1986 and the mid nineties, the Council of Ministers issued a stream of Decisions and Directives - the latter to be adopted in national legislation - which mandated the use of the MAC-packet family of systems for satellite broadcasting within the European Community (as the European Union was then called). In its later revisions of the original Directive, prompted by European industry, it ruled that only HD-MAC may be used for non-digital HDTV transmissions; that only D2-MAC may be used for non-digital 625-line transmissions in the 16:9 format; and, in a highly interventionist stipulation, that all 16:9 receivers must incorporate a D2-

MAC decoder from 1 Jan 1994. A decade later, when all-digital technology was at the same state of development, and the possibility of similar mandation of digital functionality in consumer equipment came round, the Commission was much more circumspect: by then such attempts at direct intervention in the market had been demonstrated as highly risky and doomed to failure. David Wood saw the Directives saga like this::

> For me the motive behind the original MAC Directive was honourable - to unite Europe with a single satellite broadcasting standard. This was a good idea that sadly failed to happen. The motive behind the revision to mandate HD-MAC was industrial, but it was ill-judged because new and better technologies were close by. I am not sure you can say that mandating standards is necessarily a bad thing, but if the judgement about the technology you mandate is incorrect you cannot make them work. Directives need good technical judgement as well as good intentions.

Nevertheless, by 1990 many in the industry also felt that HD-MAC's time had come. Phase I of the Eureka95 was complete and Europe had its candidate system for a world standard, although by now it was clear that there was no way to create a world standard that would bridge the 50Hz/60Hz divide, and - rather like the 1950s divide between 525/60 and 625/50 - all that could be done was to align the parameters of each as closely as possible to permit the design of switchable studio equipment which would operate on either standard. But for Europe the HD-MAC system promised an evolutionary route to high definition. Its signal was divided into blocks of picture information, arranged so that a non-high definition MAC receiver could display the picture in standard definition. This held out the possibility of a much wider potential audience for the programmes which would be made in high definition, and at great expense (the equipment was costly, bulky and in short supply), because they could be viewed on the larger numbers of ordinary receivers which would appear sooner in the market and were expected to be sold in greater numbers.

Meanwhile some broadcasters and manufacturers, particularly in the UK and Germany, had another wheeze. If those same high definition programmes could be used, downconverted to widescreen standard definition form, for broadcasting to analogue terrestrial PAL receivers as well, the financial obstacles to ramping up fully-fledged high-definition programme making could be further mitigated. Of course, 16:9 widescreen pictures, usually films originally made for the cinema, had often appeared on ordinary television screens, but they suffered from being the 'wrong' shape. Either the broadcaster filled the 4:3 frame with the centre portion of the wider picture - risking the loss of action towards the edges of the original frame, or they transmitted the whole widescreen picture in 'letterbox' form - which left areas of black at top and bottom of the 4:3

screen. While letterboxing was not uncommon, it suffered from lower quality, since instead of (in Europe) a picture with 576 active lines, only 432 could carry actual picture information. If consumers were to be persuaded to buy new widescreen sets, only to find the detail in the picture, when expanded to fill the 16:9 screen, much worse, widescreen TVs would get a bad name.

So a consortium led by Philips Consumer Electronics developed a system known as PALplus, in which the missing detail was coded digitally and buried in the unused black lines of the letterboxed display. New PALplus TV sets would have a decoder which would automatically restore the detail so that full definition widescreen pictures filled the wide screen. By 1991, the first receivers appeared at the IFA consumer electronic show in Berlin, and within a few years broadcasters in Germany and elsewhere, including Channel 4 in the UK, had begun broadcasting some PALplus programmes on their terrestrial networks, and a trickle of receivers were selling.

At Channel Four, Chris Daubney's foresight in building a serial digital infrastructure in the new Horseferry Road headquarters gave him the potential to provide a PALplus service:

> My interest in PALplus came because of the nature of Channel 4: to appeal to minorities. We tended to show films from all sorts of different parts of the world - Chinese seasons and Indian seasons - which had been made in Scope or something much wider than 4:3, and the Channel had a policy of showing them with a rather large letterbox. So I thought, we're transmitting this material, why the hell aren't we transmitting it in PALplus? It was relatively easy to do because we'd already started transferring things in widescreen on tape: to transmit it in widescreen if we had PALplus coders was easy. Non-PALplus viewers would get no worse a deal than they otherwise got, PALplus viewers got the benefit of the PALplus signalling system. So we went down the PALplus road, and of course set manufacturers thought this was the best thing since sliced bread, particularly our friends at Philips, because they could see this as a new opportunity to expand in the market. [But] PAL plus wasn't going to last very long and because of the rate at which digital broadcasting came ...

Again, the European Commission responded zealously and, in 1991, proposed a Memorandum of Understanding which envisaged a ECU 1,000 million fund to help with infrastructure and programme-making costs for 16:9 MAC programmes. Behind the scenes, not all national governments agreed with the headlong rush to HD-MAC. Programmes made for MAC or HD-MAC had to be made in analogue component form, in which the luminance and two chrominance signals had to be kept in their separate components until the point of encoding for transmission. This resulted in more complex studio equipment and, while many installations took place, component facilities were capricious in use and never fully satisfactory. Many broadcasters and facilities houses preferred to stay with the new digital PAL equipment which was more reliable, more flexible and - they judged - gave perfectly acceptable quality for PAL broadcasting. In the UK, the Department of Trade and Industry took exception to the UK being asked to stump up its share of the proposed fund, and attacked the proposals. At a bad-tempered meeting of the Council of Ministers during the UK Presidency, the proposed Action Plan was turned down. This time the UK lobbyists, amongst them the DTI, had been able to exploit a difference of opinion with the normally united Franco-German partnership: the Germans saw that the way to go was digital, the French stayed wedded to MAC. The French were outvoted. Eventually, the Commission watered down the scheme to a ECU750m fund for widescreen programme-making in which PAL widescreen production was included.

By now, however, the landscape of the new European television technologies was beginning to look rather cluttered with candidate systems. There were the incumbent SECAM and PAL systems, the MAC variants D-MAC and D2-MAC, and HD-MAC coming over the horizon. But across Europe, in the broadcasters' research laboratories, in the research departments of countless universities, and in the more far-sighted manufacturers, there was a growing realisation that, before long, an all-digital system of television production and broadcasting would become feasible, and that the goals of better picture quality and more services might be better served by developing these technologies and leapfrogging the analogue MAC system altogether.

By 1989, the doubters in Europe could point across the Atlantic to the United States, where the regulator, the Federal Communications Commission, had put out a call for proposals for a US HDTV standard, and had received no fewer than 20 candidate systems: almost all were analogue, and a number of systems were under active development. Proposals were being made for direct broadcast satellite services.[37] In Europe, some work was going on with the aim of developing an all-digital HDTV system for production and distribution, but not for broadcasting. One project, involving the BBC, with two French partners Thompson and the research institution CCETT and others, were doing work on digital compression which was seminal to the development of digital video coding systems. Elsewhere Italian and Spanish researchers were working separately on the same challenge.[38] Generally, however, interest and research activity was not particularly widespread or co-ordinated.

---

[37] in 1990, Hughes Communications, NBC, News Corporation and Cablevision Systems announced plans for Sky Cable, a high-power DBS service. The partnership became troubled, however, and the plans eventually landed in Hughes' hands. The impetus for Sky Cable eventually became DirecTV
[38] The first was EUREKA95 HIVITIS; the second EUREKA256 DIGTRANS

But digital compression was the key to digital broadcasting. As the eighties turned to the nineties, work had begun to harness the power of microchips and mathematics to achieve the very considerable reductions in the bandwidth needed for a digitally encoded television signal. The ball was beginning to roll. The dream of digital broadcasting was less than ten years away from reality.

Part Two

The Building Blocks

5
Compression and Carriage

As the trend continued towards using digital processing within devices and connecting devices together using digital signals, there was a parallel interest in reducing the amounts of data which needed to be stored, or manipulated, or transmitted. If sophisticated techniques could be used to reduce the amount of data required to carry picture information - without any perceptible loss of quality - then great economies could be made. Digital technology would make such compression both necessary and possible. The story of digital compression begins with what was possible with analogue, through the exploration and application of a range of tools for digital compression, to the emergence in the 1980s of a compression system for digital audio, which in turn paved the way for the creation of the MPEG family of compression standards in the late eighties and early nineties. Together with the innovative COFDM modulation system, the two essential building blocks of terrestrial digital television broadcasting were put in place.

The concept of compression was not new. The original pre-war analogue 405-line system, and the NTSC and PAL systems that succeeded it, used a simple form of compression to make transmission of large amounts of picture information more efficient. The lines that made up each picture frame were not transmitted sequentially, but in two 'fields': in the first field all the odd lines (1, 3, 5, etc) were transmitted, followed by a second field with all the even lines (2, 4, 6, etc). The complete picture was made up of the two fields 'interlaced', but the fields were transmitted 50 times a second, resulting in a full frame every 25 seconds, but with a reduction to the viewer's eye of the 'flicker' so characteristic of film projected in the cinema and particularly noticeable when there is rapid movement in a scene.[39] In the jargon of the engineers, this was 625/50: 625 lines at 50 fields per second.[40] Interlacing can be thought of as a 2:1 compression (by sub-sampling).

The digital processes which had been developed for use in studios, and to digitise signals for long-distance circuits, used straightforward PCM (Pulse Code Modulation) which did not compress the signal. The resulting data rates were therefore high. Digital PAL occupied 140 Mbit/s, and digital component signals needed 270 Mbit/s. These high bit-rates had the disadvantage that the cost of digital storage - itself a difficult enough technology - was very high: circuits to carry these signals required bandwidths much higher, and therefore much more expensive, than were required to carry native analogue PAL. There was a clear incentive, therefore, to look for some way of reducing the bandwidth required.

The principle of any digital video compression method is to reduce the data needed to build a picture by removing redundant information. Each frame of a television picture is made up of the 576 lines[41] which actually carry picture information, and as we have seen, the uncompressed Rec 601 digital coding samples each line 720 times. This gives 720 x 576 = 414,720 'pixels' - or discrete sampling points - to each picture.[42] In any picture there are areas in which there is a high correlation between the sampling values of any given pixel with those around it. Think of the 'talking head' interview shot: in the background there might be a plain office wall with very little variation to the brightness and colour over considerable areas of the picture. Fully coding all the pixels which go into making up that picture is not necessary - there is 'spatial redundancy', and much data can be discarded. Again, the information describing much of the 'talking head' sequence of pictures changes very little from frame to frame, so there is 'temporal redundancy' and more data can be discarded. There is also what engineers call 'entropy redundancy' in which short codes are used to describe frequently occurring values and longer codes to describe those which appear less frequently. (Morse code employs entropy redundancy: the most frequently occurring letters of the alphabet, E and T are assigned the shortest codes - one dot and one dash respectively, while the least frequently used are given the longest codes: Z, for example, is coded with two

---

[39] This is what gives 'live' television its immediacy and explains why it is so good at covering sports and other live events; conversely, the flicker inherent in the 24 or 25 frames per second of film helps to distance the viewer from reality, so aiding the cinematic art of story-telling and other impressionistic purposes.

[40] The figures given are for the European system: American television used a field rate of 60 per second giving a frame rate of 30 per second. Hence the shorthand 525/60 for the American television standard.

[41] In a 625 line picture, 576 lines carry actual picture information: the others are used for technical 'housekeeping' and in analogue systems to carry Teletext

[42] The values given are for the European 625/50 system; they are different for the American 525/60 system, but not dissimilar.

dashes and two dots.). Finally there is psycho-visual redundancy - meaning the way in which the human brain registers what the eye sees. The human ability to distinguish fine detail is limited when the eye is tracking fast movement, or when there is an abrupt chance of scene as occurs frequently during a movie or television programme when a shot change takes place.

Research began in the 1970s - long before Recommendation 601 was put together - and concentrated on the digital compression of a PAL signal, using a technique known as Differential Pulse Code Modulation. DPCM is a way of reducing redundancy, to reduce the amount of data. It works by coding not the absolute values of each sample, but only the differences between the actual value and a predicted value. This predicted value is not arbitrarily chosen (because it would be wrong too often) but is at any moment a value based on the actual values from one or more adjacent samples[43] and, in some implementations, in one or more adjacent picture frames. The prediction is made by a version of the decoder incorporated into the coder.

Using DPCM, researchers were able to make useful reductions in bit-rate, and succeeded at various times in coding digital PAL at 34 Mbit/s, and component signals at 140 Mbit/s. Bob Ely worked on digital systems at BBC Research at Kingswood Warren in Surrey and remembers:

> Kingswood had a major success at the 1978 IBC when my colleagues Paul Ratliff and Jon Stott gave a stunning live demonstration of a 34 Mbit/s coder/decoder during Paul's paper. At 34 Mbit/s the picture quality was excellent and even down to as low as 7 Mbit/s the pictures were recognisable.

This was a major triumph for the BBC. The IBA research teams were working on a similar project. Gordon Drury:

> Our objective was to produce a demonstrator. The IBA was under pressure with its relationship with BT at that time to go digital in the networks and needed a codec that just did the job simply and economically at 34 Mbit/s. We were not required to use more sophisticated methods to get down to 7 Mbit/s, well not at this time anyway.

The BBC's Kingswood Warren research department was considerably bigger than the IBA E&D whose size and budget was watched jealously by the funding programme companies. The actual research was confined to about 40 people and it was this number that survived privatisation. Gordon Drury and his colleagues also looked wistfully at what appeared to be better funded competition.

---

[43] For monochrome and component picture signals the previous sample is a good first-order predictor of each sample; for composite PAL, NTSC or SECAM colour picture signals the impact of the colour subcarrier must be taken into account in the design of the predictor.

We envied the BBC's roving thinkers and specialists who seemed to be encouraged to do deep thinking because we could not afford that kind of overhead. We would daydream at lunchtime and the like but could not always spare the time to take things through. What we therefore had to do was choose carefully what we put our limited resources into and hit it as hard as we could. Over the years we got good at selecting what was important. What we could do was use arguments based on these key targets that mollified the budget makers so it looked like we were punching above our weight. But each case had to be argued. Our perception was also that the BBC had much better political clout because they were a more unified body whereas we had internal conflicts between IBA and the companies and among the companies themselves.

At the same time, the IBA Research Department always seemed to Bob Ely and his colleagues at the BBC to be better funded than Kingswood. What the two establishments certainly shared were the constraints of having a limited budget, which may have helped rather than hindered their work by forcing both to use their ingenuity to devise elegant implementations using standard off-the-shelf components.

With digital PAL coded at 34 Mbit/s - a system which later went into widespread use - researchers now turned to the trickier business of coding digital component signals. The first time that long-distance transmission of digital component at 140 Mbit/s was achieved was in 1984, by BBC Research in collaboration with BT on a link between London and Birmingham. In the mid-eighties, DPCM was the 'state of the art' compression system, but by that time other techniques had been proposed which seemed, to some at least, to be potentially more powerful. Bob Ely:

> A debate started between those who thought the way forward was DPCM and those who said, actually we're not really getting to the heart of the matter: what we need is some form of transform.[44] My former Kingswood colleague, Chris Clarke built real-time Hadamard video transformation equipment in the early 1970s. Although, because of its complexity, it was not a practical bit-rate reduction technique for video at that time, Chris's work indicated its potential.

Indeed, Chris Clarke's 1975 Research Department Report[45] is, says Bob Ely, prophetic in identifying many of the techniques which would, some 20 years later, be included in the MPEG video coding standards. Nevertheless, during the late 1970s and throughout the 1980s Kingswood decided to focus its small video coding team not on transform coding but in the development of DPCM techniques which were simpler to implement and

---

[44] A transform is a mathematical process which alters the terms of an equation without affecting its validity.
[45] Clarke, C.K.P., 'Hadamard Transformation: Walsh Spectral Analysis of Television Signals' BBC Research Department Report 1975/26

therefore capable of more immediate application. But by the late eighties, the capabilities of chips had improved and the use of some form of transform coding at last became viable.

Of the various candidate transforms, one - Discrete Cosine Transform (DCT) - eventually became established as the transform of choice for video bit-rate reduction (although other transforms were championed and are still used[46]). Used in tandem with DPCM, it was the key that unlocked the considerable advances in compression that would follow rapidly. "The stroke of genius," says Bob Ely, "Was to combine the two."

DCT helps to remove spatial redundancy. It does this by taking the time variable changing values of the data stream and re-describing them as a spectrum of frequencies which can then be analysed and only the more important ones passed on. The more important ones are the higher frequencies, which represent the rapid variation in information which is describing detail; the lower frequencies representing - for example - the blank wall behind the 'talking head' interviewee - can be largely discarded. This process is carried out on a block of 8 x 8 pixels within the picture, and which continues in a zig-zag pattern across the whole picture. A number of other processes follow including the allocation of the variable length coding to reduce entropy redundancy, and a buffering process to even out the resulting variable bit-rate. Very busy pictures, like a shot from a cameras panning up a football field as the goalkeeper clears the ball to the opponents' half, produce high bit-rates representing rapidly changing information: the talking head produces a low bit-rate. If the buffer is becoming full, because there is a continuing sequence of busy pictures, a feedback loop instructs the preceding quantifier to operate in a coarser mode. Despite the lower detail in the picture which results, the eye and brain remain content because of the rapid changes taking place in the scene.

DCT made it possible to achieve harder compression, and its appearance was timely: by now everybody had realised that digital PAL was at a dead end, and that digital component was the future. But digitising component video meant starting with the much higher native bit-rate of 270 Mbit/s, which compounded the problem. Bob Ely:

> The first goal was to get that down to 70 Mbit/s for contribution quality. There was a demonstration [of that] to the EBU. [After that we got down] to 34 Mbit/s component which was quite a struggle, using by that time a DCT-based technique.

The contents of a potentially very powerful toolkit were beginning to become available. One of the first to realise that video could be compressed

---

[46] MPEG-1 Layer-2 audio, as transmitted with digital TV and DAB radio uses 'sub-band coding' in which the digitised sound signal is split into many frequency bands and the energy in each band is separately coded with a variable number of bits per sample.

to a very much greater extent if a number of the available techniques were combined in the right way was Leonardo Chariglione of the Italian research institute, CSELT.[47] Many engineers were sceptical of his assertion, including Gordon Drury:

> I first met Leonardo Chariglione ... in '86, and I had an argument with him about picture quality. And he was adamant that you could do decent PAL at 5-10 Mbit/s, and I was saying no, no you can't. This is not my personal view [I told him], this is the collective view of European engineers. And he said you're wrong.

Some American researchers similarly surprised European visitors by claiming that they were developing techniques which would allow them to code standard definition at as little as 8 Mbit/s. Henry Price, then at BBC Research, was sceptical:

> Somewhere like '86 or '87, I was asked to join a colleague from BBC Worldwide, the BBC's commercial arm, at a meeting with a consultant who offered the possibility of putting several [digital] TV services on one satellite transponder. So the 30 Mbit/s satellite transponder could carry perhaps - this person was saying - four television services. I just said well at this stage this is nonsense. We're just in the process of managing to do 34 Mbit/s and here's this man talking about doing it in 8 Mbit/s! I said, no, no: he must be crazy! As it turned out, I was the one that was crazy because it wasn't long after that we started to see demonstrations of coding systems that would very shortly form the basis of the MPEG systems. The proposal to BBC Worldwide was probably coming out of an American R&D lab[48]. In fact the service offered never materialised maybe because they were a bit ahead of their time, but clearly the people behind it were already seeing that such things could be done.

The European engineers to which Drury was referring were, like Henry Price, from the broadcasting community. But Chariglione worked for a telecoms company, and telecoms companies had been ploughing their own furrow for a decade or more in order to create and nurture compression systems suitable for very low bit-rate use in applications like video-conferencing, which needed to use 64 kbit/s telephone circuits. For some time, there had been a disconnect between researchers working on broadcasting technology, and their opposite numbers working for the big state-owned telephone companies across Europe. Bob Ely remembers that while BBC Research continued to concentrate upon building real-time hardware for its work on video and audio compression (the data-rates involved were

---

[47] CSELT: Centro Studi E Laboratori Telecomunicazioni S.p.a. - founded in 1964: the Telecom Italia Group's Company for "study, research, experimentation and qualification in the field of telecommunications and information technology."

[48] From the mid 1970s to the late 1980s Arun Netravali's team at Bell Labs in the USA was widely recognised as the leading innovator in digital video coding and bit-rate reduction techniques.

far too great for real-time software-based solutions at that time), the Post Office research people at Martlesham had taken the lead with software-based processing for low bit-rate applications (at around 64 kbit/s). And:

> ... perhaps there we lost connectivity because [the relationship] between Martlesham and Kingswood somehow it never gelled. There was always the CCITT [responsible for] telephony standards, and the CCIR doing radio standards, and no good information exchange. And it was really down to the industrial labs who were working on both to say, hang on a minute, what we are doing for the telephony guys for videoconferencing if scaled ... would solve the problem of digital television. And that came about in the late 80s, early nineties.

The early pioneering telecoms work which had produced a standard called H261, which was based on DCT: if scaled for the higher data rate of television, and with the benefit of the other techniques, developed since, for manipulating data, H261 might, it seemed, just provide the basis of the solution. And so it turned out.

Chariglione was the architect of the Moving Pictures Experts Group, an international body which between 1988 and 1993 produced two standards: MPEG-1 and MPEG-2. Their starting point was the earlier work of the Joint Photographic Experts Group of the International Standards Organisation. The compression method for still pictures, JPEG, together with its cousin Motion JPEG, allowed the digital information describing a picture or series of pictures to be greatly reduced by varying amounts which could be decided by the user according to the desired picture quality and the size of the data file required. MPEG's first published standard, MPEG-1 was intended for use in CD-ROMs and other digital storage media. It found widespread use not only for non-interlaced picture formats of the kind which computers use, but also in at least one early digital television system - applied by the simple expedient of coding only one of the two fields of the interlaced television picture.

In 1991, a second phase of work began to develop MPEG-2 supported by the European Commission under the Eureka625 VADIS[49] programme. MPEG-2 was designed at the outset to handle broadcast quality pictures and to reduce the bandwidth required for their transmission to levels which could be accommodated in the existing broadcasting channels. Many candidate techniques were understood when the group started work, and many had been demonstrated - individually or in various combinations - over the preceding ten years or so. The task now was to gather together the most effective of them to define the best possible overall system. The resulting set of MPEG-2 standards was first published in 1993.

The usual short definition of MPEG-2 is that it is a 'motion compensated hybrid DCT' algorithm. Hybrid refers to the combination of

---

[49] VADIS: Video/Audio Interactive System.

DPCM and DCT which is used, and to which the technique of motion compensation is integrated. This combination of techniques - and the international collaborative nature of the Group - was the key to MPEG-2's success.

In principle, motion compensation recognises that a huge amount of data is redundant and can therefore be discarded from the datastream describing a series of moving pictures if only the differences between one frame and the next are sent. The receiver can then undertake the task of rebuilding a frame from the small amount of 'difference' data correlated with the complete picture which preceded it. The system adopted in MPEG is motion compensated interframe prediction, and makes use DPCM. This allows the content of a frame, and the direction of movement of objects within the frame (motion vectors), to be predicted from the data of an earlier frame. This 'forward prediction' can be effective when the changes in the frame are easily predicted: Pinocchio's nose will continue to grow: it is unlikely suddenly to stop and get shorter again. But this kind of prediction breaks down when the unexpected happens: the racing car entering the left of the picture will suddenly appear, and there is nothing in the earlier reference frame to tell that it was coming. So MPEG offers a second method, 'backwards prediction', in which the frame is 'predicted' from the information carried in a subsequent frame. An 'interpolated' frame gives a prediction based on the averages from forward and backward prediction.

To do this, the MPEG-2 coder includes its own copy of the decoder, which supplies the input to the predictor. The coder's final output - called the 'transport stream' - is in the form of a 'group of pictures' (GoP). There are eight in a so-called 'long GoP', the first of which is called an 'I' frame, and its data is more or less uncompressed. There then follow a series of seven frames, two of which are 'P' frames, coded with references to a previous I or P frame, and five 'B' frames, coded with reference to both the previous and the next I or P frame. To do this the coder needs to re-arrange the order in which these frames are sent, and this involves a certain amount of digital storage-and-read-out, which takes a finite amount of time. In the decoder, the reverse must take place, taking more time. It is because of this that a 'digital delay' of about half a second is noticeable when comparing analogue and digital transmissions of the same programme.

MPEG-2 defines four levels ranging from relatively low quality but which - for simplicity of implementation - makes use of a reduced selection of tools from the tool-kit, through 'main level at main profile' intended for good quality broadcasting, to a high level suitable for high definition. Its specification also describes only the syntax (language) of the bitstream and the decoding process. This leaves a manufacturer's designers free to compete with different implementations and gives them scope to devise better and more effective coders as experience of using MPEG accumulates over time - a form of future-proofing.

The achievement of the MPEG-2 standard is demonstrated by its adoption for digital television systems throughout the world, across terrestrial, satellite and cable distribution, its use in long distance point-to-point circuits for contribution and distribution, and its emerging use as a production and post-production signal standard which may one day supersede Rec 601.

MPEG-2 had provided a crucial breakthrough: it was now possible to code good quality standard definition pictures at around 4 Mbit/s, and high definition pictures at around 18 Mbit/s. At these levels, it was now possible to envisage fully digital broadcasting by satellite or terrestrially: the numbers would fit. What was needed now was a digital transmission system.

The second technology that proved to be key to the eventual success of digital terrestrial broadcasting was the method of transmission, known by its acronym COFDM[50] (since its full description, Coded Orthogonal Frequency Division Multiplexing, leaves any speaker a bit short of breath). It wasn't a new technology, in the sense of having been developed specifically for digital television: in fact its origins were in radio, or more correctly, in Digital Audio Broadcasting (DAB).

At BBC Research, the team that had developed the NICAM stereo sound-for-television system (successfully launched in 1984) had tried using a version of the system for radio broadcasting, but without success. But, as Ian Childs of BBC Research remembers, one of the team, Paul Ratliff, discovered that there was a European Commission-funded project - Eureka147 - which had been started to look at a possible digital sound broadcasting system:

> The project had originally been set up in Germany. The Germans wanted a replacement for their [analogue] satellite sound broadcasting system which didn't have many channels; their aim was to make a better system with more capacity. But Paul realised that some of the technology they were working on might be applicable to terrestrial radio as well. So we joined the DAB project as the only UK participants in 1987. Basically there were three major contributors to the system that the project eventually developed. IRT[51] in Germany contributed the sound compression system MUSICAM

---

[50] COFDM is one of the principal characteristics of the European DVB specification for digital terrestrial television. In the American ATSC equivalent, however, a more conventional modulation system is employed.

[51] IRT: The Institut für Rundfunktechnik is the research and development institute of the public broadcasters of Germany, Austria and Switzerland.

or, as it later became, MPEG-1 layer 2; CCETT[52] in France contributed the modulation system COFDM; and Paul's small team at the BBC contributed the 'glue' that brought it all together into a practical broadcasting system, and [the] idea of using it terrestrially as well as for satellite.

In January 1990, the first trials of Digital Audio Broadcasting using the Eureka147 COFDM system were carried out from the Crystal Palace transmitter in south London. The tests confirmed that DAB, using COFDM, could deliver excellent sound virtually of CD quality, that it was immune to interference to a very much greater extent than FM, and could accommodate several programme channels in the spectrum occupied by one FM service. Using a second transmitter nearby, the tests also confirmed the principle of a single frequency network (SFN) in which several transmitters at some distance from each other, but with overlapping service areas, could use the same transmission frequency, resulting in more satisfactory coverage. This was in sharp contrast to analogue AM and FM transmission systems, where if reception from two transmitters using the same frequency had been permitted the result would have been an unintelligible mishmash of sound.

The early work on the use of COFDM was undertaken at the research centre of CCETT in Rennes, Brittany, but it had its origins in even earlier systems which used a large number of carriers spread across the transmission bandwidth, developed by the US army and, separately, by the Russian defence agency. Following the pioneering CCETT work, which culminated in a paper describing the work published in 1987, the COFDM multi-carrier concept formed the basis of a highly successful digital radio broadcasting system, now widely adopted. But already, in the late eighties, it was sufficiently well advanced for researchers to believe that, with the adjustment of some transmission parameters, COFDM held out the prospect of bringing all these advantages to digital television broadcasting.

The way that COFDM carries the data to form the picture and sound information is unlike anything that had been used before for public broadcasting systems. In conventional methods, the transmitter generates a single radio frequency signal called a carrier, which has a particular frequency: low for AM radio on long, medium or short waves, higher for VHF FM radio, and higher still for UHF television. Some of the figures may already be familiar from the on-air network announcements we are familiar with. Radio 4 on (amongst other frequencies) 198 (kHz) Long Wave, for example. (Television services are recognised by their channel numbers in the UHF band rather than their frequencies.) At the transmitter, the programmes - a radio service or a television service - are placed piggy-

[52] CCETT: A joint venture between CNET (the R&D centre of France Telecom) and TéléDiffusion de France (TDF).

back fashion on this radio frequency signal. This is called 'modulating' the carrier, and the result is that the space in the radio frequency spectrum occupied by the modulated carrier spreads by an amount that depends on the volume of information being carried. This spread is referred to as 'bandwidth' and is accommodated in a radio frequency 'channel' whose width is allowed for when transmitter frequency allocations are being planned. So the AM radio channel that, for example, carries BBC Radio Five Live occupies about 9k Hz and the higher quality stereo FM channel that carries Radio 2 occupies about 300 kHz. Because television pictures contain so much more information, the analogue UHF channel 26 that carries BBC-1 in London, to take another example, occupies no less than 8 MHz.

COFDM introduced a quite different way of using this 8 MHz bandwidth by employing a very large number of carriers equally spaced (but very close together) and spread evenly across the 8 MHz allocation. Current television COFDM systems use either 2,000 or 8,000 of these carriers. The MPEG transport stream is distributed between them: that's the FDM bit, which stands for Frequency Division Multiplexing. As for the 'O': adjacent carriers are 'orthogonal' to one another, meaning that although the spectrum of each digitally modulated carrier overlaps with those adjacent to it, it does so in a particular way which ensures that there is no interference between them. As the bandwidth of each individual carrier is about 1 kHz, the amount of data each can carry is very low. This, however, produces a bonus in that the signals now have a very high tolerance to interference. Finally the 'C' stands for 'coded' meaning the employment of 'forward error correction', in which the stream of data is pre-processed to enable the receiver to reconstruct data bits missing or corrupted due to interference or loss during transmission. COFDM employs a powerful cocktail of highly sophisticated error correction coding techniques all based on advanced mathematical concepts whose descriptions are well beyond the scope of this book.

The process by which the two or eight thousand carriers are modulated employs another sophisticated mathematical process. Conventional analogue modulators superimpose an audio, video or other information stream on to a single radio frequency carrier wave as a prelude to transmitting it. Clearly with two, or eight thousand carriers of a COFDM system, it would be wasteful to employ two or eight thousand modulators. Instead, COFDM employs what is known as a Fast Fourier Transform. Fourier - Baron Jean Baptiste Joseph Fourier, to give him his full name - was an early nineteenth century French mathematician who in 1807 published the theory which bears his name. A Fast Fourier Transform (FFT) is a mathematically efficient way of applying one of the properties of Fourier Analysis, which can analyse the spectrum of a signal and render it into its component parts: to put it another way, an FFT is a tool which can convert the rendering of information between the frequency domain (the spectrum of the over-the-air signal) to the time domain (the original MPEG datastream), and vice versa. The mathematics is elegant, but the demands of doing such calculations at the speed and in the volume required by digital television taxed the ingenuity of the pioneering chip manufacturers, and meant that a two thousand carrier system became feasible several years before the alternative, eight thousand carrier, system.

Because the signal consists of so many carriers equally spaced across the 8 MHz channel bandwidth, COFDM is inherently a highly efficient form of transmission because the transmitted energy is spread evenly across the bandwidth of the channel it occupies - unlike a conventional analogue transmission spectrum which is peaked around the carrier frequency.[53] A COFDM signal is much more rugged than an analogue TV signal and can therefore be transmitted at a fraction of the power of an analogue signal for the same area of coverage. This opens up the possibility that digital broadcasting could use 'taboo' channels - the adjacent channels to an existing analogue transmission normally left vacant to avoid interference and consequent loss of quality.

There is another remarkable property in COFDM which is important: it is immune to the multi-path interference which causes 'ghosting' on analogue television reception. Ghosting occurs when two or more signals from a transmitter reach a receiving aerial by different routes. This occurs frequently in cities, where an aerial might receive not only the signal directly from a transmitter, but also a number of other signals reflected from adjacent tall buildings. Because a reflected signal has taken a longer path to the aerial, it will have suffered a time delay, which shows on an analogue TV screen as a second, fainter, picture offset to the right. The more reflections the more paths - as in 'multi-path' - and the more 'ghost' images. Anyone who has juggled with a set top aerial in the student digs or in that twenty-something pad in town, will be only too familiar with the problem. But COFDM is largely immune to this: in fact, it derives tangible benefit from multi-path propagation of the transmitted signal.

Each COFDM carrier is loaded with information in bursts, known as 'symbol periods'. The period between bursts is termed the 'guard interval'. Provided the extra time taken by the 'ghost' signal to arrive at the receiver is less than the duration of the guard interval, the receiver can add main and ghost signals together, actually enhancing reception rather than ruining it. This extraordinary quality brings another innovative feature to COFDM: because the receiver can cope with multipath signals it can also handle reception of the same service in the same channel from two or more transmitters. This opens up the concept of a 'single frequency network' (SFN)

---

[53] A conventional analogue TV signal is modulated using "Vestigial Sideband" modulation so the carrier is close to one end of the spectrum of the modulated signal.

in which an entire region - or a whole country - can have a digital multiplex of services delivered using only one UHF channel. Nothing like that is possible with analogue transmission. Obviously, this option can be of very considerable benefit to frequency planners faced with a crowded spectrum and an increasing demand for access to the airwaves.

Not all of the elements of COFDM as just described were necessarily present in some of the early experiments in adapting the DAB implementation for television use, but the CCETT development of COFDM for broadcast transmission of digital audio became the point of reference for those on the lookout for a modulation system suitable for digital television broadcasting.

By now, at the end of the eighties, more and more people were beginning to think that digital broadcasting was going to be possible sooner rather than later. But there was yet no coherence to the growing ranks of those who thought they saw this. Individuals preoccupied with more immediate tasks in their organisations, perhaps, read the erudite papers from the conferences where such things were discussed, but then conferences always do throw up fascinating blue-skies technology ideas and who was to say whether any of them would fly or whether they were simply 'vapour-ware' - to use the contemporary and pejorative term. Maybe they thought about digital broadcasting quietly or shared their opinions with others of a similar conviction over lunch or tea breaks. Many thought, yes, it will come one day. Few thought, now is the time to start doing the work. There was not yet a critical mass of opinion; no widespread consensus, yet, that the time was ripe.

Within a short while, this would all change.

6
Digital Broadcasting: The Big Idea

If you ask a British broadcasting engineer at what point he or she became convinced that digital television broadcasting to the home was going to be feasible, most will give you a date and a place: September 1990, at the International Broadcasting Convention in Brighton. There, amongst the exhibition stands and in the accompanying conference, a number of organisations were talking about real advances along the road to digital broadcasting, and some of them were showing experimental equipment. None of them yet represented a system that could be turned into a practical and economic consumer system, but the signs were there that a critical mass of expertise now existed. Many of the engineers who visited IBC that year went away convinced that they had glimpsed the future, and were determined to start work themselves to learn more about it. Some went away, similarly convinced, but knowing there was now an urgent need to co-ordinate efforts in Europe to devise a workable system. Just six months later, a small group of industry leaders in Germany took the first steps towards forming an organisation, the DVB, which would go on to create the all-important technical specifications for a successful digital television broadcasting system.

The International Broadcasting Convention - IBC, then a biennial event, had, by 1990, already outgrown the venue of its formative years, the Grosvenor Hotel in London. It was now fast becoming one of the broadcasting world's three most important international industry exhibitions and conferences. America has NAB - run by the National Association of Broadcasters - and Broadcast Asia was beginning to be a 'must-go' diary entry. In the exhibition halls, manufacturers put on show their latest products, their prototypes, or their ideas for harnessing new advances in technology. In the conference, erudite technical papers were read by research engineers and product development managers to an international audience of their peers. IBC lasted for several days. By 1990, the ability of Brighton to supply enough hotel rooms for the exhibitors, visitors and conference delegates who flocked there was becoming stretched, and the exhibition itself overflowed on to the shingle beach below the Grand Hotel, where the capricious weather which sometimes blew in from the English Channel did it no favours. It would be the last year that IBC took place in Brighton. For the 1992 event it decamped to Amsterdam where, now held annually, it continues to grow larger.

Interest in MAC was still running strongly. British Satellite Broadcasting had launched its five-channel offering five months earlier - late, but successfully. In the same month as IBC took place, its second satellite was launched, and the company announced a major marketing push for the run-up to Christmas. MAC service launches were planned in Germany and in Scandinavia. HD-MAC developments were also being closely followed, and there was much interest in the interim widescreen PALplus system.

The protagonists may have felt that the MAC system was established, and that HD-MAC services would follow as the remaining work to perfect the system was completed. But if they looked carefully elsewhere at IBC, the digital technology that would all too soon supersede it was in evidence.

In retrospect, the event at IBC '90 that had most influence on the way digital television would develop in Europe was the presentation, in the conference session, of a paper entitled *Digital Television to the Home - When will it come?* It was written by three IBA engineers, Arthur Mason and two colleagues, Gordon Drury and Nick Lodge.[54] It described many of the features that the digital terrestrial television broadcasting system now has, exploring for the first time how a combination of low bit-rate compression combined with digital modulation using OFDM could deliver multiple additional television services from existing transmitter sites while co-existing with the incumbent analogue services. It was based on theoretical work only, but was remarkable in the manner in which the work started in the first place and why the paper came to be presented in that year.

The Conservative government of the time was determined to introduce more competition in broadcasting and to increase the choice of television

---

[54] Arthur Mason's specialism was frequency planning and radio frequency engineering; Gordon Drury was specialising in compression technology; Nick Lodge, also an engineer, and with a profound knowledge of image compression, was at the IBA but later, after its privatisation, which had been in process since late 1988, became the ITC officer who commissioned the work carried out by Mason and Drury and contributed significant ideas to it.

channels: in 1988 it published the White Paper, *Broadcasting in the '90s: Competition, Choice and Quality,* which amongst other things, envisaged a new analogue terrestrial channel, Channel Five, and the expansion of cable and satellite services. At the IBA, Arthur Mason decided to have a fresh look at the way in which analogue television broadcasting in the UHF band was organised.

> And I started to look at the old PAL TV system and I realised that the PAL colour TV system was all invented back in 1961, and the Stockholm UHF TV plan was produced in 1961, actually at the end of the valve era. So the interference protection ratio assumptions about receivers all date from the valve era. So I felt that the whole broadcasting spectrum scenario is living in the dark ages. How can we bring it into the modern world, with new technology? So I actually postulated a high performance receiver that had much better adjacent channel interference performance, much better co-channel interference performance, much better image channel performance. And I didn't actually say what it was, and I certainly didn't necessarily think it was digital at the time.

Mason had recognised a market requirement from, he says, the contents of the 1988 White Paper, and was trying to answer the question, how are all these new channels going to be delivered? He was also "trying to save the UHF band". He was one of the first people to realise that the introduction of satellite television broadcasting might eventually lead to broadcasters having to give up the UHF spectrum:

> The UHF band and the VHF band - we were actually sitting on large chunks of it as broadcasters - was the prime spectrum you could possibly have for portable, mobile, communications, indoor reception, that type of thing. Whereas with satellite you needed a dish and you could only point it in one direction. So I felt that to give up the UHF band for broadcasting would have been an absolutely devastating step for it and I felt very strongly about that.

But the way the analogue spectrum was used, based on the 1961 frequency plan, was that for four national networks, nine blocks of 4 frequencies had to be re-used in a patchwork across the country. A transmitter had to be three service areas away from another before you could reuse the same block of four. So there were unused channels, but unused because otherwise they would cause interference: they were the 'taboo' channels. Mason realised that if you could shorten the frequency re-use distance you would gain an enormous increase in capacity.

> So if I could make better receivers, change all the frequency planning assumptions, then we could do much bigger things with it. So I started down that route. I had some students looking through all frequency numbers and things like this, and making certain assumptions I had ass-umed you could make, how many more channels could you find and we actually we had a report which said yes we thought it was possible to build

better receivers and do something and have more channels and these were the various options.

Mason and his colleagues also investigated what new technologies might offer in advanced modulation schemes, and published his team's initial findings in an internal IBA report.[55]

> It took a digital approach, it looked at an analogue approach - precision offset - and it also looked at hybrid analogue-digital approach. And we did some experiments in the laboratory, three or four of us. In actual fact, the hybrid digital-analogue receiver at the time actually came out best, interestingly, but we felt, having considered the whole thing and looking at it a bit more that perhaps an all-digital approach might be more suited to the modern world. And that's eventually the route we went down. We had this OFDM thing - obviously, I latched on to that, and I kind of pinched the idea from DAB really - my contribution was the frequency planning assumption and RF hypotheses. So I nicked the OFDM technology from the DAB people.

The other essential element in the IBA's emerging strategy was the use of advanced compression. Gordon Drury and the team of engineers working on coders were sure that they could build a compression system that would reduce 270 Mbit/s digital component signals to around 12 Mbit/s. The video compression system used a motion-compensated DCT system which, says Gordon Drury - whose speciality was rapidly becoming compression - owed a lot to the ideas of a colleague, Nick Lodge:

> Nick, being Nick with a PhD in image processing and all that, had some ideas about how a compression engine would be put together ... We were playing with technology in the lab, hooking ideas together, simulating it, deciding what to do and then implementing it.

The MPEG work on compression for CD-ROMs and other digital storage media - MPEG-1 - was then in its early stages: MPEG-2 was still several years in the future: it was pioneering work.

The IBA were reluctant to publicise the work done by Mason and the team, fearing a backlash from the ITV programme companies who paid for their research effort. More channels were bound to be seen as a threat to what was still a very comfortable and profitable monopoly. But by the time that IBC were putting out a call for papers for the September 1990 conference sessions, Mason and his colleagues were facing a serious predicament. The Broadcasting Bill which was published in December 1989 included provision for the privatisation of the IBA's transmission arm together with

---

[55] *Exploiting the Redundancy in the UHF TV Plan to find Additional Channels, using Modern Receivers,* IBA E&D Confidential report EDCR1/89, A. Mason, first issued November 1988 and reissued with additional information September 1989.

the research team's base, the Experimental and Development Department. The spectre of redundancy loomed ominously. Arthur Mason felt strongly that the people and their ideas deserved to survive:

> The one motivating force that certainly kept me going during the time that IBA was coming to its close was the fact that I firmly believed in the people in the lab and that IBA E&D was rather special in its ability to be creative and inventive and that we should not lose this group at any cost. I think this was the overriding factor that caused me to stake digital television as the labs future - as we needed something radical that people could not ignore in order to survive. We really did not have anything to lose by putting forward a radical proposal - and I guess I was staking my reputation on my idea in saying it publicly - in the hope that it might save the lab!

Gordon Drury remembers the anxiety of the times only too well:

> We realised we were at risk as a research group - we might well be chopped. We realised that from day one, and our attitude for the following two years was, we could be chucked out; we have got to look in the cupboard and look at our resources, skills, knowledge base, what can we do and how would we apply it. And we did realise, not fully, but we did have the nous to realise that we were sitting on two significant bits of technology: one called low bit-rate TV / MPEG style knowledge and this early work on terrestrial digital, and other forms of modulation for satellite and cable and all those things. And we felt that was where our future would be.

Mason, Drury and Lodge went public. Arthur Mason delivered the IBC paper.

> We felt that we had nothing to lose - we were probably all going to lose our jobs anyway, so we might as well say it. Publish and be damned! I actually prepared the talk very, very carefully. I actually wrote a script, which I very rarely do, I normally just ad lib. I made all the points in the short time you had to do it. And at the time of course there was the PALplus project which was the competition. So I went on after the PALplus project and you could tell the audience were really warmed up about it and the Head of Research at CCETT actually came up and thanked me afterwards for saying it.

This was fascinating stuff to other researchers - the application to television of the techniques being developed for digital audio broadcasting. Ian Childs remembers:

> That aroused a lot of controversy at the time because effectively what they were doing was taking the technology that DAB had developed and saying, "If this were applied to television, what would it do?" And I think that a lot of the team who were active in the DAB area felt that it was a bit like having their clothes pinched. But, even so, it aroused a lot of debate.

The importance of this paper should not be underestimated. Mason and his team may not have been the only researchers to be thinking about these issues or investigating their potential. But they were the first to work out a coherent and practical application for them, and most important of all, they were the first to publish these ideas.

Arthur Mason and his team later christened their baby SPECTRE, one of those acronyms that engineers seem so fond of. It stood for Special Purpose Extra Channels for Terrestrial Radiocommunications Enhancements, but the inspiration for the acronym might equally well have originated in the nervousness they all felt personally about their future prospects.

Elsewhere at IBC that year, not in the conference hall but out in the exhibition halls, was something that would make a stronger immediate impression. The American company General Instruments gave a demonstration of an HDTV compression algorithm which they called 'Digicipher' - a name which the company also used - confusingly - for their whole digital terrestrial system.

In the United States, the approach to developing a new technical standard was then, and is now, quite different to that in Europe. The Europeans like to gather together experts from all interested parties who will collectively argue the toss about technical detail, and eventually settle on a compromise which suits everybody involved. This was the process by which MAC had evolved, and the way DAB and MPEG were being developed. In the US, the responsible authority - the Federal Communications Commission - stages a beauty contest of technologies developed in isolation by individual companies or separate small groupings of companies, and in due course announces a winner. Stung by the emergence of the Japanese MUSE system for analogue high definition, the FCC in 1987 made a call for proposals for an all-American high definition system to replace NTSC, the incumbent standard definition system. By 1990, the original twenty-one candidate systems had been whittled down to nine: all were analogue proposals except one - the all-digital system being proposed by General Instruments, Digicipher.

The GI system did not use COFDM or, indeed, anything like a multi-carrier system, but instead used a modified form of analogue transmission. But the aspect of Digicipher which caught the imagination of those who saw the demonstration was that the system compressed high definition pictures into what was then the astonishingly low bit-rate of 19 Mbit/s, with tolerably good results. Bob Ely says that:

> Digicipher amazed European researchers at the time by showing good quality at 19 Mbit/s at a time when European were advocating 140 Mbit/s for HDTV! However, it is probable that the Digicipher simulations shown at IBC-90 exaggerated the picture quality due to limitations of the simulation technique used. Real-time codecs later produced by GI did not achieve the same quality. Their simulations were better than the reality.

Nevertheless, what they put together was essentially an HDTV coder and decoder pair working at 19 Mbit/s. Like many of the engineers who saw it, Bob Ely had never seen anything like it, and was curious to find out if there was a fundamental breakthrough which had made it possible.

> Was it better motion estimation? a better predictor? a better transform? The answer was none of these. It eventually turned out there was nothing in Digicipher that had not already been considered for the emerging MPEG-2 standard. It was, perhaps, simply very good overall engineering of the codec. [But] the trouble with the overall Digicipher system was that although GI had good codec technology they seemed to have relatively little experience of digital terrestrial transmission systems.

Ian Childs was similarly impressed, describing IBC 1990 as a "seismic moment for me personally."

> Digicipher really I think showed the possibilities for digits. Detractors were saying they'd chosen the pictures deliberately to be easy to code. And it was true that they didn't have a lot of texture in them, so they *were* easy to code. But it was the first time that somebody had said, "Actually we think the technology is good enough now that we can achieve digital transmission inside consumer bandwidths" - it really put digital on the road-map.

And Norman Green remembers the excitement:

> It was a little bit of a catalyst because, I remember quite well colleagues from the IBA saying to me, you must go down and look at [it], and everybody was scuttling off to have a look at it.

David Wood was impressed, but regarded their work as derivative rather than original:

> I think they took a lot of their ideas from work which had been done at the IBA, BBC, the RAI[56] and RTVE research laboratories in DCT compression. They did have the foresight to see how the ideas could be used for low bit-rate broadcasting, so they still should be congratulated, but when I saw it, all I could think of was that, "We could have done that first in Europe, if we had tried."

Arthur Mason recognised that there was clearly some parallel thinking going on between his team and the GI team. But the fundamental difference between them was crucial: Digicipher would not use OFDM modulation:

> When I saw what they were doing later on I saw that their RF side was based upon adaptive filters - equalisation[57] - using a single carrier approach

---

[56] RAI: the Italian public service broadcaster
[57] An adaptive equaliser is a method used by a receiver to compensate automatically for changing distortion of the received signal which may occur at different frequencies within the channel being used. One disadvantage of the technique is that implementation is wholly in receiver manufacturer's hands, and good design is expensive to implement.

which I decided was not going to be such a good approach particularly if you're going to have mobile. And also solving the problem of making [adaptive filter techniques] work is not a simple task, so I felt that their approach was actually technically wrong. I felt that the OFDM approach was the right approach. And there was lots of punch-ups with the Americans on that whole subject many years after that.

The Digicipher system's public exposure made a more immediate impact on more people than the IBA's SPECTRE paper, but those who were at that IBC were left in no doubt of what tomorrow's technology would look like. IBC 1990 had changed the thinking fundamentally. No longer was digital broadcasting all the way to the home something for the far future, for a time when technology had developed and understanding had progressed. The technology and the understanding were now very much in evidence, albeit in an embryonic form. Digital was the future. Ian Childs summed up the feeling as the delegates left Brighton that September:

> There was a significant lobby that went away and then said, look, actually this is a better way of doing it than MAC. We should focus on this for the future.

With the minds of so many talented research engineers from all over Europe now sharing that view, it was only a matter of months before the ramifications began to take effect. Having seen HDTV being compressed by Digiciper more or less successfully into the surprisingly low bit-rate of 19 Mbit/s, it was obvious to many that the door had opened on a way of transmitting a new generation of high quality television channels over existing terrestrial transmitters.

Until now, the prime focus in Europe for research into high definition had assumed that any system which came out of the process would be used for satellite broadcasting. Now it had been shown that it was possible to compress a television picture by enough to get it into a terrestrial 8 MHz channel - a much more constricted bandwidth than was available on satellite. This was new and ground-breaking stuff, and it set many research minds thinking: was the time ripe for a co-ordinated effort to develop such a system for Europe? In laboratories in the UK, Scandinavia, Germany, France and Italy where the informed debates took place the answer seemed to be 'yes'.

Meanwhile, back in the commercial world, MAC was in trouble.

Just four months after IBC, in January 1991, the UK's MAC platform, BSB, ceased transmissions following its merger with Sky. BSB's surviving programme content - and not much did survive apart from its movies and sports contracts - were then broadcast in PAL over the Astra satellite by the new company British Sky Broadcasting. There were many contributory causes of the end of BSB. It had exceptionally strong competition with Sky TV whose owner, Rupert Murdoch, had deep pockets; it was financially profligate and pitching public service broadcasting values into a thoroughly commercial marketplace. And many consumers who quite fancied more channels held back from investing in either satellite system, fearing - rightly as it turned out - a repeat of the VHS versus Betamax format war that bedevilled early sales of consumer videocassette recorders.

But the MAC technology didn't help. The set-top boxes were more expensive than Sky's because of the newer technology involved. BSB were late coming into the market - behind Sky TV - because of problems making the early receiver chipsets work. Claims of superior technical quality - cited frequently by the BSB marketing people as they sought to differentiate their product from that of Sky (with its PAL technology) - simply didn't materialise in practice: the trained eye of the engineer might see the difference, but not Joe Soap. Ian Childs and his colleagues at BBC Research had seen that part of it coming:

> Now I think the judgement here at Kingswood [was, there's] absolutely nothing wrong technically with MAC; it was a step forward from PAL. However it wasn't a sufficient step. I think our view was that most of the audience wouldn't notice the difference (just like the Part Committee, if you like) and that the additional cost of the equipment would put people off buying it. We felt that technically there were some benefits, but in business terms there were huge disbenefits and the one didn't outweigh the other.

Across Europe, the introduction of MAC satellite broadcasting was patchy, to say the least. The services that did start were confined largely to Germany and Scandinavia. Other countries were much less enthusiastic. The manufacturers for their part, with only a few exceptions, shied away from involvement in the all-important consumer equipment. As Chris Daubney put it:

> That was one of the mistakes we made with MAC, we'd done too much of it on our own - on the broadcasting side - without talking to industry, particularly the receiver industry. Bear in mind that the investment at the consumer end of television is vastly greater than it is in the broadcasting end. So you do things at the broadcasting end that don't interest the receiver end at your peril.

With the potential of all-digital systems so dramatically demonstrated it was inevitable that MAC was doomed. Later, there was a last ditch attempt to save the high definition variant: At the 1992 Barcelona Olympics - in a rather desperate final push to gain credibility for HD-MAC - Philips promised 225 hours of HD coverage using 40 HD cameras, and to deploy 1,000 HD-MAC receivers. Standard definition MAC services were short-lived in the UK, but survived a little longer in Germany and Scandinavia. But the impetus had gone, the interest was now elsewhere.

General Instruments' Digicipher system had a similar galvanising effect in the United States. The US regulator, the Federal Communications Commission, had set up an advisory committee three years before with a remit to investigate 'Advanced Television', which was generally understood to mean high definition broadcasting. At the time, satellite direct-to-home systems were being devised and seemed, as in Europe, to offer the possibility of delivering greatly improved picture and sound quality. There was also a wish to develop some means of delivering HDTV over terrestrial transmitters, and doubt as to whether the bandwidth-hungry signal could be accommodated in the 6 MHz channels used for analogue NTSC broadcasting in North America.

Two alternative approaches had been discussed: to broadcast in a new channel a signal which would augment the existing NTSC service, leaving the latter unaffected, but enabling new high definition receivers to collect and combine the two signals to give full HDTV. The second proposed a new system, incompatible with NTSC, which would 'simulcast' a second, high definition, version of the existing NTSC service. The Advisory Committee received some 23 different proposals from companies inside and outside the US, and set about evaluating them. Some proposed the augmentation approach, other proposed a simulcast: all were analogue.

The choice would be made by testing and evaluating each system in turn, whittling the candidate systems down to a short list, before declaring a winner. It was a beauty contest, and one being held for high stakes. Testing the hardware was placed in the hands of two laboratories in Alexandria, Virginia: one was the Advanced Television Test Center, a private, non-profit organisation put together jointly by American broadcasters and industry, and the Advanced Television facility of Cable Laboratories, Inc, the research and development consortium of the American cable television industry. The facility became known simply as 'CableLabs'[58]. In 1990, the FCC decided that it preferred a simulcast system and selected a short list of a handful of the original proposals. Their plan was that a choice could be made by the end of 1991 and high definition services would begin six years later.

At which point one of the five short-listed system proponents, General Instruments, put forward a completely new proposal for an all-digital system. Three of the four others immediately announced that they intended to submit their own proposals for all-digital systems. The remaining proponent, the Japanese broadcaster NHK, stuck with its analogue proposal, and eventually dropped out. The Advisory Committee's schedule was now delayed by two years as a further round of hardware testing and evaluation of the new proposals took place.[59]

---

[58] A third laboratory in Canada carried out further subjective testing.

[59] The proponents were: a consortium including the David Sarnoff Research Center, the broadcaster NBC, and two manufacturers, Thomson and Philips; Zenith, AT&T, NHK, and

So, almost overnight, the United States became fully committed to a digital terrestrial future. The point was not lost on the Europeans.

Europe at the beginning of the 1990s could boast an impressive spread of centres of excellence working in the field of broadcasting technology. In Britain, of course, there were the research laboratories of the public service broadcasters: BBC Research at Kingswood Warren in Surrey, and the IBA's research base at Crawley Court in Winchester which was privatised along with the IBA's nationwide network of television transmitting stations and bought initially by an American company and became part of NTL. In France there was CCETT, a co-operative establishment formed by the transmission authority Télédiffusion de France and others, and based at a modern facilities on the outskirts of Rennes in Brittany and in Metz in Eastern France. In Italy, the public broadcaster, RAI, had an established and highly competent research arm in Turin. In Germany, there was the Institut für Rundfunktechnik (IRT) based in Munich. And in Scandinavia, the Swedish public broadcaster SVT together with others was also active. All at various stages would contribute materially to the creation of the European digital television broadcasting standard, DVB, each bringing to it the fruits of their own researches and their own specialisms.

All now shared the view that any real technological advance for application in Europe must involve a high degree of collaboration between their opposite numbers in the other countries of Europe. There was no future for the national rivalries that had bedevilled the early arguments about line standards in the 1950s, the arguments about colour systems in the 1960s, and the schisms of the MAC system which occurred in the 1980s. Too much was at stake: there had to be one digital system for Europe and, if possible, one that could be adopted worldwide. The obvious consequence of that thinking was that there needed to be a pan-European - or better still - world forum in which the new standard could be argued over and decided. The biggest obstacle to turning that concept into reality was politics.

New television technology in the early 90s was a political hot potato. National governments in many countries had an interest, and so did the European Commission. In fact the Commission was ahead of the game, much to the chagrin of some national governments, particularly that of the United Kingdom. More than anywhere else in Europe, the stark reality of what happens when altruistic ideals applied to new technology (MAC) collide head-on with established technology (PAL) combined with free-market entrepreneurism (for example, Sky TV) was all too plain. It was too early for the free-market ideas of Britain's government to gain credence in

---

another consortium in which General Instruments teamed up with the Massachusetts Institute of Technology.

much of Europe. And crucially, the Commission was still gung-ho for MAC, and particularly for HD-MAC, which it saw as the saviour of the European lead in television broadcasting technology, and which it sought to promote at every juncture.

The result of all this was that, no matter how eminent your research was, no matter in how high regard your research institution was held, no chief executive was going to recommend publicly to anybody that the Commission were barking up the wrong tree and the future really lay in some work as yet seen and understood only by a relatively small number of experts. No: things - if they were going to move on - had to do so behind the scenes.

7
The Early Collaborative Projects

The early years of the 1990s saw the start of a number of collaborative projects in which the emphasis swung away from the development of high definition television for satellite broadcasting towards the investigation of multi-channel digital terrestrial systems. A broadly similar view of the future began to form in the minds of research engineers in many European laboratories: MAC was a dead end, HDTV would come eventually, but not until display technology improved and came down in price. Long before that happened, digital television broadcasting would be possible and necessary, and would be multi-channel. The Americans had shown their determination to develop a viable digital technology for both satellite and terrestrial television. Europe needed to get going. The European Commission was prepared to give financial assistance to some research projects, even if at the top political levels, MAC and HD-MAC were incontrovertibly for now and digital was for another day.

The IBA's SPECTRE research programme was, of course, already running in the late 1980s, but it was perhaps the last major research project undertaken by a single organisation in isolation. The important work of the 1990s would now largely be done in collaborative projects, and NTL - now continuing the SPECTRE work - would participate in several. In 1990, the Swedish public service broadcaster SVT set up the HD-DIVINE project, which drew participants from elsewhere in Scandinavia. German industry joined together in a national collaborative programme, HDTV-T. And in 1991 two important international projects were set up under the European Commission RACE II programme, HD-SAT and dTTb. All would make material contributions to the system of digital television that would emerge later in the same decade.

When, in the course of 1990, the Independent Television Commission was formed, the old IBA transmission and research arms were sold to NTL. An agreement was brokered whereby the ITC would contract NTL's research arm to continue with certain research projects which included frequency planning and, crucially, the further development of work on digital compression and modulation - the core of the SPECTRE concept.

Up until that point, all the work that Arthur Mason's team had done had been theoretical:

> We had done experiments because, you know, an OFDM modem [capable of working at the bit-rates needed for digital television] didn't exist[60]. The video compression ideas were modelled on the computer really just using students to hack it together, and OFDM things were sort of simulated. But I think I proved it would all work in the laboratory based upon my theoretical assumptions. But it was still a big hypothesis. There was still the thing, would it interfere with analogue? All that was a little bit of an open question.

Arthur Mason was confident in his prediction that, using just a fraction of the power of an equivalent analogue transmitter, a digital OFDM transmitter would give roughly equal coverage without interference. But there was only one way to find out: to try it for real. Now, with a guarantee of funding for a few years, it would be possible to do so. However, negotiations went to the wire, as Arthur Mason recalls vividly:

> It was 1st January 1991 when the IBA formally came to an end and all the contracts should have been be signed. [But] the contract wasn't signed, and I remember phoning up my boss who was Mike Windram at the time and saying, "Do I need to come in? Do I have a job in the morning?"

Fortunately for the early development of digital terrestrial television, the old IBA researchers had both jobs and funding. Arthur Mason and his team immediately set about the construction of a modem - the OFDM modulator and demodulator pair, and a codec - the compression coder and decoder pair. Their first modem was limited to 512 carriers, because that was as much as the available chips could reasonably cope with, and had no error correction.[61] It was built, remembers Arthur Mason, to allow changes to be made as experience in practice might require:

---

[60] COFDM modems for DAB radio had been developed several years previously but had a maximum bit-rate of about 1.5Mbit/s

[61] Hence OFDM: there was no "coding" as in COFDM which DAB and later implementations of DTT modems included.

When we first designed it we chose to use DSPs which are basically highly parallelised computers - so it was a whole stack of computers in parallel. So we could always change the software. So for instance when we went from 512 carriers to 2k carriers to 8k carriers - whatever we wanted - all we had to do was to change the software, we didn't actually have to change the hardware. At the time as a research prototype - because obviously I'd done a lot of research over the years - and I'm always very conscious about the fact that the only thing you know about research is that it's going to change, so we designed it in a way that was easily changeable. Easily: it might have been a year's worth of software you had to write, but it was do-able, and you didn't totally have to start from scratch.

The modem allowed a payload of 13 Mbit/s - 12 Mbit/s for vision and 1 Mbit/s for audio. A source of pristine digital component pictures to feed the coder was sought - and found. Arthur Mason:

At the time ITC had purchased a Sony digital television tape recorder - D1 - which was brand new technology at the time. It was 270 Mbit/s uncompressed and we plugged it into our digital compression coder and we compressed it down to 12 Mbit/s and we transmitted it and decompressed it back up to 270 Mbit/s then put it into this TV and fed it in RGB so it never went through PAL. [Using PAL] would have been something we wanted to avoid like the plague.

The next stage was to find a suitable site to carry out the field trials. Arthur Mason identified Stockland Hill, a transmitter which serves much of Devon, as a promising location. Towards the edge of its service area lay Exeter which would offer suitable venues for demonstrations. It had the advantage of being near the coast so that potential interference over the sea from French transmitters could be studied, and it could use the same channel as one of the analogue transmitters at Rowridge, on the Isle of Wight, which would allow study of low-level co-channel interference. Much of the western side of town was shielded from the main Stockland Hill transmitter to the East and reception was provided by a low power analogue relay. The site therefore had prospects for studying digital relays. But Arthur Mason adds mischievously that there was another reason for choosing a transmitter in the West Country for his first experiments:

In fact the reason why I started in Stockland Hill rather than in London - which I think was the BBC's approach later on which was to start from the most high-profile transmitter - I actually started at a very low-profile transmitter so that if I did cause interference I could just quietly slide away and hope no-one would notice.

There was great concern on everybody's part that there should be no interference to the analogue services in the area. The Radiocommunications Agency, which had granted the temporary licence to the IBA experimenters to use a vacant UHF channel, had a representative present when Arthur Mason's transmitter was first switched on. They wound the power of the

OFDM transmitter up very slowly indeed, with all eyes glued on an analogue receiver in case any interference became visible. But the computer predictions that Mason's team had made were accurate. There was no interference.

They put a receiver and measuring equipment into a Renault Espace with a telescopic mast to raise a receiving aerial to the standard height for measurement of ten metres, and hitched a generator trailer to the back. This trundled round the coverage area - up hill and down dale, behind trees and in amongst buildings, near and far from the transmitter, stopping from time to time to look at the signal they got and the pictures it gave them, measuring the levels of interference between the digital and analogue transmissions in adjacent channels. At a second transmitter, Beacon Hill, which lies twenty-odd miles further west from Stockland Hill, they installed a second transmitter so that they could measure interference between two COFDM digital signals. Later, they changed the Beacon Hill transmitter from being a deliberate interferer to form a single frequency network with the main transmitter, and did a new set of measurements. And they took their results back to the laboratory and compared them with the theoretical models.

Arthur Mason was still worried about interference with analogue, especially under abnormal conditions:

> If you have anomalous propagation conditions, which only occur say one per cent of the time, where you get say foggy days in November, temperature inversion layers or humidity inversion layers, you can actually have television coming right in from Germany, so obviously we had to design the system to work in the most difficult environments. I remember driving around in the fog in November at Stockland Hill trying to find interference and we couldn't find any. We were very concerned at the time that people would come down like a ton of bricks on us, and say you're interfering with analogue, you've got to switch it off, you can't do anything. In fact that never happened, and I think we came to the conclusion that we were actually much more conservative about the interference into analogue than we ever needed to be. We could probably have bumped the power up by 10dB and nobody would have noticed.

In one crucial set of measurements, NTL demonstrated one of the great advantages of digital terrestrial transmission: with the power of Stockland Hill's experimental OFDM transmitter just *one hundredth* of the power of the permanently installed analogue transmitters, they measured a comparable coverage area.

It was time to trumpet their achievement. In January 1993, a series of demonstration was mounted at an hotel in Exeter to which the great and good of the industry, together with regulators, civil servants and politicians were invited. The results impressed the visitors, although the technical parameters were still far from being the mature set of later research demonstrators. The primitive OFDM system transmitted an MPEG-1, QPSK-modulated bitstream, although the desire to move to 16-QAM was even then being expressed.

For a few years after that, NTL's work on SPECTRE did little more than tick over, following developments elsewhere and contributing to collaborative work on DTT. Arthur Mason delegated more and more, and sent his deputies to international meetings. The company now had other priorities. The ITC five year funding for SPECTRE - and the other work which NTL was contracted to undertake for its erstwhile parent - was set to diminish over the period. So Mike Windram, now head of this surviving team within NTL, together with Gordon Drury and his colleagues, started putting together a business plan for their unit and looked for clients who wanted to start digital television broadcasting. They looked particularly to the less fully regulated areas of the world and shortly identified one potential customer in M-NET, a Dutch company operating out of South Africa, which had some terrestrial analogue stations and a regional analogue satellite service covering southern Africa. M-NET wanted the ability to broadcast more services, and were looking for the digital technology to do it. Gordon Drury remembers:

> So we found them, we did this deal, we signed a contract, there was a development programme in which we would develop the technology to their requirements and fitting in the conditional access elements and .... we had to find the chips. We had to go to California and talk to C-Cube and say, we really want these chips, we're not joking: here's the funding, here's the deal ...

At around the same time, NTL received an approach from News Corporation who were looking at the feasibility of starting a digital satellite service themselves, although Windram, Drury and their colleagues did not - then - know where in the world that might be:

> We were working in '92-3-4 on this development programme in secret - because we had to keep the M-Net people apart from the News [Corp] people. But we knew that each knew the other was about, and they both knew there was benefit in having a developed technology which they could both use.

Eventually, BSkyB's UK digital satellite service would use MPEG coders developed by Gordon Drury and his colleagues, but not before NTL's research arm had been sold on to News Data Communications, NDC - another Murdoch company which supplied his analogue broadcasting system with its vital conditional access technology. The marriage was an obvious one for News Corporation. The merged companies were shortly to become News Digital Systems, NDS.

But SPECTRE continued to operate, with various modifications, for some years. Forward Error Correction - the 'C' in COFDM - was added, and the modem was adapted to be configurable between three modulation modes - QPSK, 8-PSK and 16-QAM, and to offer a payload not only of 13 Mbit/s as it had to begin with, but the choice of 24 Mbit/s as well. Gordon Drury's compression engine too, was becoming more MPEG-like as he and his colleagues joined the collaborative effort to define the MPEG-2 standard. Towards the end of its life, SPECTRE was moved to a London transmitter in the run-up to the launch of a public service in the later 1990s, to begin transmission of a DVB compliant multiplex.

Arthur Mason was able to return to IBC in 1992 to give a paper on the Stockland Hill trials. But by then, he shared a day's conference session with speakers describing other parallel projects: there was a paper on the collaborative VADIS project which was working on MPEG-2 coders, a paper from the French laboratory CCETT on their STERNE modem, and from the manufacturer Thomson on the mathematics of COFDM. And a paper from General Instruments on developments in their Digicipher system.

In Sweden, back in 1990, the origins of the HD-DIVINE project were quite different from those of SPECTRE. The similarity was that the progenitor of HD-DIVINE was SVT, the Swedish public service broadcaster, which like the IBA was part of the public sector, and had an established and well-regarded Research and Development department. SVT's decision to investigate digital terrestrial television was taken in the Autumn of 1990. It followed an unfruitful period in which their labs had tried to develop a PAL-compatible high definition system which, in the end, turned out to be a complex system with poor picture quality.

SVT felt that the approach of the Eureka95 HDTV project - which had its sights set firmly on satellite broadcasting - had missed the point. SVT's view was that terrestrial public service broadcasters need to provide regional programmes, and that terrestrial transmission is the natural home for them. Like many others, the SVT team had been impressed with the General Instruments Digicipher system demonstrated at IBC earlier that year. But SVT formed the firm view that any new system should be suitable for all delivery systems - and that included terrestrial.

By 1992, they were able to demonstrate an initial system at IBC, and by 1993 their system had some added improvements. Like SPECTRE, HD-DIVINE used a home-grown compression system, using the available techniques of motion compensation and DCT: their COFDM modulation parameters were 512 carriers at 16-QAM which gave a gross payload of 27 Mbit/s - again not dissimilar to SPECTRE. In one respect, however, their approach was innovative: the system employed four coders each of which compressed incoming standard definition to around 6 Mbit/s, allowing it to carry four services in a multiplex, but could also be reconfigured to code a single high definition picture by dividing the HDTV picture into four vertical stripes and sending one stripe to each coder. In the receiver, the four decoder output were stitched together to reconstitute the HDTV picture.

The approach in Germany was different again. There a national collaborative project, HDTV-T, was set up under the chairmanship of the Heinrich Hertz Institute. Other participants included another research institute IRT, the manufacturing companies Bosch, Grundig, Seimens and Thomson Consumer Electronics, and the chip-maker ITT-Intermetall. Its remit was to investigate possibilities for digital television and HDTV broadcasting over terrestrial channels, satellite channels, and over broadband cable networks. It concerned itself with a flexible approach to using the data capacity of a COFDM multiplex, and did work on hierarchical modulation: it took the use of COFDM as a given, and put its main efforts into looking at source coding, relying heavily upon, but also making important contributions to, the work then under way in the Moving Pictures Experts Group to develop the MPEG-2 compression system.

Two more important projects started in 1991, HD-SAT and dTTb, and both were set up under the aegis of the European Commission as part of the RACE II programme. This EC programme recognised what visionaries were beginning to call 'convergence', a thesis that said that once you had converted your messages or your information into digits, then no matter whether the data represented sound, pictures, or any other information, a digital means of transmission could handle them all, and that future technology design should therefore reflect that and allow for sufficient flexibility to cope.

So RACE II had the far-sighted purpose of funding research into the eventual bringing together of telecommunications, broadcasting and personal computer services. It also sought - successfully as it turned out - to foster pre-competitive co-operation between major companies (as it were, to collaborate on writing the rule-book and marking out the playing field before competing for the sporting trophy), and sought common functional specifications across separate delivery mechanisms. It naturally wished to promote open standardisation to encourage wider use of any eventual outcome.

HD-SAT's specific purpose was to investigate studio quality high definition satellite broadcasting - how to devise a system which would deliver to a receiver pictures as good as those leaving the high definition camera.

It also set out to find a solution to the problems of what became known as the 'digital cliff'. When an analogue signal becomes weak, the television picture becomes noisy and grainy in texture. The weaker the signal, the more indistinct the picture detail becomes. With digital transmission things are different: as the signal level decreases and the noise - or interference - becomes significant, there comes a point where the picture freezes or disappears altogether. What, the project asked itself, could be done to mitigate this? They answered the question by proposing, and then investigating, a system whereby the very high bit-rate (45 Mbit/s) high definition signal was accompanied by a standard definition copy at a much lower bit-rate (5 Mbit/s) which could be made to be more robust and therefore receivable when the high demand high definition signal failed. The receiver could then automatically switch to the more robust but lower definition copy.

HD-SAT also included in their programme research into suitable modulation schemes for terrestrial and cable, and the proposed MMDS microwave local distribution standard that was being talked about, and future cable distribution systems based on a technology known as Asynchronous Transfer Mode.

Of these early collaborative projects, the one in which the thinking was perhaps moving closest to the way in which DTT in Europe would finally be implemented was the dTTb Project. Also set up in 1991 under the RACE II programme, and led by the French research laboratory, CCETT, the Digital Terrestrial Television Broadcasting programme ran from 1991 to 1995. A number of research establishments with activities in the field from across Europe were represented: they included from Britain the BBC and the ITC, from Spain the transmission company Retevision, from France, CCETT and Télédiffusion de France (TDF), from Germany IRT and from Italy the research laboratories of RAI, the Italian public service broadcaster.

The CCETT laboratory in Rennes had independently taken forward their earlier work on COFDM for DAB, and had developed a system the called STERNE (Système de Télévision en Radiodiffusion Numérique) designed for use in 8 MHz transmission channels and to deliver picture and sound quality no less good than D2-MAC. This, together with ITC/NTL's SPECTRE work, formed an important initial contribution to the dTTb project.

The dTTb's remit was to define a digital terrestrial broadcasting system based on 64-QAM COFDM for use in the existing European UHF broadcasting channels. The stipulation of 64-QAM is an interesting one, because it implies a wish for the highest feasible data capacity in the transmitted multiplex. There was no doubt that dTTb was aiming for a high capacity multi-channel digital terrestrial system, and that it had no particular interest in HDTV. Many of its preliminary concepts - of using COFDM to facilitate single frequency networks, of a hierarchy of parameters for picture quality and for robustness of transmission, of using statistical multiplexing (in which the complexity of a picture at any moment in time determined the bit-rate allocation), and of the need for digital transmissions to co-exist with analogue transmissions in a crowded European spectrum - would form the mould from which the eventual European DTT system would be cast. But first, there were the differences of opinion amongst participants.

Work during the first two years had led to the point where there were two contending systems, one proposed by CCETT and the other from Philips. Bob Ely, from BBC Research, was involved in the project and remembers how it was decided to resolve the serious division of opinion within the Project:

> In the end the project was in danger of falling apart because of this tremendous rivalry between these two systems. And I was appointed to the very unenviable task of actually achieving a single system. The original proposal was that I should supervise a shoot-out between the two systems. I decided that that was going to be a futile waste of effort, because both systems had got good features, and probably the best way forward was to merge these two systems.

Bob Ely's proposed approach was not what the Project had in mind: rather it expected an intensive period of testing and measurement of the two systems, an evaluation and a comparison of the results, and the declaration of an outright winner. This was the approach in America, where Cablelabs had been set up at huge expense to test the various contenders for the ATSC system. Within the dTTb Project, the BBC labs at Kingswood Warren had been given, as Bob Ely put it:

> ... the scraps of test and measurement. It was the time when about half the staff were made redundant, and all the traditional facilities like the workshops, drawing office and so on were all abolished ... I simply didn't have the time to set up the European equivalent [of Cablelabs] because Kingswood was going through its most severe period of restructuring and redundancies.

The differences between the two systems was down within the detail. CCETT were very keen to include a recently developed concept of 'turbo-codes', which were another of the very powerful error correction tools for use in COFDM. In the end, Bob Ely says:

> Turbo codes were not adopted. They would have been better, but a) they were not tried and tested, and b) a much bigger obstacle was patents: there was going to be a huge negotiation [over] royalties.

Another issue had to do with the system of synchronisation and equalisation. Synchronisation between receiver and transmitter is required in order that correct demodulation of the signal can be carried out. In those days, the preferred approach included the use of 'cazacs'[62], in the

---

[62] Constant Amplitude Zero Autocorrelation Code.

transmitted signal which assists synchronisation in the receiver. Similarly, to assist the receiver to 'equalise' (i.e. compensate for) the impact of multipath propagation, 'nulls' (unmodulated carriers) were periodically inserted into the transmitted signal. So far so good: but, as Bob Ely found, the trouble was that the two groups had very different proposals as how to implement the 'nulls' and 'cazacs' and how to extract that synchronisation information, and compounding the difficulty was that everybody had simulation results but no actual hardware results.

> It was difficult therefore to actually evaluate the systems as you would have done normally in the field, and therefore you really had to take very much an uninformed guess as to which system was going to provide the right balance of complexity and performance. Certainly for me again that was a watershed, because up to then I'd been working on systems which I knew inside out, I could test in my own lab, and there was no .... unknown. I was now working with systems which nobody at Kingswood understood properly, we'd never built a COFDM modem of our own, we didn't have resources available to check the simulations that the other labs who were working on it did, and so the only way in which I could actually determine who to believe was by interrogating them and working out whether they were really telling the truth!

In the end, the project succeeded in merging the two alternative approaches into one agreed specification. In doing so, the project demonstrated that there was a good alternative to the 'shoot-out' principle of resolving differences. The merging together of good, workable ideas - rather than choosing one or the other - very often results in a solution which is better than the separate constituent parts. It also ensures acceptance of the agreed solution by the owners of the intellectual property rights which are included, and avoids the risk that the losing side in a shoot-out might be tempted to pick up their toys and go home - only to develop their own competing system.

Within months, the agreed approach had been turned into hardware - a working COFDM transmitter and receiver. The dTTb specification, and the test and measurement results which came from a real working system, provided one of the principal inputs to the development of the future European system definition.

In the summer of 1995, the dTTb system - not yet DVB compliant - was demonstrated at the Montreux Symposium. In those days, the Montreux event took place on alternate years from IBC. It was still a different animal to the trade show that was IBC. Montreux, an Edwardian spa town on the bank of Lake Geneva, was the place for research teams to present papers and give demonstrations of their current work. The 1995 demonstration, which also involved the HD-SAT consortium, was an ambitious one: it set out to demonstrate the combined technical and service proposition that a digital television future would hold. A high definition channel was broadcast over satellite to the venue, and a terrestrial multiplex of four standard definition services was broadcast in an SFN from transmitters at Thollon, on the other side of the lake, and from another near Montreux. The HDTV and SDTV signals were also distributed to the venue over the Montreux cable television network. Digital satellite, cable and terrestrial.

Andrew Oliphant of BBC Research, and one of the prime movers in organising this highly successful event, wrote with justifiable confidence that "we believe we have shown the future of television in Europe." HDTV in Europe was then still eleven years away as a commercial service, but Oliphant was right: everybody now knew what the digital future would look like, and that it would work.

But all those early projects, SPECTRE, STERNE, HDTV-T, HD-SAT and dTTb, were research programmes. They looked at what was desirable and whether it was possible: they investigated different technologies, and each had particular aims. Their purpose was to advance the state of under-standing by doing theoretical work, certainly, but also by building experimental equipment that would substantiate - or otherwise - the theor-etical predictions. None of them pretended to be trying to set a standard, or to be setting the parameters for consumer equipment design.

That required the creation of a quite different project.

8
Towards a European System

In the few years before the seminal events at the 1990 International Broadcasting Convention, the idea of devising a standard for digital television had cropped up from time to time within the European Broadcasting Union. Even to the enthusiasts, however, the way forward was not obvious, and to begin with there was less than universal support for such a project. There were a number of issues that could not, to begin with, easily be resolved. There was the changing nature of the industry in which the broadcasters and the manufacturers to a greater extent than before had to think of their market-place as European rather than national. This new view was being encouraged by the European Commission, sometimes with Directives and increasingly with funding for research into new technologies within international collaborative projects. And the recent introduction of the MAC system, again with strong Commission support, made manufacturers in particular unwilling to contemplate another new technology and another range of consumer products so soon. So, in the late eighties, the prospect of creating a standard for digital television was bedevilled by complexities which went beyond the undoubted complexities of the technology itself.

Until this time, many technical standards for broadcasting had been devised largely by European Broadcasting Union: draft standards would be agreed by the membership and passed to other international bodies - the CCIR or the ITU - for formal adoption. The EBU had been founded after the second world war and, following the end of the Cold War, had merged with its eastern European equivalent, the OIRT. EBU membership consisted almost exclusively of state regulated public service broadcasters and their regulators, often bound by domestic government policy. Consequently, the draft standards it proposed for adoption were those devised by broadcasting engineers and often took little account of the views of manufacturers. (Or, for that matter, the new kids on the block, the satellite broadcasters.) The Irishman George Waters, who was Technical Director of the EBU during the 1980s, recognised that this had to change:

> When I became Technical Director of the EBU I think there might have been some separation - if that's the right word - between the industry and the broadcasters, and if you go back some years I would even say the broadcasters were perhaps too arrogant in their approach to the whole issue because the broadcasters would dictate exactly what should be done and the industry would follow. And I think that was wrong.

Waters and his technical colleagues decided to form a closer relationship with the industry, and set up regular meetings with EACEM, the European Association of Consumer Electronics Manufacturers.

In a separate development which recognised the same need to broaden the base of industry representation in decision-making, a new standard-isation body ETSI - the European Technical Standards Institute - was formed in 1988. Its inception was driven by a British civil servant, Stephen Temple of the DTI, with encouragement from the European Commission. In future, European telecommunications and broadcasting standardisation would be the remit of this broader-based organisation, working in partnership with the global equivalent, the International Telecommun-ications Union (ITU).

The EBU quickly established an EBU/ETSI Joint Technical Committee which held regular meetings and reinforced the dialogue between the broadcasters and the rest of the industry.

It was therefore with the background of this newly established and improved but more complex framework of necessary liaison with industry that the idea of a project to develop a digital television standard first arose within the EBU. David Wood remembers one discussion on the subject:

> SVT suggested in 1989 to our Working Party V that we should have a European equivalent of the ATSC to devise a digital broadcasting standard. We discussed this in the EBU Technical Committee, and these ideas, and those of others, eventually led to the DVB Project. Everybody realised that the time was right to have a project. But at that time it was seen as a project to develop a digital terrestrial television system which was probably going to be high definition, rather than a satellite system.

One difficulty was that digital television meant different things to different people. Was the discussion about devising a studio standard, a high definition extension of the recently introduced Recommendation 601 for digital standard definition, to be used in studios and other production areas, or was it about a system for broadcasting digital signals to the home? As George Waters says,

They really are two separate things and they very often got confused in the arguments that were going around at that time.

For a while, the discussions in the EBU were positive. But only for a while. George Waters:

During those meetings there was a small sub-group set up by the EBU under the chairmanship of John Forrest - Working Party V - which was responsible new systems and services. And he came back and reported that the industry was very interested in collaborating with the EBU in the development of digital television. During the course of that meeting and probably subsequent meetings some disagreements developed between some members of the Bureau and that project was left hanging for a while.

Later, the topic was discussed in the EBU/ETSI/CENELEC Joint Technical Committee, then under the chairmanship of Charlie Sandbank of the BBC, but again, no initiative was undertaken. Then the German Ministry of Posts and Telecommunications laid on a big meeting in Brussels with the same idea. Ed Wilson was there, and remembers the meeting as ...

.... trying to build some understanding with the European Union, with the Commission, inviting broadcasters and consumer manufacturers along, trying to bring them into an environment where they would naturally, spontaneously see that there was some progress that could be made here. The chairman at that particular meeting, Armin Silberhorn, I recall very distinctly, was annoyed when his agenda was taken over by the consumer manufacturers who were saying, hey, just a minute, we don't want to go all-digital yet, these things take time and in the meantime we're much more keen to roll out D2-MAC equipment. After all we've invested a lot of development into this, we've got standards in place at ETSI; this is a market-place we need to exploit first. It was a verbal hijacking of the meeting, but obviously there was momentum building up on the all-digital front which wasn't going to be stymied in that way.

Back at the EBU Technical Committee, in April 1991, George Waters tried again:

I reintroduced the subject at a later date and it was decided that we should then again attempt to do something about digital television. And almost at the same time we were told that industry had taken the initiative.

The meeting which did resolve to take the initiative was a small, private, and rather clandestine gathering of seven mostly German industry executives which took place on the third and fourth of May 1991 at the Schloss Hotel Schönburg - a converted castle overlooking the Rhine in Southern Germany.

The seven men were all friends as well as colleagues, and frequently met as members of the PALplus Board. Two were from Germany's public service

101

broadcasters ARD and ZDF, and five from major manufacturers, Grundig, Nokia, Philips, Thomson, and the chip-maker Intermetall. Five were German, one a Dutchman and one came from Belgium.[63] From their at times heated debate came a resolve to start the process which would eventually lead to the formation of the Digital Video Broadcasting Project.

Professor Ulrich Reimers now runs the Institute for Communications Technology at Braunschweig Technical University near Hamburg, but at the time of the Schönburg meeting was Director of Engineering at Norddeutscher Rundfunk (NDR) the public broadcaster for northern Germany:

> The background of all this lies in the fact that its the same individuals who were instrumental in the PALplus in those days, knowing that HD-MAC would go nowhere And that was the incentive. So we got together and we tried to find a way out - mainly for European industry. With D2-MAC and HD-MAC we had entered a dead-end street, some of us more than others saw the wall at the end of the dead-end street, but Europe was still running at full pace. The seven of us saw that this would not become successful and therefore we got together for a very secret meeting over a weekend in a castle on the Rhine river, by invitation of the Director of Engineering of ZDF.[64]

The secrecy was crucial, as were the many meetings which took place in the months ahead. Reimers explains:

> Now the secrecy was due to the fact that when we met there it was a dangerous meeting for some. Can you imagine for example our friends in Thomson and in Philips of course at that stage still fully behind the HD-MAC project - they'd got all kinds of millions of Euros from the Commission in support of the activities to develop the HD-MAC system. So the meeting which they attended which did look at things beyond the HD-MAC strategies agreed by the boards of their companies at that stage really was a little dangerous.

Their judgement was that MAC would not become a major new trans-mission standard because PAL was already being used for direct-to-home satellite broadcasting. They believed that high definition television was at least five to eight years in the future as a mass consumer proposition (it turned out to be very much longer), and they knew that digital compression technology was coming on by leaps and bounds, and its feasibility as a consumer proposition was not many years away. They agreed that work on

---

[63] The six were: A Ziemer, Director of Engineering at ZDF, the second German television network; Hans Georg Junginger representing Grundig; Theo Peek representing Philips; Erich Geiger from Thomson; Charles Schepers of the chip-maker Intermetall; Helmut Stein, representing Grundig; and Ulrich Reimers, Director of Engineering at Norddeutscher Rundfunk (NDR) the main public service broadcaster in Northern Germany, but representing ARD which is the federation of regional public broadcasters.

[64] Zwei Deutsche Fernehen, Germany's second public service television network.

the standardisation of digital video broadcasting in Europe should begin as soon as possible.

To succeed, they concluded, the work would have to be collaborative, and to involve as broad a spectrum as possible of representatives from across the whole industry and from all over Europe. The failure of MAC had been, at least partly, judged to be the consequence of a lack of broad industry consensus during its development stage. Standardisation for a new European digital system needed to avoid that trap. So the first task that faced the six was to bring together as many interested parties as they could. It took a long time, nine months, as Reimers remembers:

> This whole time was totally spent with trying to familiarise people, to help our friends in France across the hurdle, try to invite our friends in the UK, to make sure that no, we're not talking about shooting at HD-MAC but we need to look at other prospects and look at what the people in the US are doing. I mean this was very helpful: the activities in the US showed that there were things beyond analogue television and that was very helpful to us because to some extent it created awareness, to some extent it created readiness to move. [But it] took us nine months or so until we had a meeting which people could attend and were not scared of being shot dead after returning to the normal office.

In the course of those nine months, the original Schönburg seven grew steadily in number until the group embraced broadcasters, network operators, manufacturers and regulators from eight countries. They set about drafting a Memorandum of Understanding stating the aims and the ground rules of the so-called European Launching Group for Digital Video Broadcasting (ELG). By the early part of 1992, the Group began to meet regularly. For many participants, as Reimers recalls, it was a slow start:

> When we all met there we were a bunch of people who at that point only knew a very little about the prospects for digital television. Very little. For example, video source coding: we all noted that we didn't know much about the possibilities and about the limits - imagine that in those days MPEG-2 didn't exist. There existed MPEG-1 but the prospects of MPEG-2 ... was known [only] by some real experts in video coding but not as much by the people who were really in the broadcast scene like ourselves. Don't overestimate what we knew at that stage. No, it was more a strategic meeting, about trying to find a way out of that dead-end street. It was very early days.

And the political sensitivity of even discussing an alternative to the European Commission mandated HD-MAC system seriously inhibited some of the participants. Reimers again:

> It was very difficult. I remember that we had a meeting in Bad Godesberg near Bonn on the Rhine river, and that meeting ... many countries had sent representatives. One of the recollections I have is that our friends in France were very much ... governed by their government position [which was that]

still the goal was HD-MAC. So it was a difficult discussion about what would we do, what would we not do, would it be allowed to work on this, and it took quite some time until we had everybody at least prepared to give it a try and to really look at what could be the potential impact and so on and so on. We all started with a fear that political repercussions, after so much money had been gone into HD-MAC, would all strike us politically or possibly even individually.

So the Launching Group worked very much behind the scenes, avoiding any publicity, and struggling to find a form for the draft MoU which would be acceptable to all its participants. Despite these reservations, things were beginning to happen. The EBU was invited to join and moved quickly in support of the initiative, but at the same time felt it had to be, as George Waters put it, "diplomatic" about the way it did so.

> There was some sensitivity. The Commission were pushing the MAC system very hard and particularly HD-MAC at that stage. Certainly from the EBU point of view - although we may not have done this officially - there was a resistance to it. I think we at that stage realised that the future for HDTV anyway was not in analogue technology but in digital technology, and I think from that point of view there was a certain amount of sensitivity in the air all right, yes.

In the Spring of 1992, the ELG set up a 'Working Group on Digital Television Broadcasting' (WGDTB) to look at the possibilities of the technology. Reimers took the chair and the first meeting was close to his NDR office near Hamburg. David Wood was the secretary and one of two vice-chairmen was Ian Childs of BBC Research:[65]

> To start off with, the Working Group was looking purely at terrestrial. We started off by trying to define what digital broadcasting should do. Absolute blank sheet of paper. Should it be HDTV? Should it be mobile? Should it be multiple channels, single channel; should it be hierarchical? And we had a whole lot of discussions to decide what it was we wanted to develop. It's interesting to look back on it now, because HDTV was definitely on the list of potential outcomes at that stage.

It was clearly a complex issue: different countries saw different purposes in terrestrial digital broadcasting. And the technology was going to be difficult to work through. It certainly was beginning to look like several years work. Recognising that this rapidly growing activity could not remain for long in low profile, George Waters wrote a carefully crafted editorial in the EBU Technical Review.[66] In it, he explained that his organisation had to give support to all valid solutions to the commonly held wish to move to "16:9, better picture quality and better sound." But there could be no answer by the EBU to the question, "how?", except by reaffirming support

---

[65] The other was Daniel Sauvet-Goichon of TDF.
[66] *Horses for Courses.* Editorial in the EBU Technical Review, Autumn 1992.

for "all valid solutions", which meant PALplus, D2-MAC, HD-MAC and "the cry from certain Members" for all-digital terrestrial transmission.

The EBU remained an important and respected body, but no longer were the public service broadcasters the sole occupants of their environment, in stable monopolies or duopolies in each country. In the late eighties the cold wind of competition was being pushed ahead by the UK's DTI and its equivalent in some other countries: there was talk of privatisation, especially of telecoms and transmission utilities. There were new commercial broadcasters. Manufacturers increasingly sought markets for their products that went beyond their national boundary to encompass all of Europe certainly, and a world market if possible.

Understandably this changing landscape preoccupied the public service broadcasters. Developing a new system of terrestrial transmission wasn't high on their list of priorities. George Waters remembers that, in the early days of the ELG:

> Certainly the public broadcasters were going through very difficult days financially, because all this new competition had come into their world and with commercial stations and satellite stations and so on, they were feeling the pinch. They didn't want to know really at that stage about anything that was going to cost them more money. So they weren't overly enthusiastic. Now they weren't anti, or anything like that, but they didn't show an awful lot of enthusiasm at any rate within the EBU and elsewhere.

But enthusiasm for solving the technical challenges, and perhaps an understanding that doing so would provide a competitive edge, was strong and growing stronger in the minds of knowledgeable engineers. In the months which followed the Schönburg meeting, while Ulrich Reimers and his group of friends were working to pull together the Launching Group, a real shift had taken place in a number of research organisations in Europe. In the Spring of 1991, the number of research programmes looking at digital terrestrial broadcasting increased markedly. The SPECTRE project, begun in the UK by the IBA, was now jointly in the hands of the ITC - the successor body to the IBA - and its privatised research contractor, now owned by NTL. At CCETT in France, the STERNE Project was taking shape, as were DIAMONDS at Thompson-LER, also in France; HDTV-T in Germany, and HD-DIVINE in the Scandinavian countries. IBC 1990 had been the catalyst, but there were two other decisive developments which added to the impetus.

Work had now started in earnest to define the MPEG-2 compression system, in the Eureka625 VADIS[67] project which involved twelve European partners with backing from the Commission. It was now generally understood that the new MPEG-2 standard, when it was completed, would be the obvious compression system for digital television. It would have the

---

[67] VADIS: Video/Audio Interactive System.

power to reduce the bit-rates of television signals sufficiently to permit them to be carried in existing broadcasting bandwidths, and produce high-quality images at the same time. MPEG-2 would also have the ability to 'multiplex' - to combine together - a number of different television programmes into a single datastream - or 'transport stream' - so that perhaps four standard definition services could be broadcast in a single channel. What was now urgently needed was the development of a modulation system for digital television: the technique by which the MPEG-2 transport stream could be 'piggy-backed' on to radio waves for broadcasting.

Much of the European work was still focussed on the terrestrial transmission of high definition television, and had more than half an eye cast over the shoulder at the fast-developing situation in the United States. There, following the appearance of General Instruments Digicipher system, competing companies were clamouring to put together their own digital system for submission to the FCC's 'beauty contest'.

But the preoccupation in Europe with a terrestrial system was shortly to change abruptly. The late eighties and early nineties had seen the launch of a number of analogue satellite direct-to-home commercial television services, principally in the UK (BSkyB), Germany (Kirch Group) and France (Canal Plus). They too were looking at the potential benefits of introducing technical systems which were digital because of the advantages it would offer them, of which the ability to offer many more channels was just one.

These commercial players had allies inside the ELG, principally Peter Kahl, a senior official of the German Ministry for Post and Telecommunication who for several years was the ELG chairman, and Stephen Temple, a senior official of the UK Department of Trade and Industry. Both had good reason to favour an extension of the ELG's purpose: both ministries were keen to see privatisation and greater competition within industry. In particular, the Germans were looking at selling off Deutsche Telekom which still had a monopoly of the country's growing analogue cable delivery systems, and would have an interest in upgrading to digital; in the UK the DTI shared the prevailing free market philosophy of the times and, like the UK government, were keen to see a successful BSkyB. SES-Astra, the company which operated the satellites that carried the analogue DTH services of BSkyB, Canal Plus and others, was planning a new series of satellites for digital broadcasting, and was talking about setting up its own group with their client companies to look at standardisation.

Ian Dixon, of the DTI, worked for Stephen Temple, and remembers the dilemma the ELG were in and the role his boss played at that time:

> Do we try to get them on board and all part of the same package or do we let them go on with their own proprietary stuff and do the work on the rest in a more leisurely way? And Stephen Temple was one of those who said

look we've got to catch them - we've got to get them. There was a lot of work done behind the scenes again from here by Stephen Temple to loop in the satellite broadcasters and to try to get them on board and try to get them to be part of this, because it was seen as being far more powerful if it encompassed all three potential methods of delivery.

The persuasion succeeded, and they approached the ELG. Ian Childs remembers how the satellite lobby made their case:

> They came to us and said, "Look, we're definitely going to do digital. We think you're not going to get to digital terrestrial yet, but we have aggressive commercial plans to roll out digital satellite. We are happy to join your club if you'll give this the highest priority but if you say no we'll go and form our own club and we'll do it anyway." So Ulrich's position was he either took them into the fold and juggled the priorities to make satellite the first objective, or he carried on as if nothing had happened and let the satellite system develop separately. And I think he took the right decision, which was to say, "Join our club - we'll put your task on the front burner, we'll put our terrestrial stuff on the back burner and we'll work together on this."

The satellite lobby held two strong cards. One was that, even then, it was known that developing a satellite system (and its closely related cable variant) would be a lot easier than working through the complexities inherent in any terrestrial system. And a satellite system could be made available much sooner. The other had to do with the cost of equipment, especially consumer receivers. If the proposed digital satellite systems across Europe could use a standardised system, then manufacturing costs would be significantly lower, because of the greater volume of production that would result. But also, theoretically at least, the three systems - cable, satellite and terrestrial - could share a number of common elements, which would imply lower production costs for any eventual terrestrial receiver as well. Anything that might reduce the start-up costs of any new digital service was good news both for the commercial operator and the public service people too. It was a winning argument. So, while the ELG itself set about yet another redraft of the MoU to encompass the expansion in membership, the Working Group's priorities also changed, as the idea of a family of inter-related standards covering satellite and cable delivery - as well as terrestrial - took hold.

Finally, in November 1992, the Working Group presented its report: *The Report to the European Launching Group on the Prospects for Digital Terrestrial Television in Europe*.[68] In it, Reimers and his team surveyed the

---

[68] Professor Reimers recalls that the title was misleading in that the report did not look only at terrestrial television. But it was a deliberate ploy in the hope that it would be less alarming to the European Commission's officials since they regarded HD-MAC as a satellite system.

available technologies, the rate at which work to refine them was proceeding, and the capabilities each could be expected to offer. Then it discussed what uses could and should be envisaged for them, and made a stab at predicting the amount of work which would be needed to define the standards, and the sort of timescale which would be needed. It was a ground breaking document.

The model envisaged was multi-layered and multi-dimensional. It recognised the need for a closely related family of standards applicable to cable, satellite and terrestrial delivery. But across each of the three delivery systems was overlaid a hierarchy of other potential requirements. The first set concerned the conditions under which the programmes might be viewed, set out in four groups: first, a large screen, with reception provided by a fixed, roof-top aerial; second, a conventionally-sized (28 inch) screen, similarly fed by a fixed, roof-top aerial; third, a 14 inch portable receiver with its own 'rabbit-ear' aerial; and finally, the potentially revolutionary concept of the hand-held receiver, or the in-car receiver which would function at high speeds. A second set of potential requirements was mapped against this: first, high definition 'studio' quality; second 'Rec 601' quality (for standard definition); third, quality equivalent to that of existing PAL or SECAM broadcasts; and finally VHS-type quality for hand-held and mobile receivers.

Once the matrix had been scrutinised, the twenty or so practical service options which resulted could then be reduced to four: high definition intended for stationary receivers (i.e. those using a fixed roof-top aerial); Extended Definition Television (EDTV), a term used to mean 16:9 widescreen at the same quality as in the studio, for stationary receivers; Standard Definition Television (SDTV), meaning PAL/SECAM quality equivalent, for portable receivers; and Low Definition Television (LDTV) - that is, VHS-like quality - for mobile receivers. (Portable and mobile reception were considered only for terrestrial use, for obvious reasons).

Looking at the various research projects by now under way, Reimers and his team took a stab at making assumptions about the bit-rates which would be needed to deliver these four levels. Given the need to set aside space for the programme audio - which might be multi-channel surround-sound, together with teletext-like data, and data required for conditional access, the Report quoted 30 Mbit/s for HDTV; 11 Mbit/s for EDTV; 5.6 MBit/s for SDTV; and 1.5 Mbit/s for LDTV (figures which would later turn out to be a bit on the conservative side). David Wood, who drafted much of the document, recalls;

> The figures were essentially derived from what we knew was possible with MPEG1 compression, which compresses a quarter picture, LDTV, into 1.5 Mbit/s. We scaled this up for SDTV, EDTV, and HDTV. In practice though, the higher qualities compress more efficiently - but we didn't do too badly.

So what, the Report then went on to consider, would that mean for transmission methods? The work of the various European research projects was throwing up a number of variants of the multi-carrier OFDM technique which, as Arthur Mason had demonstrated, could co-exist with the incumbent analogue services. Looking first at terrestrial, and noting the public service broadcasters' continent-wide obligation to provide over 97 per cent population coverage, the Report concluded that the use of single frequency networks - as demonstrated in the DAB system - would be required. That implied the use of OFDM or COFDM. For satellite use, where transmitter power was very low and interference in the form of electronic 'noise' had to be countered, a related but simpler system, QPSK[69] looked better on paper.

The Report also registered the bewildering number of options available in the many parameters from which the system might be constructed: the number of carriers; their relative spacing and phase relationship; the possible levels and complexity of error correction and the related implication for payload - the usable amount of bandwidth which would result. And it identified a potential hierarchical structure for the content of a broadcast channel, in which various combinations of HDTV, EDTV, SDTV and LDTV could be chosen according to the service requirement: the concept was one of 'degradability' in which the coverage areas of the lower definition versions would be wider than for the higher definition; reception would be progressively more robust for the lower definition services; and receivers of different capabilities - principally in terms of picture quality - and therefore with different degrees of complexity, would be available at a whole range of different prices. The method of combining two or more variants was envisaged as one in which the lower definition variants were embedded within the higher definition variants, sharing common data. This would be more economical in bandwidth than the more obvious - and certainly the more straightforward - alternative of simply multiplexing together completely separate versions of the same programme. This ingenious concept has yet, fifteen years later, to be used anywhere in the world in regular public service, but survives in the DVB standard as a option which from time to time is taken out, dusted down, demonstrated again, but always put back on the shelf for another day.[70]

The Report met with widespread acclaim and interest. If anybody still felt that the time was not yet right to begin to define a set of standards for digital television broadcasting, this document dispelled such caution. But

---

[69] QPSK: Quadrature Phase Shift Keying.
[70] For an authoritative summary of the Report's conclusions, see: Reimers: *European perspectives on digital television broadcasting: Conclusions of the Working Group on Digital Television Broadcasting (WGTB)*, EBU Technical Review Summer 1993 (reprinting the Reimer's NAB paper of April 1993).

looking back on it now, Ulrich Reimers is almost disparaging of the work he and his group did:

> And still that thing, if you look at it now with hindsight, was very vague and very shaky. It was vague because we didn't know better. That was one of the real reasons. We just didn't know better in many areas.

But in truth he and his team had, in the European Launching Group, laid the foundations for the present-day DVB Project and, in the Working Group which Ulrich Reimers chaired, had set in train the thinking that would result, within a very short time, in the successful DVB family of standards. The political sensitivities about supporting a potential rival to the Commission's beloved HD-MAC were still potent, and would remain a constraint for a while yet. But the Reimers Report was another nail in the coffin, if one were needed, of any European hybrid analogue system.

9
Enter the DVB

In the autumn of 1993, the European Launching Group had reached a watershed. The membership had greatly expanded, and for much of the preceding twelve months, the commercial satellite operators - including SES-Astra, BSkyB, Canal Plus and others - had been participating in the work of the technical groups and in the main assembly. The tricky wording of the Memorandum of Understanding had now been completed more or less to everyone's satisfaction. The consolidation of the ELG into a new entity would be the formal beginning of a major international collaborative effort which, within a remarkably short space of time, would produce effective and lasting specifications for digital television broadcasting.

The formal ceremony took place in Bonn, hosted by the German Minister for Post and Telecommunication. Eighty-three organisations from all over Europe signed the Memorandum of Understanding. They represented the four constant sectors of the industry: broadcasters, network operators, manufacturing industry and regulators. This was the first meeting of the General Assembly of a new organisation, formally called the European Project for Digital Video Broadcasting. After signing the MoU, the assembly elected a Steering Board, with Peter Kahl of the German Ministry of Posts and Telecommunications as its first Chairman.

Membership of DVB was initially limited to European organisations, and those non-European companies who could demonstrate proper commitment to the new organisation's purpose by virtue of their membership of either the European Broadcasting Union or the European Telecommunications Standards Institute. Some associations were granted a place on the Steering Board, but without voting rights: they included the public service broadcasters' 'club', the EBU, the cable association ECCA, the manufacturers association EACEM, the manufacturers standardisation body CENELEC, ETSI, and the European Commission.

Right from the beginning, the DVB's objective was to come up with systems for digital television broadcasting which were open, interoperable and market-driven. The definition of these three conditions itself serves to define the DVB's philosophy. The concept of a technology system being

111

open means that it is available for all manufacturers to produce: this is the key to the so-called 'horizontal' market, and implies a freedom for manufacturers, retailers and consumers to choose from a range of competing products at every level in the value chain. Interoperability in this context means ensuring that across the three platforms of satellite, cable and terrestrial, there is as much commonality as possible in the architecture of the system so that the equipment can share the maximum of generic elements, and that equipment from different manufacturers' implementations should function correctly when interconnected. Being market-driven means that the systems should satisfy the requirements of the business planning of the organisations involved - which in effect means that the products must be ones that people will buy, and not simply what technical experts decide is good for the public.

This last stricture was one of the most important conditions laid down by the commercial satellite operators before they would agree to join the ELG, and later to sign the MoU to become full members of the DVB. The principle was therefore embodied in the way the DVB organised its committee structure from day one. Before work on a specification could begin, a Commercial Module must have agreed the terms of a set of commercial requirements, and have it endorsed by the DVB's executive body, the Steering Board. Only after that, can the Technical Module and its working groups get down to work. Reimers himself has no doubt of the importance of technical work being driven by commercial reality:

> The thing which I personally find extremely important is that we always have, as we say in Germany, a 'four eye' principle. So there are always four eyes looking at a thing. That means two eyes which may be the techies, and two more eyes which are the commercial [people]. That is very important: I think it is one of the keys to the success of the DVB.

Vassilis Seferedis, then working in Britain for the manufacturer Toshiba, attended many DVB meetings:

> You have the Commercial Module dictating the direction it's going to be ... A very German approach: we define, you do, kind of thing. But it works very well because that is exactly what was required. If you leave the technical people alone, they'll go on for ages.

Deciding to separate the two sets of decision-making processes, commercial and technical, was an inspired insight which would prove crucial to the DVB's success.

It was certainly true that there was, on the surface, a very strong element of German leadership, first in the early effort's of Ulrich Reimers' Schönburg group to create the ELG, then within the ELG and now in the new DVB: the Chairman of the DVB, and of its Steering Board, Peter Kahl, was

German, so was the chairman of the Technical Module (Reimers): Germans also held other key chairmanships, including that of another early module responsible for communications and promotion, led by Helmut Stein and A. Zeiemer.[71] In truth, there had been a strong British presence in the ELG from very early on, and many other countries contributed experts. There was something truly international about it, even from the beginning. Ian Dixon, of the DTI, believes that the fact of German leadership was useful and necessary

> The Germans were central - we were probably next in line. The French had problems because of their involvement in MAC, but there were one or two key people there who were as supportive as they could be in the circumstances.

In European eyes, the British had proved unreliable in the debates on the mandating of MAC and the proposal for massive subsidies from the European Commission to encourage its introduction. The UK Treasury refused to countenance such expense, and vetoed any British contribution. In Brussels, the DTI lobbied hard in the Commission, and at the Council of Ministers, Britain's representative took an intransigent stance. Ian Dixon played his part in that battle, and remembers the fall-out from it:

> It was a very difficult time when the reputation of the Brits in particular went through the floor so far as a lot of [the] people we normally got on well with were concerned. And anything we said was taken to be a spoiling tactic. And we came out of the MAC debate victorious in the sense that our views had prevailed, but very severely damaged in terms of our relationships with others, and our ability to bring them along to do anything. So I think the German lead [in the DVB] was not only opportune but necessary. It could not be seen as the Brits trying to delay things - suggest other things - do anything else to stop MAC getting off the ground. These were very much Germans who were very much pro-MAC who had shown themselves as being good boys who were actually leading the discussion and took key places in the DVB that was leading this forward. So they were credible leaders: other people could rally round them. At that time, I don't think we'd have had that possibility.

In fairness, the German leadership in no way amounted to domination of the agenda. Many other countries were represented in chairmanships of the growing number of working groups, bringing with them their expertise and that of the organisations they worked for. Individual points of view and national agendas got a fair hearing. The principles of collaboration and consensus that were embodied in the MoU needed no enforcement: the will to co-operate and to agree was general, even if some of the battles were

---

[71] Even the administrative support for the DVB initially came from the German Ministry of Post and Telecommunication. Before long, the support moved to the EBU headquarters in Geneva, which established the DVB Project Office. It remains there today.

hard-fought. For its size and purpose, no other international body had yet worked quite like this. Chris Daubney, then at Channel Four, thinks the model might have come from the international group which put together the basis of the GSM mobile telephone system (another RACE European collaborative programme), in which DTI had been involved:

> Outside the broadcasting world what is now the GSM mobile phone format had been done as a collaborative process between players and manu-facturers and governments and network operators and so on. And so this very key concept of all the competitors - be they broadcaster competitors or receiver manufacturer competitors or what have you - all sitting round the same table pooling their interests to get a common standard and then go off and compete fiercely with each other... against a common standard - is in everyone's interest.

And Chris Hibbert, then working for the ITVA, and for many years chair-man of one of the DVB groups, agrees:

> DVB members who've been in DVB a very long time - as opposed to some of the new ones, who have to go through a bit of a learning curve - have learnt that you may be sitting round the table with your rivals, but if you can come up with something that works for all of you, you can then go out and be competitive in the market place with service, content, pricing. As far as I'm concerned, the DVB is a proven model. And Europe is way ahead in digital broadcasting with all the different markets in Europe - different cultures, different administrations - we're working to the same technical format. That means the manufacturing process is greatly simplified - and the consumer market, of course, must benefit.

But before those benefits could come, there was much argument and hard work to be undertaken.

When the commercial satellite operators agreed to join the common effort, they made another condition: that work on a satellite standard would take priority over work on a terrestrial version. This was not necessarily an easy prospect for some of the other members. Because the original purpose of the ELG had been solely terrestrial, and because terrestrial was largely in the hands of heavily regulated public service broadcasters, it was they who had dominated the original membership line-up, and continued to do so in the new DVB.. What's more, they all perceived to a greater or lesser extent that the biggest threat to their privileged position in their own countries was the emergence of strong competition from lightly regulated, and highly combative commercial satellite operators - the very people now admitted to the DVB's councils. Ian Childs:

> I think it was thought of as treating with the enemy, actually, to some extent. So there were tensions there. Equally, I'm sure that there were tensions on the Sky side of things. I mean they were very, very suspicious

of the public broadcasters - it was quite visible in meetings. Also they were not given a very long amount of rope by their bosses; they came into a meeting with a definite agenda of stuff that had to be agreed whether it was sensible or not, and so the table got thumped very hard on occasions during meetings: by which I mean that some of the meetings were quite tense and quite hard fought.

To make things run more smoothly, two parallel commercial modules were set up, one which concentrated on satellite and cable systems, the other exclusively for terrestrial. This reflected not only the different timescales to completion being demanded, but removed the much more complex - and at times politically loaded - discussion of the terrestrial requirements to a separate forum. Urgent work on the satellite and cable systems could then proceed without distraction.

The operators of the growing number of analogue satellite services broadcasting in the early nineties lived in a much simpler and sparser regulatory climate than their earth-bound and predominately public service competitors. Introducing digital satellite systems needed financial investment and a suitable technology, but it did not need legislation by national governments. Technically, the system would be simpler than any terrestrial equivalent, since there would be no problems of complex transmitter networks with attendant reception problems, and no requirement to cater for portable or mobile receivers. Commercial and market judgements had it that an early start to digital services was essential. Led by BSkyB, Canal Plus and Kirch, the Commercial Module had, by November 1993, put the finishing touches to its satellite commercial requirements, and put great pressure on the Technical Module to complete the work in the shortest possible timescale.

The urgency gave additional rationale to one of Ulrich Reimers' golden rules: that if a technology existed there was no need to invent another one. So the way the DVB went about selecting its toolkit was to start with a 'call for technologies' to its membership. In other words, is anybody out there working on a suitable technology, and would they be prepared to bring it to the DVB? If the technology ended up as part of the DVB specification, then the sourcing organisation retained the IPR rights, but agreed to make the licensing of it available to all on equitable terms.

This made the DVB's choice of a compression system straightforward. The working group in the International Standards Organisation had finished its work on defining MPEG-2, and the standard was approved in November 1993. MPEG-2 provided a tool-kit which allowed the compression of a video signal into any desired bit-rate, of combining all the components of any programme - the video, audio, text, and control data - into a 'single programme transport stream', and the multiplexing together of any number of them into a multiple transport stream. This combined transport stream - the multiplex - would then be modulated on to a radio frequency carrier wave for transmission, first from ground station to satellite, and finally from the satellite's transponder to a terrestrial receiving dish. The big job for the Technical Module was to choose a suitable modulation scheme.

Fortunately, quite a lot of preliminary work had taken place inside the Reimers technical group during the nine months since the satellite operators had joined the ELG. Some members were active in the multinational RACE HD-SAT project, where there had been progress on a modulation system intended for use in the 20 GHz part of the broadcasting spectrum. The interest had now moved to another band of frequencies, around 12 GHz, and a number of potential service providers were looking at commercial and technical models. At the RAI Research Centre, a team under Dr Mario Cominetti had considerable experience of work on proposed satellite broadcasting systems, and were contributing to the HD-SAT programme. Cominetti took the chair of the satellite modulation group in the DVB Technical Module.

Direct broadcasting satellites are in geostationary orbit above the equator, where they occupy a fixed point above the earth's surface,[72] parked at an altitude of 35,900 km (22,300 miles). So the signal broadcast by the satellite back to earth must cover this distance at least (and - if it is to be received at high latitudes - a greater distance through the atmosphere which may attenuate the signal significantly if the sky is not clear.) The power of the satellite's transmissions is limited by the size and weight of the satellite and particularly by the capacity of its solar cells to collect sufficient energy from sunlight, and the capacity of the on-board batteries to store enough power to sustain the satellite in operation during its occasional journey through the earth's shadow.

While terrestrial transmitters can use tens or hundreds of kilowatts of power, a typical broadcasting satellite must make do with very much less, typically 50 to 100 watts or thereabouts for each transponder.[73] Although the signal path is a long one, it is at least 'line-of-sight'. The satellite's weak signal is therefore unaffected by the reflections and absorbtions of ground objects between transmitter and receiving aerial that bedevil terrestrial transmissions. But the satellite signal, being so weak, is particularly prone to a form of interference which degrades the signal, and which communications engineers term 'noise'.

For that reason, the modulation scheme chosen for satellite is different from the COFDM systems that would be used in terrestrial broadcasting.

---

[72] 'Fixed', by virtue of the satellite's orbital speed, chosen to keep pace with the earth's rotation.

[73] A satellite transponder receives the signal beamed up from the earth station, changes its frequency, and retransmits it to earth via a directional aerial which provides a 'footprint', or coverage area on the ground.

A much simpler system, Quadrature Phase Shift Keying (QPSK - also known as 4-PSK or 4-QAM) is used. In QPSK, the modulation of the carrier by the digital transport stream produces four distinct states of the single carrier wave, well separated from each other in phase, and therefore easily distinguished from each other by the receiver and so capable of being accurately decoded. Since the carrier in each QPSK 'symbol' can be in one of 4 possible states, each symbol can carry 2 bits of information.[74]

Of all of the choices available for digital modulation, QPSK (or, equivalently, 4-PSK or 4-QAM) provides the greatest immunity to interference caused by noise[75], combined with the optimum data carrying capacity - or payload. As a further precaution, powerful error correction techniques are employed.

In putting together the modulation system, the DVB recognised the need for a range of options built in to the technical parameters to take account of the way the system might be required to work in a practical, business-friendly way. For example, satellites could be constructed to operate at different channel bandwidths (which would directly affect the payload capacity); they may be used to serve different geographical areas, or with different power outputs (which would affect their resilience in the presence of noise); and they may be designed with the intention of being received on the ground by different sizes of receiving dish (which would affect the power-gathering ability at the receiver, with a knock-on effect for transponder power requirements). Other business considerations which would affect the technical choices made included the extent to which the service was required to remain available to the customer if the receiving dish were misaligned, or if adverse meteorological conditions could be expected to affect transmission for a given amount of time.

So the specification included a choice of five different levels - or code rates - for error protection.[76] High levels of error protection give a corresponding reduction in payload capacity but yield a greater immunity to noise: the difference in payload between the highest and lowest levels of error protection specified is nearly two-to-one. In practical terms that

---

[74] QPSK is identical to 4-QAM (Quadrature Amplitude Modulation). In this mode there are two carriers which are in quadrature (i.e. at $90°$) to each other and each carrier is 'modulated' (by inverting or not the carrier) by the digital transport stream in such a way that in each symbol there are four possible states: (i) neither carrier inverted; (ii) one carrier inverted; (iii) the other carrier inverted; and (iv) both carriers inverted. 4-QAM is unique amongst the family of QAM modulation systems in that the amplitude of both carriers remains constant; in higher-order QAM systems such as 16-QAM and 64-QAM the amplitude as well as the phase of each of the two quadrature carriers is modulated by the digital transport stream be conveyed.

[75] 2-PSK/2-QAM has the same immunity to noise, and occupies the same bandwidth, as 4-PSK/4-QAM but conveys only 1 instead of 2 bits per symbol. Hence 2-PSK is used only in special circumstances where its particular properties such as its relative immunity to phase distortion are key or where simplicity of the demodulator is an over-riding consideration.

[76] described as Code Rate 1/2, 2/3, 3/4, 5/6 and 7/8

represented the difference between transmitting, for example, five pro-gramme services with the highest resilience compared with nine with the lowest resilience.[77]

But choices like these were for the end-user's business plan, where the judgement lay between offering a cornucopia of choice and variety laid against considerations of quality of service - and therefore customer satis-faction. The job of the DVB as they saw it was to provide a system specification which had useful set of options applicable to most event-ualities, and from which the business planners can select the most appropriate.

Under Mario Comminetti of RAI, the work on the modulation system progressed rapidly, to the point where, just three months after the formation of the DVB proper, the specification was finalised and submitted to ETSI for standardisation. It had been hard work: not all the differences of opinion were technical in nature, as Ian Childs remembers:

> RAI did most of the work in developing the DVB-S spec. We had all sorts of hard fought arguments about whether we should use this particular digital coding method or that particular digital coding method for the error protection. Actually there was frequently little technical difference between the systems being debated - the real issues lay underneath, as so often. There was a clear intention to try to have as much in common with the standard that DirecTV[78] intended to use, and I guess there were patent arguments as well. So there was a clear incentive to see the DVB-S choose one parameter option rather than another. In fact I think the situation we eventually got to was where the DirecTV spec wasn't exactly the same as the DVB-S spec, but it was sufficiently close that it could be considered as a sub-set. So, if you like, a lot of the argument wasn't really technical - it was dressed up in technical clothes, but it wasn't really technical.

As part of the specification, a great deal of work went into designing a structure for 'service information' or SI. This is the 'glue' that holds together the system. SI consists of a set of information fields in the multi-plex which identify to the receiver the correct constituent parts of each individual programme within the transmission. Without such extensive labelling, the receiver would be unable to find a desired service, nor know the parameters to use when decoding it. Service Information therefore carried an elaborate hierarchy of information which identified, amongst other things, the network carrying the programme, its title and running time, the title of the programme which would follow on from it, together with the date and time of day.

---

[77] On the benefit side, most satellites used for TV broadcasting operate in the 10-12 GHz range, which permits a much wider channel bandwidth (27MHz) than can be practically accommodated in terrestrial use.

[78] DirecTV: While the DVB-S specification was being discussed, DirecTV Inc. - a US consortium - was planning a direct broadcast digital service. It launched in 1994

From early on, the DVB had envisaged that digital television receivers would be built to receive services carried by any or all three platforms, cable, satellite and terrestrial, serving the receiver's locality. It followed that transmissions by each means should carry common structures of service information, so that a receiver would have the necessary information to be able to identify any programme being carried in any multiplex on any of the three platforms, and to be able to tune quickly and easily to whatever service the viewer selected. From this came the requirement to 'cross carry' service information about other services besides the ones in any particular multiplex. Tuning to a service would be made using an on-screen display of available services, constructed using the information carried in the service information.

The concept of service information existed already in the structure of MPEG-2 single and multiple programme transport streams. The DVB took the concept, and extended it to satisfy these requirements. It was an enormous task and a complex process of logic, but one which has proved of lasting worth. It works well, and has a considerable degree of future-proofing built into it.

With the satellite specification (DVB-S) completed, the technical teams now turned to the cable specification. There were common elements with the satellite version: the use of MPEG-2 transport streams, the concept of multiplexing, the service information, and so on. But cable required a different modulation system.

Historically, cable systems had been constructed to redistribute local over-air broadcasts. At the cable head-end, the company received broadcasts from all the local transmitters, and re-broadcast them over its cable network to its consumers. As a result, cable systems were generally designed with the same channel bandwidth as the over-air broadcasts, 8 MHz in Europe. This cable bandwidth remained, even though cable companies made increasing use of programme feeds from communications satellites, and progressively upgraded their networks to optic fibre.

Cable presents a relatively benign environment for the transmission of digital television signals: there is little problem with noise, as amplification can be provided along the way wherever necessary. However, in upgrading an existing cable system to carry digital signals, there will be an interim period during which both analogue and digital services must share the same distribution path. For that reason, care was needed to design a digital cable system which did not interfere with the analogue system, and which maximised the payload of each digital multiplex. For these reasons, the cable system differs from the satellite system in that it uses, instead of QPSK modulation, a choice of 16-QAM or 64-QAM, with higher options also available.[79] 16-QAM allows 16 carrier states to be used, which are differentiated from each other not only by phase difference - as in QPSK - but also by a number of different amplitude states.

The DVB-C cable specification was completed in March 1994. It offers one optional configuration which allows the transport of exactly as many bits per second in one cable channel (38.01 Mbit/s) as a typical satellite channel will transport to a cable head-end. This simplifies significantly the re-transmission of satellite signals via cable.

The DVB next turned its attention to an essential requirement of cable and satellite broadcasting, but one which was to strain to the limit the co-operative ethos of the organisation. Some form of scrambling of signals is required, together with secure conditional access arrangements to ensure that only those customers who pay their subscription can view the pro-grammes. The security of such systems is of paramount importance to operators: once the code is cracked they stand to lose their income. Increasingly rights owners, particularly of Hollywood films, required assurances that a cable or satellite broadcaster were maintaining highly secure conditional access systems before they would agree to sell them broadcasting rights to their intellectual property. So one of the company's greatest potential risks is that its conditional access system is not secure, a constant concern underlined by the knowledge that most, if not all, of the analogue era conditional access systems had been cracked by 'hackers' and many major operators estimated that they were losing between 10% to 30% or more of their revenue from such piracy.

Traditionally, secrecy of the algorithms used by the conditional access system had been seen by the operators to be an important part of the system's security[80]. The details were shrouded in extreme secrecy. So when discussions started within the DVB on whether it was possible or desirable to produce an open standard conditional access system for use by all, the going was tough. Ulrich Reimers:

> One of the areas where, in the very early days of DVB, people did not want to work on open standards was the conditional access business. So there was even a time when the DVB ran a special group on CA systems, which was chaired by a representative of the EU: it was something like a group of

---

[79] The later, revised, DVB-C specification offers QAM options of 16, 32, 64, 128 and 256.
[80] The fallacy of this was well known to experts in cryptography - a fundamental assumption in cryptanalysis, first enunciated by the Dutchman Auguste Kerckhoffs in the 19th Century, is that secrecy must reside entirely in the key and not in the algorithm. Unfortunately, Kerckhoffs' law is so counter-intuitive that even today non-experts still sometimes place undue reliance on the secrecy of algorithms. It is, however, now widely acknowledged that the strongest cryptographic algorithms are open standards such as the US Government's Advanced Encryption Standard (AES) which have been peer-reviewed by the world's community of experts.

people deeply involved in the CA business talking among themselves about how we could create the next generation of the market place exclusively for themselves. Totally exotic situation. Totally out of the typical working methodologies of the DVB. It was because strong partners had been able to organise a kind of closed shop inside of DVB which would define what CA - conditional access - means, and what DVB would do in this area, and what DVB would not do in this area.

A conditional access system, to simplify rather, consists of a lock and a key. The 'lock' comprises 'scrambling' of the transmitted picture and sound signals in such a way as to render them unintelligible unless they are 'unlocked' (i.e. descrambled) by application of the appropriate key. The key is usually made up of two or more parts which must be properly combined cryptographically to operate the lock: one part is secretly stored inside the receiver or in a secure device such as a 'smart' card plugged into the receiver; another part is sent with the transmitted signal to ensure that the 'lock' is effectively changed every few seconds - so that making duplicate static 'keys' will not be sufficient to hack the system.

The idea that any of these things could become common elements as part of an open standard worried a lot of people, not just in broadcasting. But there was an exception. In the DVB discussions, the conditional access vendors could see the advantage of a common scrambling algorithm, because the manufacturing costs of the complex chipsets required could be reduced if they all shared in volume production. Ulrich Reimers:

> And imagine that in these days Kirch in Germany, Canal Plus in France, NDS, Sky, Irdeto, all these people who are really offering CA systems were part of that camp. So the conclusion was, "The only thing we really require is a scrambling system which can be implemented in all of the set-top boxes and which we can address with our CA. So we need a unified scrambling system, and the rest we will take care of privately."

Any scrambling algorithm would need to be carefully vetted by the authorities, GCHQ in Britain and their equivalents elsewhere, to ensure there was no risk to national security. At that time the idea that a common scrambling algorithm should be freely available via the DVB specification worried them. In the end, access to the DVB specification for the Common Scrambling Algorithm was carefully controlled: Reimers was satisfied:

> The work on a common scrambling algorithm resulted in a fantastic system: not openly standardised but you can get hold of it, of the specifications, in a very open mechanism. And I am still full of respect for its stability and commercial success over so many years.

The DVB's algorithm is now used by virtually every conditional access supplier in the world. Chris Hibbert believes it to be one of the DVB's big success:

... a major achievement amongst rivals. To have the Common Scrambling Algorithm, which was agreed by the major suppliers of CA systems, who were competing against each other - [all used the] common scrambling algorithm - meant that manufacturing was cheap, and they could go out and be competitive on the business side, and on the secret key stuff which differentiates them from each other, and the manufacturers only have to put one descrambler in the box: that was another example of the DVB at its best.

A year after the common scrambling algorithm was finalised, in March 1995, the DVB agreed on a specification for a so-called 'common interface' for conditional access. This described the requirements for a socket for receivers which had no conditional access built in to it, but into which a plug-in module could be inserted which carried the conditional access chip. Later, the European Commission would mandate its use in integrated digital television sets, principally to address the terrestrial market.

In its eighteen months of existence, the DVB had come a long way. It had produced major achievements in the specifications for satellite and cable broadcasting systems, and for aspects of conditional access. These specifications were now going through the formal process within the International Telecommunications Union which would give them the status of worldwide standards. Fifteen years later, DVB-S and DVB-C systems are in use on every continent of the world, even in the US: very few installations use anything else.

By September 1994, membership of DVB had risen to 147 organisations. The status and reputation of the organisation was growing and, crucially, the European Commission were beginning to accept that digital television broadcasting was the future. Officials were starting to talk about digital, and the emphasis on MAC and HD-MAC was waning. The political sensitivities so keenly felt inside the DVB had eased. Reimers:

> My personal recollection of this is that when we had finished DVB-S I felt
> we were purely on the winning side and it was clear we were the winners.
> And from that time onwards I didn't feel any problems any longer.

With the pressure to complete DVB-S and DVB-C now off, the Technical Module could turn its attention to proposals for a digital terrestrial system, and to pick up the commercial requirements that had by now been finalised. Meanwhile, interest in digital television broadcasting had spread beyond the technical people, to the national broadcasting administrators and the politicians. And of all the countries in Europe, Britain was thinking about launching services sooner than anybody else.

Part Three

Britain's Digital Adventure

10
The Momentum Builds

The British Broadcasting Corporation has a peculiar and long-standing relationship with Government. It is constitutionally independent from, but in practice ultimately dependent upon, the government of the day. It is established under a Royal Charter, which gives it its editorial independence. But the Charter runs for a fixed term, usually ten years. The renewal of the Charter and the crucial element within it, the amount of the licence fee which funds the BBC - a flat-rate tax payable by the majority of households in the country which operate a television receiver - is at the behest of the government. The relationship is one, therefore, of stable equilibrium - a device much favoured in British public life - even if it doesn't at times look like it. It was a form of national institution semi-detached from government which was much employed in the 1920s with the creation of the likes of the Central Electricity Board. The BBC, when it was turned from a company owned by radio receiver manufacturers into a corporation in 1927, was one of the first.

This quasi-independent status is tested periodically. Government will signal its intermittent interest in the nation's premier public service broadcaster in a number of ways. Criticism of its editorial policy, particularly with regards to its news and current affairs coverage of politics, comes and goes. As Charter renewal time comes round, the issues become wider in scope. There's always the question of value for money: whether the BBC is making proper and efficient use of the licence fee. The Treasury counts it as part of the Public Sector financial reckoning, and any suggestion of an increase sits uneasily with them. And justifying any rise usually involves, amongst other things, the BBC agreeing to provide enhancements to the service it is obliged to provide to all households, but which the government of the day can also claim to be improvements to the national well-being and in harmony with its current political and electoral strategy. Usually, the enhancements are also chosen to fit the BBC's own best interests. For the sixth Charter in 1964, the deal included a BBC commitment to introduce local radio; in 1981 the BBC agreed to accept a 25 per cent quota of programmes made by independent producers, and to the eventual sale of its transmitter network. For the eighth Charter, in 1996 it was, amongst other things, digital television.

By the time that John Birt became the BBC's twelfth Director-General, at the end of 1992, an understanding of the implications of digital television was beginning to move outward from the corpus of research engineers into the strategic thinking of the Corporation. Digital technology, it was realised, would bring both potential benefits and potential risks for the established broadcasters. Among the benefits identified early on was an end to the scarcity of broadcasting spectrum which would allow greater choice of programmes for the viewer and an opportunity for the BBC itself to expand into new television services. Among the risks identified was the understanding that in a digital future, with a very broad choice of services on offer from the terrestrial, satellite and cable platforms that were sure to develop, the dominance of the traditional broadcasters would be undermined. The signs of this change were already present. BSkyB's analogue satellite service had, in the year leading up to John Birt's appointment, signed an exclusive pay-TV deal with the Premier League, and with subscriber numbers rising, had reached operating profit for the first time. A digital future in which a largely unregulated and monopoly satellite service might entirely satisfy the public appetite for television, without the presence on its system of the established broadcasters, was a nightmare scenario both for the BBC and for the government. Doing nothing was not an option. One way or another, the BBC had to embrace the emerging digital technology.

With John Birt's arrival at the helm of the BBC, widespread changes took place in the way senior management was organised. Many of the engineering departments, including Research and Development, were transferred to a new division, BBC Resources, under a new chief executive, Rod Lynch, who had been with Air Europe and Forte Hotels. Suddenly, the BBC no longer had an engineer at the highest level of seniority in the Board of Management. The post of Director of Engineering was abolished. In its place, two more junior positions were created reporting to the Head of Policy and Planning. The creation of a Policy and Planning Department within the BBC's corporate centre was one of John Birt's first creations, and under its ferociously capable and politically skilful Head, Patricia Hodgson, it would play a central role in developing the BBC's digital strategy.

But relationships between the corporate policymakers and the engineers of the Research and Development Department were far from good. It was not just that the adjective 'engineering' would rapidly be replaced by 'technology' in the organisation's official usage, much to the dismay of the many BBC employees with professional engineering qualifications: Henry Price, who moved to the corporate centre as a technical advisor, expresses a view commonly held at the time:

> I think Birt had little regard for BBC R&D, and Patricia was particularly unimpressed with it, and I think if it had been left up to them they would probably have tried to sell it, but I don't think they ever thought it had much value. It's just my personal opinion, but I believe they thought that nothing any use had ever come out of Kingswood. Only bad advice.

Famously, back in the late 1980s, the BBC's R&D experts had confidently predicted that the medium powered Astra satellite would be incapable of providing a commercially viable direct-to-home service, and the only satisfactory technology was the proposed high-powered DBS satellites. With the success of Sky, which used the former, and the collapse of BSB, which used the latter, that advice was proved resoundingly wrong.

Phil Laven, who had become Controller of Engineering Policy within the corporate centre, frequently found himself having to defend R&D and as a result had a difficult relationship with his boss, Patricia Hodgson. Certainly the days when the recommendation of a Director of Engineering might be accepted by Board members at face value had gone. Under the new regime, the views of Phil Laven and his colleagues were constantly challenged and scrutinised, and sometimes found wanting. Research and Development perceived, rightly or wrongly, that their existence was under threat. A new Head reorganised its structure in what many felt was preparation for privatisation. On the research side the effects became obvious, as Henry Price remembers:

> They'd spread their gold quite thinly over quite a lot of topics, and they were doing a lot of work on things that were relatively obscure rather than being quite focussed on just one or two topics. The trouble was, I believe, in defending R&D the people who were involved in a way didn't want to start giving ground, because I think one of the things they felt was that once you start to give up and retreat, what can [start] as a retreat can become a massacre. Also I think, because of the structural changes that were taking place in the BBC, the management of R&D were much more involved in making sure that the place survived rather than focussing on what was the best thing to be doing in terms of research.

Nevertheless, the body of knowledge within R&D was profound even if, at that time, the cutting edge research into digital television broadcasting was being done elsewhere. And that knowledge remained useful to the corporate centre.

As the Board of Management became increasingly preoccupied with the review of the BBC's Charter in advance of its renewal due in 1996, a process of assessing current and future technologies took place the better to inform the Board's strategic planning. Phil Laven prepared for them a paper on digital broadcasting:

> I pointed out that you could use digital terrestrial television or digital satellite television. And my hint in the paper was that digital terrestrial is relatively difficult - it hasn't yet been defined - but we think we know how to do it, but digital satellite is probably going to be easier. And I remember John Birt saying, "But wait a minute, we're terrestrial broadcasters, why should we want to be satellite broadcasters?" And I said, "Well I think in the future we may have to be on all platforms." And he disagreed with me very strongly, I remember. He said we need to be strongly terrestrial.

The BBC's first instinct was to embrace the new digital technology on its home ground - terrestrial broadcasting - and to position a digital terrestrial 'platform' as a competitor and counterbalance to the monopoly digital satellite platform that was likely to emerge. For a time that view prevailed. Michael Starks, later to lead the BBC's Digital Broadcasting Project, had participated in the technology review process:

> There were at least a dozen task forces doing various things and I chaired the one on technology. And we certainly encountered the possibility - I don't think it was more than that - of digital terrestrial, at that time, by taking a look at what was going on elsewhere and picking up the fact that this was on the agenda in the United States.

Ian Childs remembers one of the major contributions made by the BBC's last Director of Engineering, Bill Dennay:

> Bill together with Phil identified I think four technical developments which are specifically included in Extending Choice. One was HDTV, one was digital television, [another was] DAB ... and basically the benefit that Phil was touting for digital television was better quality and more channels.

Michael Starks regards Phil Laven as the BBC's visionary: the man who first identified the real and imminent promise of the new technology

> I think he realised the potential digital television could have - I think he'd probably been quite influenced by what had gone on on the digital radio side ... but I think he realised that it could turn the key to more channels and take the BBC into a future which he was pretty sure was going to happen in a technology - terrestrial - with which it was familiar. And I think he worked on Patricia Hodgson - his boss - and anybody else to whom Patricia opened the doors to get that vision established.

Gradually, the vision was established. Phil Laven:

There were various events where we talked to the Board of Management and the Board of Governors and so forth about the future. Eventually it culminated in a BBC initiative about digital terrestrial television.

By the middle of 1994, the BBC was writing to a senior official at the Department of National Heritage outlining its proposals. They included digital widescreen versions of the two existing analogue services BBC-1 and BBC-2, and envisaged a 24-hour news service and a channel carrying parliamentary coverage. And a sense of urgency appeared: the BBC offered to complete a feasibility study within months and suggested that services could be launched in 1997. The urgency, thinks Michael Starks, was ....

... with an eye to what might happen on the satellite side, in the sense in which nobody wanted too much time slip by and find that the digital world had become dominated by digital satellite.

Then the BBC took their ideas directly to Ministers. A high-level delegation - which included Phil Laven - went to see the Secretary of State for the Department of National Heritage (DNH), Peter Brooke, and the President of the Board of Trade, Michael Hestletine. The DNH were receptive, but the surprise of the meeting was the support of Hestletine whose ministry, the DTI, while keen to see new technologies such as digital broadcasting energetically pursued by British industry, were much less keen that they should be pursued by public service organisations like the BBC.

Events began to move rapidly. In July 1994, the DNH announced a plan for "as many as 12 digital terrestrial television services" with perhaps analogue switch-off in 2009. In the same month, the government published a White Paper *The Future of the BBC* which included this summary of the BBC's position:

Provided questions of technical practicality, and of costs, can be satisfactorily resolved, the BBC would intend to begin experimental digital terrestrial television broadcasting services during 1995, entering into discussion with equipment manufacturers on the availability of receivers and investing in studio equipment to produce programmes in a widescreen format. It would aim to launch digital services, which could be received in widescreen or conventional format, by autumn of 1997.

Within Independent Television, interest in digital terrestrial television was also growing. The ITV Network was a federal structure of sixteen regional companies - large and small - each separately licensed by the IBA. But the Broadcasting Act of 1990 heralded fundamental changes to the ITV system. The Act abolished the IBA and established a new regulator, the Independent Television Commission. The ITC began statutory life in the same week of November 1990 as the Sky-BSB merger. It was designed to be a new kind of regulator for a more free-market era, less paternalistic and with a lighter touch. One of its first tasks was to place the ITV companies under a new relationship - by auctioning their licences. In January 1993, the ITV companies ceased operating under their old contracts with the IBA, and now operated under the new ones. In the process, four of the old programme contractors failed to win one of the new licences, including the London weekday company Thames which was replaced by Carlton Television, run by the entrepreneur Michael Green. London Weekend Television and the Manchester-based Granada retained their licences.

Barry Cox was Director of Corporate Affairs at LWT, and was one of many people from ITV who, along with representatives from the rest of the industry and from government, were invited to Exeter to see the ITC's SPECTRE demonstrations from the Stockland Hill transmitter. Cox was immediately struck by the significance of what he was shown. He had become familiar with many of television's new technologies, born out of a visit to America some years before when, as Head of Current Affairs, he'd seen the new Electronic Newsgathering system being used, imported it to LWT and did a pioneering deal with the company's unions to use it. Now, along with his engineering colleague Ken Sheppard, he returned to the States to look at their work on digital television:

> The USA, which had been behind everybody, suddenly said, we're going to do digital, and it was having these competitions. So Sheppard and I went over and we did a tour on the East Coast talking to both the manufacturers and some of the broadcasters and the regulators. And from that emerged the idea - their idea - of simulcasting: we fastened on to that.

Almost immediately, Cox and his opposite number at Carlton, John Egan, wrote to the ITC saying that they believed that they could use buffer frequencies in London to develop a digital service, and asked for dis-cussions on the proposal. Barry Cox remembers the reaction:

> My memory tells me that Gary Tonge [at the ITC] told me that that put the wind up the ITC and they instantly had a consultation ... quite quickly. We felt that we'd semi-precipitated this and that was really the start of the process that led to the 1996 Act. I was not very aware at that stage what the BBC were up to. Indeed, we thought we were ahead of the game - we obviously weren't, but that's what it felt like to us. The combination of Gary Tonge at the ITC and the enthusiasm of LWT and Carlton to get on with this, we thought was what was driving it.

Barry Cox says that LWT and Carlton had another reason for acting quickly. They had become aware of the stance being adopted by the Dep-artment of Trade and Industry:

> The other driver was Stephen Temple at [the DTI]. NTL had latched on to him and he was constructing a plan which would really have given the terrestrial broadcasters nothing. In his view they shouldn't get anything,

they should just get no scope for extra services at all. So we didn't like that one. He seemed to think that the only people who could do digital were going to be Sky and NTL. So the battlefield shaped up quite quickly into an ITV alliance - the other ITV companies [felt] let's just get on with it.

The DTI's drive is understandable: they were very keen to ensure that the UK could gain a technology advantage by an early start of digital television. Those who strode the corridors of power in Parliament and in Whitehall agreed, but those on the political right did not at that time consider either the BBC or ITV to be appropriate agents for such change. Both broadcasters already occupied dominant positions and what they needed, so the thinking went, was not the empire-building of additional channels, but more competition. Launching digital television would require heavy financial investment and the marshalling of competent technical and marketing resources by a determined management. Better, therefore, to trust in risk capital and the focussed, almost driven, approach of a News Corporation. It was not, as it turned out, a point of view fully shared by the Department of National Heritage.

The proposal for "as many as 12 digital terrestrial services", announced by the National Heritage Secretary in July 1994, was not a number plucked out of the air. The DNH had done its homework, and had taken advice on what was possible, given the current understanding of these things, from specialists.

It was the job of the specialist frequency planners at the BBC and ITC to work out where transmitters could be sited, what channels they could use, and at what power, in order to give whatever coverage was desired. In doing this, they are constrained by the need to work within international agreements - transmissions from one country 'leak' across borders and seas to affect transmissions in other countries. For digital terrestrial transmission, the planners were further constrained by the fact that the UK already had a very crowded spectrum: across the country, 1,100 UHF transmitters of low, medium or high power were broadcasting four television services to more than 95 per cent of the population. That was what had been planned at the international conference in Stockholm in 1961, and very few spare frequencies were left over. But the planners also had a bonus: the nature of the COFDM transmission system which was envisaged for DTT. Already, enough was known about the characteristics of COFDM for the planners to know that they would be dealing with a different animal, and could use different rules as Arthur Mason had pointed out in his seminal IBC paper.

In the analogue world, the four programme services being broadcast from any particular transmitter have to use frequency channels spaced one full channel apart from each other to avoid interference between them.

Other transmitters - particularly those operating at a high power - within a radius of perhaps up to a hundred miles, must use yet other frequency channels, again to avoid interference. But COFDM signals use the radio frequency channel in a much more efficient way, which not only means that a similar coverage to that of an analogue transmission can be obtained at greatly lower powers - anything from 50 to 100 times lower, but also can use channels adjacent to those occupied by an analogue transmitter at the same site, again without causing interference. And then there is the remarkable property of COFDM which is that of a single frequency network - or SFN - whereby a chain of transmitters up and down to country can all operate on the same frequency even if their coverage areas overlap (provided, of course, they all broadcast the same service). With these properties it became possible to identify a much larger number of channels available for digital use.

Surveying the use made of the spectrum by analogue, the planners knew of four UHF channels which were not used for television broadcasting - channels 35, 36, 37 and 38. Of these channel 38 was - and is - reserved for radio astronomy[81] Channel 36 was in widespread use for radar, but channels 35 and 37 although with some radar use, could be cleared for television broadcasting. These clear channels nationwide would have been ideal for COFDM single frequency networks. But politics changed all that.

In the late 1980s the Conservative government, having tried and failed to find a way of privatising the BBC or turning it into a subscription broadcaster, had turned its political artillery on ITV, famously described by Prime Minister Margaret Thatcher as "the last bastion of restrictive practice".[82] The 1990 Broadcasting Act introduced a bidding process for the award of licences to ITV companies in an attempt to bring the reality of the market to commercial television and to encourage a new breed of management with greater financial prudence. The Act also paved the way for a new national analogue broadcaster, Channel Five. Frequency planners now had to plan for Five's new analogue transmitters while at the same time preserving as much spectrum as they could for digital.

The government's decision was a compromise: Channel Five would use channel 37, one of the two empty channels, together with a spattering of other channels where they could be found. Channel 35 would be reserved for digital terrestrial television (DTT). When the licence first advertised in 1992, the bidders immediately found that it would only be able to reach half of the UK population, and worse, that in the areas where it was to broadcast using channel 37 any licensee would face a massively expensive

---

[81] The frequency spread of channel 38 covers frequencies emitted by pulsars and used by very long baseline interferometer observatories.

[82] A reference to the excessively generous pay of ITV technicians, and the apparent inability of ITV managements to rectify the situation.

programme of helping householders to retune the output of their VCRs, many of which had been set to that channel in the factory. Unsurprisingly, there were no takers. It would be three years before the ITC tried again, this time successfully, to interest bidders in the UK's last analogue franchise. By then, plans to use channel 35 for a digital single frequency network had been abandoned, and that channel was now on offer to Channel Five (in addition to channel 37) for analogue broadcasting.

The plan for "as many as twelve" DTT services was based on the use of just three digital UHF channels at each transmitter, each broadcasting a multiplex of four services.[83] One network was to be a single frequency network using the remaining clear channel, 35, while the other two would use 'interleaved' frequencies - different ones at each transmitter, just like analogue. The effect of this was that regional variations would not be possible on the four services carried by the SFN. Nevertheless the BBC, despite being a regionalised broadcaster, was very keen to acquire the SFN for four national services: BBC-1 and BBC-2 (in widescreen but presumably without the regional news and other 'opt-outs') and two new ones. Once they had started to think seriously about it, both the ITV companies and Channel 4 were insistent on networks using interleaved channels: ITV's federal structure then ensured a much greater degree of regional content than the BBC, and Channel 4, while it did not have regional variations in its programmes, did regionalise its advertising content.

The more that ITV thought about it, the more unsatisfactory the proposed plan for three multiplexes seemed. As the detailed content of the Broadcasting Bill was worked up the original proposal would be much modified, as would the BBC's initial preference for an SFN.

In 1994, Barry Cox moved from LWT to become the Director of the Independent Television Association, which effectively spoke for all the ITV companies. One of his principal responsibilities was to pursue the ITV interest in digital terrestrial television, and one of his first acts was to bring into the ITV's Network Centre more engineering expertise. Chris Hibbert was Chief Engineer of Carlton when he got a call from Cox:

> ... and he said, look you're the obvious guy to come over and work with me 'cos I need a technical person. We've got to think about how ITV's going to implement digital terrestrial, we've got to get our lobbying in to the DCMS because ... this was the land-grab phase.

Like other organisations, ITV was reducing the influence of its senior engineers, as the cult of management became dominant. Some old hands moved on, including Norman Green, who had run the ITVA's engineering

---

[83] a fourth digital network had been planned

arm for a number of years. But for Barry Cox, first rate engineering know-how was crucial:

> I enhanced the engineering committee - I effectively ran it - and that was where we formulated our policy - it was very much an engineering thing, and the key people were Sheppard and Vince Flanagan and Chris Hibbert. Those three were definitely very key. It was at a time when ITV Chief Engineers were in retreat, but there were still enough of them around doing a decent job: [they] understood everything, they were very good. We were very lucky that they were there, frankly, that understood the damn thing.

Hibbert had already started going to DVB meetings, where he sat on the Commercial Module, so he was as aware as any of the possibilities the technology could offer. He participated in the growing lobbying effort to ensure that ITV had as much of the DTT action as possible.:

> Barry and I would go off to the DCMS. We said, let's see if we can get the whole lot, so we put forward a proposal for high definition. Why? Keep out the opposition! So we cooked that one up: it didn't get very far. The DCMS said, go away, we're not talking about that, we're talking about multi-channel.

Barry Cox says that high definition was never a serious proposal:

> Carlton had a vision of the use of [DTT] for pay, that was absolutely clear, they were well ahead of the game in that respect. And I suppose at the ITVA my concern was simply to ensure that ITV got extra capacity, I wasn't involved in what we were going to use it for except very indirectly and informally in my relation with John Egan. I was perfectly happy with what they were proposing, so my pitch was make sure we maximise the opportunity through the lobbying. They will decide what to do with it, you just get it, to be blunt, that was basically it.

When the ITV's game plan later became clearer - nothing less that the creation of a terrestrial pay service to rival that of Sky's satellite offering - it would become obvious that maximising the number of channels that DTT could carry was of prime importance. For a time, that would cause a certain amount of friction between ITV and the BBC.

11
Winning Hearts and Minds

Suitably encouraged by the outcome of their discussions with government, the BBC set up, in August 1994, the Digital Broadcasting Project under a senior Controller, Michael Starks. The terms of reference set the project the task of conducting a feasibility study, with "a related experiment" into BBC digital broadcasting "based on terrestrial transmission", together with a range of consequential issues which ranged from programme content, through various technical, commercial and financial factors, to the impact on the licence fee. It was required, too, to provide a briefing for the BBC's response to the government White Paper which had been published that summer. Michael Starks remembers:

> The most urgent questions was, was the whole thing [DTT] feasible? And what was the feasibility of doing what the BBC was proposing to the government to do, which was to launch a service, and to do a sort of experimental or pilot service first? And that had both a technical and a financial theme to it, as well as of course ... a policy view that encompassed all of that. When I started, I didn't know if it was possible to do a demonstration. So the idea of doing a demonstration came in a bit later ... I didn't know at the outset how far this technology was still on the R&D workbench and how far it was workable ... I didn't know if there were receivers!

Over at the BBC's Research & Development arm, many people were involved in one or other of the international collaborative projects which were then looking at digital broadcasting technologies. At their head-quarters, a nineteenth-century country mansion in Surrey, many were already aware that in the summer of 1994 of the interest in digital broad-casting was gaining ground at Broadcasting House. Earlier that year, John Birt's office asked for a half page explanation of 'digital compression' and what it was and 'should the BBC be doing it on its channels?'. This somewhat garbled request ended up on Bob Ely's desk.

> I failed miserably to answer the question - not realising, of course, that the baseline of understanding of 'digital' amongst the BBC's top echelons was so low. However, it did alert Kingswood to the fact that digital was now firmly on the agenda at the top and ... we mobilised accordingly.

What did come as a surprise to Kingswood was the creation of a Digital Broadcasting Project as a creature of the corporate centre. Bob Ely was given the role as its R&D contact:

> The Digital Broadcasting Project rather came out of the blue and certainly the first thing I knew about it was Phil Laven rang me up and said go to a meeting in White City [with] this guy called Michael Starks - who I didn't know ... And the DBP project itself was at that stage very secret, so I certainly wasn't empowered to go back and say, hey guys I got this fascinating project can you give me the resources to implement it.

Under the tutelage of Bob Ely and his R&D colleagues, Michael Starks embarked on the furious intellectual challenge of understanding the poten-tial of digital technology and, together with consultants and the BBC's own experts, coming to grips with the ramifications of it across a whole raft of strategic and commercial issues, in order to tackle the full feasibility study required of him. By the autumn of 1994, Starks had decided that the 'experiment' referred to in his terms of reference could and should be a demonstration of working digital television. But it was not to be simply a demonstration of the technology: it would also model the BBC's service proposition and the viewer experience which might be expected.

It was at this stage that the author became involved. Michael Starks wanted a producer to stage the demonstrations[84]; his job would be to prepare content, to create a theatrical demonstration area, to put together a foyer

---

[84] Bob Ely recalls: "This was in itself a significant and important innovation: although producers had often been involved in making programmes or tapes for technical demonstrations, until that date the demonstrations themselves had nearly always been designed and presented by engineers rather than by programme makers or professional presenters - with sometimes less than happy results. Another important innovation was the use of corporate affairs professionals to manage the invitations lists and shepherd the various VIPs attending."

exhibition, and - crucially - to work closely with the R&D engineers on the practical details of presentation. I had for many years worked frequently in the BBC's outside broadcast events department in a culture in which almost every programme was different and where close liaison with engineering colleagues was crucial: just the background, perhaps, for such an unusual assignment as the Digital Broadcasting Project's demonstrations. And I was in the right place at the right time. In the autumn of 1994 I had put together a videotape demonstration which explored the issues surrounding widescreen production and the problems of simulcasting: it was paid for by the Digital Broadcasting Project. Now I was being asked to stay on to produce the digital broadcasting demonstrations. It was October 1994: the demonstrations were to take place in March 1995, five months away.

Initially, the research and development people were all for a simulation, and were aghast at the prospect of doing it for real. Michael Starks was determined to have the real thing:

> My view was, I had been asked to carry out a feasibility study, I'd been given a deadline, I could be in one of two situations: one was I was able to say, here is a technology which is mature enough to be demonstratable, you can see it and that gives you confidence that the basis exists for going forward, and the other one is you say actually we tried to do a demonstration, it was impossible, or this bit or this bit or this bit were missing and so you need to be aware that this technology is not very mature and therefore if you are wanting promises about launching services in year X or year Y, you've got to allow for the completion of this work. And I think in a way by undertaking the demo we were taking a snapshot of the degree to which the technology was ready.

Michael Starks got agreement for the real thing. The difficulty was that the BBC themselves, while active in a number of digital broadcasting research programmes, owned no appropriate experimental digital transmission or reception equipment of their own. Following the BBC's financial crisis of the late eighties, says Bob Ely, it was:

> ... [an] era of belt-tightening .... there was a consolidation... We focussed the very limited resources we had available for digital TV into collaborative projects such as RACE HIVITS - to do digital HDTV at 140 Mbit/s - RACE dTTb and the Eureka VADIS[85] project. Very much the message was, participate in international groups because that is a good way of being a fast-follower, leveraging a limited investment. But what you can't do is lead, and that was a very big culture shock for Kingswood because obviously it had been the leading research lab and whilst some researchers enjoyed the new dimension of international collaboration and travel others found it difficult to adjust to this new way of working.

---

[85] VADIS: Video Audio Digital Interactive Systems

The BBC - not for the first time - asked its international research partners if it might borrow some of their equipment.

A key part of the proposed demonstrations was for four lengthy videotape sequences, each representing one digital widescreen service, to be multiplexed together, and broadcast digitally from the London transmitter (at Crystal Palace) to be received at the demonstration venue for display. To do this required coding and multiplexing equipment, and a COFDM modem - modulator and demodulator. Of the four or five research programmes going on around Europe, two - HD-DIVINE and STERNE - had potentially suitable equipment. HD-DIVINE was a Scandinavian project, while the STERNE equipment was owned by CCETT in France, with whom the BBC, together with other organisations, were collaborating in the European RACE dTTb Project. Both organisations were approached by Andy Bower of BBC R&D in October 1994, and by December the demonstration team knew that the STERNE equipment was available, that it could do what was needed, and that CCETT had generously agreed to send a team of their own engineers to London to operate it. Negotiations with the Radiocommunications Agency resulted in a licence for the short-term use of a spare UHF channel at the Crystal Palace transmitter where a temporary transmitter and transmitting aerial were installed.

The demonstration area was in an unused boardroom on the top floor of the BBC's new White City building. While the STERNE modulator was installed at Crystal Palace, the rest of the French equipment was located in a room next door to the demonstration venue. For the outgoing signal, coders and a multiplexer produced a multiple programme transport stream which was relayed to Crystal Palace by landline and microwave radio link. Back at White City, the STERNE demodulator, demultiplexer and decoder received the broadcast signal and gave outputs of each of the four programme streams. That was the extent of the real demonstration of digital terrestrial broadcasting. But elsewhere in the next-door room, out of sight of the demonstration audience, was a mass of equipment and operators. Videotape machines played out the four programme streams; others provided a closed-circuit replay of a sequence to demonstrate five-channel surround-sound. An electronic programme guide was simulated and played out from laserdisc. A vision mixer and a sound mixing panel were installed, together with extensive monitoring facilities, to create a seamless presentation. Under Dave Perrottet, a team of R&D engineers tended their own sensitive equipment, while stalwarts from OB engineering operated the conventional TV kit, and a group of quiet, purposeful, French engineers nursed the STERNE equipment.

In the demonstration area, four widescreen sets showed the four programme streams. A fifth set, centrally placed on a bookcase flanked by armchairs to suggest a living room, showed a choice of source controlled by a custom-built infra-red remote control. It looked real, and in the important elements it was real, but there was quite a lot of furious pedalling going on out of sight.

The DVB specification for digital terrestrial was still incomplete, and the parameters of the STERNE modem were slightly different from those which eventually were agreed on, but in most respects it functioned well. The performances (for such they were) included one sure-fire show-stopper: Because the venue was on the fifth floor and had almost line of sight with the transmitter, the received signal was, despite the very low power of the DTT transmissions, quite strong. Phil Laven discovered that a cheap set-top aerial, if carefully positioned, gave almost unwatchable pictures from the analogue transmissions (due to multipath/ghosting) but perfect pictures via the digital system (which, of course, due to the use of COFDM, was immune to multipath). To demonstrate that the set-top aerial was really in use, he would at one point disconnect it and then reconnect it: the pictures would disappear and then reappear. This extraordinary feature of COFDM DTT - perfect pictures from a cheap portable aerial, and so graphically demonstrated - caused the sceptical and normally taciturn technical journalist Barry Fox to utter an involuntary shout of "Christ!".

Over a period of two weeks in March 1995, Michael Starks[86] and Phil Laven (sometimes Henry Price deputised for Laven) gave a 40 minute presentation to audiences which included government advisors, broadcasting and industry representatives, and others, as well as BBC management. The messages were carefully crafted. There was an emphasis of course on the benefits of widescreen and an increase in the number of services that the technology could handle. There was also emphasis on the possibility that because of the commonality of much of the technology across terrestrial, satellite and cable, digital receivers could be made which were capable of receiving all three platforms. And when it came to the content, Michael Starks remembers that:

> During the Digital Broadcasting Project the BBC was very coy about wanting new channels for itself, and was positioning itself as investigating the potential of new technology, it wasn't positioning itself as - shall we say - looking for imperial expansion. And so, when we were demonstrating the possibility of extra channels we were rather firmly instructed not to present them as BBC channels. So this wasn't a bid to expand the BBC's capacity, because I think politically it was too soon for that, but I think there was a realisation that multichannel was going to come and to be stuck with the old technology and no access to multichannel was not necessarily wise.

---

[86] Michael had started out as a programme maker in the BBC and was a skilled presenter; Phil Laven and Henry Price were also good at talking to non-specialists..

So by April 1995 the feasibility of digital terrestrial and many of the advantages that it could offer had been amply demonstrated, albeit with experimental and non-standard equipment, but against a background of growing international efforts to establish a definitive specification. Many must have left those demonstrations with much to ponder - certainly that was the impression that Michael Starks had:

> At that time we put quite a lot of emphasis into quality, and I think the BBC might have been ambivalent about whether it wanted to expand into extra channels, but it was not ambivalent about wanting to see beautiful pictures on BBC-1 and BBC-2 in widescreen. And I think other broadcasters reacted the same way. So we weren't pretending at that stage that everything was mature, we were just saying that it was possible (and that there was a room full of equipment next door), but what we showed people was a compelling consumer proposition - a combination of extra quality and extra services, and I think that had a very important enthusing effect. I wasn't worried that ITV or Channel 4 would walk away from this, one of the reasons they didn't was because they were caught up in this enthusiasm and what it could do for their services.

These carefully constructed demonstrations presented industry with a cogent and convincing picture of what digital terrestrial television could be, not just in technical terms, but in the commercial and service opportunities which it could offer to all corners of the industry - broadcasters, manufacturers and retailers. There is no doubt that for many of them, and to some extent for the government, the BBC's vision was an important catalyst to their thinking.

With the successful demonstration of March 1995 complete, the BBC's own timetable - set out to government the previous summer and summarised in the White Paper that it wished to demonstrate the feasibility of DTT in March 1995 (which it had done emphatically) and that it wished to start a service in 1997 - now looked realistic.

To coincide with the demonstrations, Michael Starks issued his internal report. It was a comprehensive document that examined the implications for the BBC of the new technology from a number of perspectives. The programme services choices, which included widescreen, additional services and whether subscription services should be contemplated; how the digital services might be distributed, which included some thoughts on satellite, cable and ADSL[87] as well as terrestrial; the practicalities of transmission and coverage; and commercial feasibility. The report concluded with a series of clear recommendations that digital television broadcasting - and digital terrestrial broadcasting in particular - was something that the

---

[87] ADSL: Asynchronous Digital Subscriber Line: the technology now in widespread use for broadband delivery to the home, but at the time in its infancy.

BBC should plan for with urgency and seriousness. The report also expressed in tentative form two ideas which were to become key elements in the BBC's digital strategy over the following five years.

The first was the thought that the BBC should join forces with other broadcasters interested in DTT to discuss with manufacturers the timely provision of suitable receivers, and that the BBC should use its technical expertise to participate "fully" in the DVB standardisation process. Both parts of this proposition represented a departure from the historical BBC attitude to the world outside: discussions with industry had in the past been somewhat cursory, and the implication (unstated) was that some kind of forum would be required. As for participating "fully" in the DVB's work, the reader's implication, borne out by the experiences of R&D engineers like Bob Ely, was that the BBC's participation in the DVB had not hitherto had the full support of senior management, and that that support should now be forthcoming.

The second lay in the discussion on distribution, and with the thought which was expressed that the BBC should look at the pros and cons of distributing its new digital services on cable and "possibly" (a highly tentative note here) on satellite. The idea that the BBC, traditionally a terrestrial broadcaster, should introduce a policy of distributing its services by satellite, was revolutionary. In engineering terms it made sense, and strategically it would also come to make sense as well, but politically and commercially it risked being seen as either imperial expansion or fraternising with an enemy.

Before many months had passed following the report's appearance both sets of thoughts would be translated into actions. Meantime, the core business at hand - the development and trialling of digital terrestrial television - continued to dominate. But it wasn't just the technical system that was unfinished; deciding on how digital broadcasting was going to be organised, funded and legislated for, had still to be tackled. Michael Starks was conscious that a lot of work lay ahead:

> I think in that first eight months between the summer we started and the March [1995] demo a lot of things that were clarified later like, how many frequencies were there going to be, how many multiplexes, the principle on which they were going to be allocated, the idea of guaranteed space of simulcasting ... were all pretty fluid actually. So I wasn't conscious at that stage [that] I was interacting with a government timetable I could see, but I was later.

In July of 1995, the BBC persuaded CCETT to bring their equipment back to White City for two days of further demonstrations. This time the audiences were senior government figures, including the Broadcasting Minister, Virginia Bottomley. In August, the government White Paper on digital terrestrial broadcasting was published. By now the legislative timetable had emerged and the government had begun work on the

Broadcasting Bill. During the drafting process, many outstanding issues would need to be resolved. From now on, if it had not been doing so before, much of the industry was engaged in thinking about the changes it would bring.

The choice of a technical standard for DTT was a given: a European Commission Directive effectively bound the UK to use the forthcoming DVB-T specification. There seems to have been also broad agreement on the use of open standards as a means of stimulating competition and innovation. The devil, however, was in the detail. What exactly, asked those drafting the legislation, can this new technology offer, and how do we best employ it? For the answers, they consulted widely with the specialists in industry. At the BBC, Bob Ely found himself drawn into this process:

> [there were] huge elements of input and drafts sent for people like me to read and comment on. In terms of process, very impressively done. There's no doubt, they got an exceedingly high quality Bill by consulting the best experts - fairly even-handedly so.

Realising that a broad industry consensus might go down well with those who were drafting the legislation and might contribute to a Bill that contained proposals which would satisfy the aspirations of industry as well as government, the major players took to discussing matters amongst themselves before putting their recommendations forward. The UK Digital TV Group (DTG) had been formed, which provided one technical forum, and in September the Minister hosted a dinner to elicit views on her White Paper's substance from industry leaders. But many meetings were bilateral: the BBC and ITV met at the senior level of policy-makers, and it was in those encounters that the most difficult differences of opinion were exposed, discussed and eventually resolved.

The major difference of opinion between the BBC and ITV had to do with the capacity that would be available on the DTT platform and the coverage that could be achieved. Capacity and coverage are determined by a number of technical factors, and are inter-related. The issue was put in sharp relief as the frequency planners began detailed work on a scheme for digital transmission.

At first sight, the original July 1994 DNH announcement of plans for up to twelve TV channels on DTT might have appealed to the expansionist-minded BBC and ITV, constrained as they were in what was then still a four-channel analogue world. Indeed, to begin with, the BBC actively lobbied for the use of a single frequency network in channel 35 which would have allowed very widespread coverage and enough capacity to simulcast BBC-1 and BBC-2 together with at least one new service. But twelve channels did not come anywhere near looking as attractive as the

150 channels people were saying would be available on a future digital satellite service. It soon became apparent that 12 channels was not going to be enough to ensure commercial success. Both ITV and its regulator the ITC wanted the terrestrial platform to offer as many services as possible. It was clear that some, if not the majority, of new services would be pay services. That would bring the platform into direct competition with Sky's satellite service. The BBC developed a similar view, believing that a strong commercial presence on DTT was essential for its success. The frequency planners were asked to think again.

As the joint BBC, ITC and NTL team set out to prepare a new plan for digital television broadcasting in the UK, differences of opinion on the relative merits of planning round one single frequency network immediately surfaced. The ITC, and their research and transmission contractor NTL, wanted all the multiplexes to use frequencies which were interleaved with the existing analogue frequencies. They wanted to use the 2k modulation option, because chipsets able to demodulate that would be available sooner than for an 8k version. To begin with, the BBC stuck to its preference for using a single frequency network and 8k modulation. Michael Starks was worried that the use of channel 35 might result in the BBC having to bear the financial and logistical burden of retuning millions of videocassette recorders which used the channel to play back to the TV set. But he had a further insight:

> The issue that I recall bringing to the table personally was to say if you were serious about wanting manufacturers to make receivers, it's no good thinking of a policy which was exclusively BBC-centred, if you want manufacturers to make receivers, they are going to have to make them so the public can get a range of services from different broadcasters, and so rather than fall out with ITV and the ITC over 2k and 8k and single frequency networks versus interleaved we might need to think about having a common position if we're seriously going to get this going. And by the way, wasn't BBC-1 regionally based, and different in different regions, and if we were doing simulcast wasn't it quite important for us to be able to do that [too]?

The original 12-channel proposal envisaged granting the BBC the one remaining clear national UHF channel to give nationwide coverage using a single frequency network. Under this proposal, 8k chips would be needed in UK receivers. Ranged against this were the arguments of those - in ITV and some in the BBC - who saw the imperative of an early launch of services. DTT would provide a counterbalance and a competitor to the growing market penetration of BSkyB, which was sure to intensify once Sky launched a digital satellite service. There was technological leadership - the DTI view - which held that early experience of new technology led to a business bonanza; and NTL, new owners of the privatised IBA transmitter network, saw a particular business opportunity. For the highly regionalised structure of the ITV network, 2k was better suited[88]. Motorola, the only company yet to make progress with the development of COFDM chips, said rather firmly that while it might have 2k chips ready for a late 1997 service launch, an 8k chip would be at least two years later. And everybody expected that by then, a BSkyB digital satellite service would be well established.

ITV were lobbying the BBC very hard to agree to the use of the 2k mode, supported by the DTI and NTL. Henry Price remembers that:

> NTL said very firmly that 8k chips would be far too costly. This was in the early days of Policy & Planning and NTL managed to convince the P&P people that they knew better than BBC. All part of the picture that John Birt and Patricia did not trust what BBC R&D told them, and if R&D told them that this was a good idea and NTL said it wasn't, they were more inclined to believe NTL.

Henry Price was present when NTL later turned up the heat on the BBC's Director of Policy and Planning:

> I was at a meeting between NTL and BBC Policy and Planning (I think both Phil Laven and Patricia Hodgson were present), where Peter Marchant of NTL said that if the decision is taken to go 8k then NTL will pull out of the project completely. That's our bottom line [he said], we will not put money into it, we will not support this project if it's 8k.

The BBC's policymakers were faced with a united front made up of most of the other major broadcasting players, and the DTI. From inside the BBC Michael Starks had made the point that 2k actually had some advantages - the continuation of regional broadcasting in digital future. The advantages of 2k that were key to the independent sector's strategy - greater capacity for services so giving a stronger and more competitive commercial proposition - played also in the BBC's favour. And the BBC was very anxious to make common cause with its competitors in advising government on the content of the Broadcasting Bill. The DCMS would be unimpressed if industry were not all singing from the same hymn sheet, and close co-operation between all the industry players would obviously be crucial in the successful launch of DTT. So in August 1995, the BBC abandoned its position, and supported the development of a frequency plan based on the exclusive use of 2k and interleaved frequencies.

That decision allowed the joint frequency planning team to begin work in earnest. Henry Price remembers the brief given to the BBC's planning team:

> The brief from Phil Laven was, "First objective, find four frequencies at every main station, number two objective, see if you can find a fifth; number three objective, see if you can find a sixth." And that's the way the

---

[88] The two BBC services also carried regional 'opt-outs'

planning went, because the initial brief really formed the whole of the way the planning was done.

Once the main stations had been planned, attention turned to the relay stations - the medium and low power transmitters that were used to extend the coverage areas of the high power main stations. Some of them served large centres of population, so work began with those serving the greatest number of homes and worked down the list. The question was, where to stop? As more and more relays were included usable frequencies became harder to identify, but there was another consideration: cost-effectiveness. The break point was found after the 81st transmitter site had been planned: the last one served 56,000 homes, and the next one on the list would have served just 25,000.

The frequency plan which resulted envisaged equipping just 51 main stations and 30 relays of the 1100-odd analogue transmitter sites for digital broadcasting. A priority was that as much of the existing analogue network infrastructure as possible should be used. If existing sites, and existing transmitter masts - even the existing aerial systems - could be used, and if the new digital signals could use similar frequency groupings and polarisation of transmission, then existing domestic aerial installations would, it was hoped, be adequate to ensure digital reception without modification. "It is important", wrote the frequency planners in a 1996 conference paper, "not to place unnecessary difficulties in front of potential viewers."

These 81 sites between them used up almost all of the available interleaved frequencies. But before building the transmitters, there needed to be one further process. The countries of Europe cannot unilaterally decide to use whatever frequencies they wish: there needs to be international agreement. Television transmission from sites in the UK can interfere with transmissions on continental Europe, particularly in northern France, Holland and Belgium, and vice versa. Interference from a high power transmitter can occur at distances up to 500 km, and more if the path is over the sea.

The frequencies used in Europe for television broadcasting were agreed at an international conference in Stockholm in 1961, long before digital television became a possibility. Frequency planners later realised that digital transmissions could co-exist with those of analogue and so, at least for the time being, no new treaty was required. In 1997, a major international meeting in Chester clarified the technical criteria and administrative procedures for introducing DVB-T transmissions in Europe. Within it, agreement for the use of a particular frequency, and the power levels to be used, are negotiated bilaterally with neighbouring countries - a lengthy but equitable arrangement. This process allowed the UK to begin to build its digital transmitter network as soon as agreements were made. In Europe's crowded spectrum, however, there had to be give and take. [89]

By September 1996, the frequency planning team had identified frequencies for the first four multiplexes at each of the 51 main stations, and the additional two frequencies at all but two of the relays. But there had to be some compromises, particularly to avoid the possibility of causing interference on existing analogue services. At a number of transmitters, new digital frequencies would lie outside the group of frequencies used for analogue broadcasting at that site, and for which domestic aerials used in that area had been optimised. This risked a situation where many homes would need to re-equip with a wideband aerial covering the 'out-of-group' frequencies before being able to receive the multiplexes being broadcast using them. And it quickly became apparent that, while analogue broadcasting continued, digital television coverage could not be brought to many areas of the populous English south coast and parts of East Anglia, while the planned digital transmitter to serve the Channel Islands has still to be built. These restrictions would haunt the industry six years later and, for a time, risk the collapse of the then nascent DTT platform.

There was one disadvantage in an interleaved frequency planning approach, however, which was that no one multiplex using a patchwork of frequencies could have the same near-universal coverage that a channel 35 SFN could offer. As the planning work proceeded, the figures emerged: it was estimated that the best multiplex would reach 93 per cent of the population, and the least good just 62 per cent, provided a rooftop aerial was used. But to achieve such coverage, the COFDM 16-QAM mode would have to be used, which would allow each multiplex only 18 Mbit/s of useful capacity - thought then to be enough for only three services. Four services in each multiplex would require the use of the 64-QAM mode which gave a 24 Mbit/s capacity. But that further reduced coverage, to 89 per cent for the best multiplex, to 53 per cent for the least good. [90]

The ITV companies and the ITC wanted to trade coverage for a greater capacity, but some at the BBC, like Phil Laven, were not. He argued his case with the Director of Policy and Planning, Patricia Hodgson:

> The technical people inside the BBC were absolutely adamant that this was a dangerous thing to do and Patricia had her arm twisted by Barry Cox and others from ITV who said, but we're going to do this, and you have to come along with us and we can't have the BBC doing something different. So there was a huge amount of pressure. Whilst accepting that the number of programmes was useful, and you couldn't squeeze them into 18 Mbit/s and have reasonable quality, the thing that had to be compromised [on] was

---

[89] Later, the International Telecommunications Union began making arrangements for a major round of meetings, to begin in 2005, to bring the Stockholm Agreement up to date by planning for Europe's spectrum use in a future when analogue transmission had ceased.
[90] These predictions later proved in practice to be highly optimistic.

coverage. And everybody to my surprise at the time - in the non-technical area - said, well, OK let's sacrifice coverage: it doesn't matter.

Meetings between Patricia Hodgson, Barry Cox of the ITVA and Frank McGettigan of Channel Four certainly resulted in a common approach. In Barry Cox's words, "We did try and co-ordinate what we were doing." Cox does not remember the issue of capacity and coverage being a source of disagreement. And for a time, it seemed that coverage didn't matter: the main population centres would be covered, and the figures looked acceptable. The business proposition looked good. It was only much later that Phil Laven was proved right, but by then he had left the BBC to become the Technical Director of the European Broadcasting Union in Geneva, while in Britain the digital terrestrial platform would be in crisis.

With agreement between the BBC and ITV on the use of the 2k modulation mode, an interleaved frequency plan for six multiplexes, and the use of 64-QAM - all of which maximised capacity with some compromise on coverage - both organisations, together with Channel Four and the ITC, could present a common position to the DCMS officials who were drafting the Broadcasting Bill of December 1995.

The Bill outlined the core elements of the future shape of digital terrestrial broadcasting. Of the six multiplexes: one (Multiplex 1) would be 'gifted' to the BBC[91], a second (Multiplex 2) would be shared between ITV and Channel Four, a third (Multiplex A) would have half its capacity reserved for Channel Five and, in Wales, the Welsh language public service broadcaster S4C. These broadcasters would be required to simulcast their existing services in digital, but would acquire room for additional services alongside them. The remaining three multiplexes (Multiplexes B, C and D) would be made available for new services provided by new broadcasters. The Independent Television Commission would be given the role of allocating licences for all but the BBC multiplex.

The Bill introduced the concept of a 'multiplex operator'. These were new business entities with a specific role unknown in the conventional analogue broadcasting world. Multiplex operators were to be positioned between the broadcasters (now more accurately 'programme service providers') and the transmission or network operators (who provided the actual transmission services). The IBA's transmitter network had already been privatised and bought by NTL. The privatisation of BBC Transmission would follow in February 1997. The proposed legislation therefore lay the basis for competition in the digital terrestrial television market at three levels - service provision, multiplex operation and transmission - to form a horizontal market.

---

[91] The BBC's multiplex was also the one with the greatest coverage. The BBC had lobbied hard for this and the DCMS Secretary, Virginia Bottomley, had agreed to it.

The Bill proposed that the BBC would act as its own multiplex operator for its 'gifted' multiplex, and that ITV and Channel Four should form a joint body to operate their multiplex. For the other four multiplexes, licences would be awarded to new companies who, it was envisaged, would act as 'content aggregators', selecting services from a range of suppliers, combining them together into multiplexes, buying transmission capacity from one of the two privatised network operators, and marketing the combined content to consumers.

The Bill would go through parliament in the autumn of 1996. Now, with the future shape of the industry becoming clear, there was a great deal for the industry to do. At the BBC, Michael Starks got agreement for the next phase of his Digital Broadcasting Project. He was to build on the recommendations of his report. In the course of the following twelve months, he and his colleagues would build alliances with broadcasters and industry representatives in the UK and in Europe and take the idea of the BBC broadcasting on satellite forward. The publication of the Broadcasting Bill imposed an aggressive timescale and spurred to action the next crucial stage of the UK's accelerating race towards digital television. Within those twelve months, the DVB terrestrial specification would be complete, and the world's first fully compliant pilot service of one full digital multiplex would be on the air from the BBC in London.

Whitehall was not, in the middle of 1995, the only place where the lobbyists were at work. Both the BBC and ITV found themselves mounting a strenuous lobby at the European Commission and Parliament as the Commission's *TV Without Frontiers* Directive was being discussed. With the rise of powerful satellite pay TV operators in various parts of Europe, often with a monopoly as BSkyB was in the UK, the Commission were keen to ensure that these operators allowed fair access to their platform for other broadcasters. The Commission proposed legislation.

Although the digital satellite television systems being designed for Europe all relied on the open standard DVB-S specification, the pay-TV operators had two technical means at their disposal which could lock out competitors' services (even if they were being broadcast independently by the same satellite), and so lock in the subscriber to the operator's own range of programmes. One was conditional access, the other was the electronic programme guide (EPG), used by the viewer to tune to a desired service.

Conditional access was necessary because when programme rights holders sold broadcasters their content, they came licensed for use only in a particular territory. So a BSkyB would buy UK rights only to, say, a popular American soap, while the German rights would be sold to, say, Kirch, and the French rights to, say, Canal Plus. Conditional access scrambled the signal so only a receiver with the correct smartcard for the region could unscramble and allow the programme to be viewed. CA also ensured the all-important revenue stream: if you didn't keep up your subscription, the card's entitlement could be terminated by an over-the-air signal. So, any broadcaster who wished to reach a satellite home had to use the same conditional access system as the pay operator. The electronic programme guide, unknown in analogue television, was a viewer's means of finding the desired service. Without agreement with the operator, a broadcaster's service could not appear on the EPG. And if it wasn't on the EPG, the viewer had no means of tuning to it.

Taken together, these two factors ensured that the satellite operator was effectively the 'gatekeeper' of his platform. The Commission was determined that other broadcasters should have right of access to such a platform on "fair, reasonable and non-discriminatory terms". The BSkyB lobbyists went into overdrive and, together with representatives of like-minded organisations, mounted a concerted effort to have the proposed directive watered down. Britain's official view was being expressed by the free market oriented DTI who, being disinclined to contemplate obstacles placed in the path of a developing and successful BSkyB, largely opposed the Commission's proposals. The BBC and ITV were becoming increasingly concerned.

The BBC was by now edging towards a policy of platform neutrality. With DTT unable to reach all of the population before analogue switch-off the Corporation, obliged to provide a universal service, needed the option of broadcasting its new digital services by satellite (and cable) as well as terrestrial. ITV too, with an eye of the market opportunities of pay TV on satellite as well as on terrestrial, wanted the same option. Both organisations sent their lobbyists off the Brussels to plead their case, and supplemented that with visits by high-powered delegations which at times included John Birt and Patricia Hodgson from the BBC and Barry Cox from the ITVA. Cox recalls:

> It was an enormous battle, We were really trying hard, and that was a very big battle which went on for a couple of years, and I can remember going to European sessions where we were almost the only people arguing against the new players, particularly Canal Plus and Sky.

The lobbying went to the top, and eventually to a meeting with the Commissioner, Martin Bangemann, who was finally won over by the public service broadcasters' case.

In the Autumn of 1995, the European Parliament issued Directive 95/47/EC which enshrined the principle of access to both a platform operator's conditional access and electronic programme guide on "fair, reasonable and non-discriminatory terms". For their part, the BBC and ITV were content that the principle of open access to a new Sky Digital platform had been established and that a proper regulatory framework had

been set up to ensure that it happened. And while BSkyB certainly resent-
ed the intrusion on its freedoms, and railed against what it regarded as the
old broadcasting establishment in cahoots with the regulators, it is not at all
clear that they actually wished to exclude other broadcasters. Indeed, well
ahead of launch they were talking to a number of operators who wanted to
put their services on the platform alongside those of Sky. When launch
came many of them would be present and BSkyB's policy of accommodating them would deny any opportunity for a rival satellite platform to
establish itself, as happened in some other European countries.

But with three years to go before any digital platform would launch in
the UK, the digital future was still one of options, possibilities and opportunities. The only certainties were that digital broadcasting was coming,
and that terrestrial digital broadcasting must play an important part in it.

12
Refining the System

With the completion of the DVB-S satellite specification in December 1993, and the DVB-C cable specification the following March, members of the DVB could now turn to its next major task, the DVB-T digital terrestrial equivalent. This was always going to be a more complex undertaking, for a number of reasons. Terrestrial transmission is a more difficult environment than cable or satellite, and the COFDM technology being proposed was highly complex and with a greater choice of parameters. The DVB Technical Module faced a daunting challenge.

It would take time to discuss the merits and demerits of the various candidate technologies, and to evaluate them - first by theoretical means, then by laboratory simulations, followed by building test equipment and proving it in field trials. But first, before this could begin, the Commercial Module had to come up with a set of commercial requirements which would form the brief for the technical work. That, too, would turn out to be less straightforward than first thought. At least to begin with, there seemed no particular need to hurry.

But the urgency which had surrounded the satellite work - because the big pay-TV operators of Europe wanted to move to digital broadcasting as soon as practicable - would soon also be present in the DVB-T work. Given the probability that digital satellite services would launch as soon as the chipsets could be developed - say two to three years - broadcasters like those in Britain who wanted an early start to terrestrial digital broadcasting knew that, to be competitive, their platforms should if possible launch no later. And the pressure to complete a DTT specification in time for that to happen would come to bear considerably on the DVB's work and cause some serious disagreements along the way.

When the members of the DVB's Terrestrial Commercial Module[92] started to look in detail at what the DVB-T specification should encompass, they faced another major complexity. There were many differing views about what a digital terrestrial television service would be used for. The original Reimers Report had recognised this to a certain extent, and had outlined a system which could be used to carry a hierarchy of services - everything from HDTV through high quality SDTV to PAL quality SDTV and to low quality VHS-type quality. This was possible because of the flexibility of both MPEG-2 coding and the COFDM modulation system. MPEG-2 provided a series of profiles for coding television pictures at different qualities, and similarly the COFDM system could be configured in a number of different ways. A choice could be made between one of a number of different forward error correction (FEC) code rates, the duration of the guard interval, or between QPSK and QAM, and between QAM rates 16 or 64, and finally the number of carriers, 2,000 or 8,000. With each came a trade-off between capacity and robustness: the more robust you wanted your signal to be, the lower the capacity and the fewer the number of services which could be carried.

But before making these choices for inclusion in the specification, there needed to be a consensus of what DTT was actually going to be used for. Ian Dixon, of the DTI was a UK representative at the DVB commercial module which, in those days, had taken to holding its meetings in the Salon Jupiter at Charles de Gaulle airport outside Paris, where ...

> ... there was a lot of sitting round twiddling thumbs and trying to think about what we wanted out of digital for terrestrial TV and nobody really had any idea. There were a lot of questions like, do we want it mobile? Do we want it high definition? Do we want it this do we want it that? There were more questions than there were answers. And everybody sat round and pondered these great things but couldn't really come up with any conclusions that had any market realities.

But as different countries worked though the market scenarios it became clear that their conclusions differed. Different countries wanted a different mix and for different purposes. For example, the German market was characterised by a high and growing uptake of analogue satellite and cable services: only a minority of homes relied upon terrestrial analogue transmissions for the main living room set. Holland and Belgium were similarly heavily cabled. Many in those countries were looking at the possibility of a new kind of terrestrial television service that could compete, and began to identify one. Early tests of the COFDM-based

---

[92] The DVB had separate commercial modules for different purposes. In 1995, there were three, covering Interactive Services, Cable and Satellite, and Terrestrial. In this chapter the title 'Commercial Module' refers to the Terrestrial Commercial Module.

digital audio broadcasting system, DAB, had indicated that it could deliver high-quality, interference-free services with reliable reception to portable receivers in boats, caravans and holiday homes. In theory at least, a COFDM-based digital television service could do the same. And there was, in their view, no particular urgency in introducing these new services.

In Britain on the other hand (and to some extent in the Scandinavian countries), the thinking was different and much clearer: it was becoming obvious that DTT would have to compete with digital satellite services particularly, and would therefore need to do so on the basis of as large a number of standard definition services as the digital signals could carry - which meant four services multiplexed together in each available UHF channel. And these signals should be broadcast from the same transmitter sites as the existing analogue services, and designed to be received on the ubiquitous rooftop aerial, just like analogue.

The single-minded clarity of the emerging UK view alarmed many at the DVB. As Ulrich Reimers put it:

> Many, many people only started to think about the introduction of DVB-T and what would it mean and how would the business models be, and so on - when you [in the UK] had clear plans. Which means that there was resistance in part of our DVB membership simply because you were so good and so well-informed and so well-organised that they felt steam-rollered by things coming out of the UK.

Standardisation work is predicated on trying to find a single standard that will do everything that everybody wants. In practice, of course, and with different agendas round the table, building options into a specification becomes the only way out of an impasse. Ian Dixon is certain that the flexibility of the DVB-T specification when it finally appeared arose from just these practicalities:

> One of the real strengths of the DVB in those early days was we all sat round the table and the Spanish would come up and say, we want the standard to accommodate this that and the other and you'd sit there thinking what on earth do they want that for? What possible reason could there be for them wanting that? And you'd go away to lunch and they'd explain why and it would turn out to be something that was particular to their regulatory situation or the fact that they had language regions and all this sort of thing which had absolutely no relevance to us but we could accommodate it without damaging our own interests. And from I think that catholic input, right across the whole of Europe - all the key countries with all their different histories and their different requirements - from that I think came the options and the flexibility and the capability.

And any worthwhile specification ought to be future-proof, to as great an extent as possible. Chris Hibbert also remembers this time at the Commercial Module:

When specifications are written for something very new the engineer's responsibility is to really look into the future and say, well, what are the likely ongoing needs? Can we make sure that this is going to have a reasonable life ahead of it? Is it going to be future-proof? Conversely, don't let's over-egg it and make it so complicated that nobody wants to build it. Always a difficult thing to do. Engineers get blamed for inventing things that people don't want. But always, always, always, at some stage they do want it and engineers know that they will want it, so you build them in. But you have to do it in such a way that it maybe can be done in a modular way so you don't have to build everything on day one but you can add bits in a backward-compatible way.

While the discussions continued in the Commercial Module, some frustration was felt by Ulrich Reimers and his Technical Module colleagues, who were sitting there ready to go, but unable to proceed without having received a set of commercial requirements. Why were the commercial people taking so long? Why couldn't it be done as quickly as the satellite requirements had been? Gordon Drury, who had by then joined the Technical Module, says that Ulrich Reimers understood the problem and is full of praise for way Ulrich Reimers handled the situation.

He managed the Technical Module supremely well. And what he was doing was keeping the engineers occupied by doing field trials, consolidating the work, trying to do in advance what he knew he would have to do in the future. So he was working on the consensus and trying to get the R&D guys to go back to their labs and say, well, he wants this and we want that, is there any way we can find a compromise on it. Go back to your labs, do a bit more work, I'm not pressurising you now, 'cos he didn't have to, he didn't have a mandate.

And there was an unexpected bonus from this lengthy process. Gordon Drury:

There was leakage, because the techy things were leaking back into the commercial discussions, and saying, well, the technology can support these things: what about this? Oh yes, we might think about that. So it informed the commercial debate, and several people were common to both modules.

Finally, part way through 1994, the commercial requirements were completed. Many, but not all, of the features outlined in the 1992 Reimers Report were incorporated. Among the principal requirements was for maximum commonality with the newly standardised cable and satellite specifications. The concept of service provision to receivers both with fixed outside aerials as well as portable receivers was endorsed, but stopped short of asking for a system that would offer reception on mobile receivers. Mindful of the need for DVB-T to co-exist with analogue transmissions in Europe's crowded spectrum, it asked that the system should be designed to make the most of existing transmitters sites (implying the need to reproduce very similar coverage areas), that it should

154

allow the use of single frequency networks - national or regional - if desired, that it should permit local and regional programming, and that it should be rugged enough to avoid interference from and to the analogue services that it would have to co-exist with in the spectrum. The Commercial Module wished also for the system to be designed so that it could be easily reconfigured by the broadcaster to trade data capacity - the number and quality of services - with the extent of coverage. Slightly implausibly, given the complexity of the system to be specified, and the envisaged difficulties of 8k processing, it wished to ensure that services could start by the end of 1997: presumably the 2k option allowed them to stipulate that and pressure from the UK forced them to do so. Interestingly, there was concern about the cost to the consumer of receivers, and the requirements stipulated a system design in which the difference in cost between an analogue and a digital TV receiver was kept to 450 ECUs (about £300) at launch, falling to 200 ECUs (about £150) two years afterwards. And crucially, it required the broadcast signal to be a 'data container'. This was to ensure that datastreams of any size and for whatever purpose could be transmitted with equal ease within the DVB-T system. This prescient stipulation opened the way to the interactive services that soon followed, and to the later DVB standards of the early 2000s which included broadcasting of content in internet protocol form.

Reimers and his team now had their brief, and the Technical Module could get down to work in earnest.

Besides the Commercial Module's requirements, the starting point for the Technical Module was the existing DVB specifications for satellite and cable. The concept of a family of standards across the three platforms of terrestrial, satellite and cable was firmly entrenched in the DVB's philosophy, and as a consequence some of the detail was readily accessible: the MPEG-2 compression, coding and multiplexing processes, the concept of error correction and service information, and others. The working assumption was that the modulation system for DTT would be COFDM: many teams, like dTTb, were working on its development, and early results substantiated the theoretical understanding that its particular characteristics were admirably suited to the close co-existence between DTT and analogue television transmissions in the crowded European airwaves. Nevertheless, when alternative ideas were offered, the Technical Module felt bound to give them serious consideration.[93]

The Technical Module went about its task by taking the Commercial Module's proposals and then making a call for proposals for technologies. The proposals were put in by a number of different European collaborative

---

[93] The detailed work of the Technical Module was conducted in a number of Task Forces or ad hoc Groups. In 1995, to take an example, there were no less than fifteen separate groups.

projects. At this stage, there was considerable input to the DVB from a group called the Task Force for System Comparison (TFSC), which had been set up - at the DVB's invitation - by the dTTb project with members also from the parallel German HDTV-T and Scandinavian HD-DIVINE projects. The TFSC, recognising the large degree of common purpose and approach of the three independent projects, set out to outline a specification for an COFDM system which drew on the features of the three projects' results. The group compared them, then distilled out those features most appropriate to the DVB's commercial requirements, and delivered its findings to the Technical Module in September 1994.

The TFSC chairman was Lisa Grete Møller, the head of broadcast systems for Tele Danmark, and who had worked on both the dTTb and HD-DIVINE projects. Bob Ely is full of praise for the way she handled her group:

> I think one of the people whose contribution is not fully realised and should be is Lisa Grete Møller, because she was chairing the DVB specification group and she was brilliant at it. She's a very modest individual, extraordinarily clever, so she could understand what needed to be done. A good choice because the Danish Radio had no particular axes to grind in one way or another, so she was completely neutral. Sometimes she had to take the various warring factions behind the bike shed and give them a talking-to, including I might say, my own colleagues at Kingswood.

Henry Price also had great praise for Lisa Grete Møller:

> I think she did an absolutely wonderful job, and she's probably an un-sung hero of the whole story. She came to a number of our [Commercial Module] meetings, very calm, quiet and very professional.

The process drew in a number of suggestions that were not taken up. A BBC researcher remembers an early DVB meeting in Germany where one company proposed an alternative to COFDM - a spread-spectrum system similarly of defence origin. After due deliberation the DVB's conclusion was that COFDM - already tried and tested in DAB - was preferable. After all, said one who was present:

> Why re-invent the wheel? It had been standardised, we know how to do it, we're just going to do it for more data at a higher rate and transmit in different frequency bands. We're going to re-optimise the parameters. Oh and by the way, we have people who really understand these technologies who we can transfer across from one project to another.

Actually, the process of adapting COFDM from its DAB application to the more demanding DVB-T environment was not entirely straightforward, as Gordon Drury remembers:

> We had a huge amount of experience in COFDM come the time we had to write this spec. We also knew what DAB had done so we knew what

parameters had worked in that arena, so we ... just imported every feature of DAB into DVB-T as a start. And then you look at it and you say ... it's all very well to do this for 1.5 Mbit/s sitting in a 1.5 MHz slot, we're now talking about 8 MHz slots ...

There was one major difference of opinion that, for a time, preoccupied many minds and raised hackles, and at one point severely threatened the cohesiveness of the DVB and strained the ethos of compromise and consensus to the limits. The argument was about the number of carriers to be adopted in the COFDM modulation system. Providing for a large number of options for error correction rate, 4, 16 or 64-QAM and for variation of guard interval was reasonably straightforward. And to begin with, settling on eight thousand carriers seemed also to be a straightforward choice.

Early OFDM implementations of the very early 1990s, like SPECTRE, STERNE and HD-DIVINE had all used 500 or 1,000 carrier systems, because that was the best that could be expected from current silicon. Better results, however, might be expected from using even more carriers. The options available (because of the mathematical nature of the COFDM) were 500, 1,000, 2,000, 8,000 and 16,000.[94] The choice followed naturally from one of the commercial requirements, that which stated that the system should be designed to allow operation of single frequency networks. In principle, a single frequency network is possible with any of the available choices (NTL had demonstrated a small SFN using the 500 carrier SPECTRE system). But the area that could be served by an SFN depended on the length of the guard interval, one of the parameters of the modulation system. Many countries represented at DVB wanted large area SFNs capable of covering the whole of a small country - like the Netherlands, or the whole of a German *Lander*, or even - as the BBC first thought - the whole of the UK. But large area networks needed a long guard interval, and only 8,000 or more carriers could provide that.[95]

The first draft of the DVB-T specification, completed in the Spring of 1995, therefore proposed the '8k system'. But the choice had a major

---

[94] There are round figures, which give rise to the colloquial usage of "2k" for 2,000 carriers and "8k" for 8,000 carriers: more accurately, the options are 2^9 (=512); 2^{10} (=1,024); 2^{11} (=2,048); 2^{13} (=8,192)

[95] In COFDM systems the symbol period is inversely proportional to the number of carriers - so the symbol period for an 8000 carrier system is 4 times that for a 2000 carrier system. The 'guard interval' is an extension in time of the period of each symbol beyond that of the active symbol: the receiver will experience neither inter-symbol nor inter-carrier interference provided that any echoes present in the signal have a delay which does not exceed the guard interval. However, the addition of the guard interval reduces the data capacity by an amount proportional to the ratio of its length to the length of the active symbol. The larger the number of carriers, the larger will be the active symbol period and thus the larger can be the guard interval. DVB-T has guard intervals in the range 7μs to 224μs.

impact on the design, development and manufacturing cost of the chipsets, which translated into the period of time needed for silicon technology to reach the capability required. In turn, this bore on the commercial feasibility of introducing the technology in the first place.[96] Modulation and demodulation of COFDM carriers is carried out in an integrated circuit using a highly complex mathematical process called a Fast Fourier Transform (FFT). The more carriers which are to be modulated, the more calculations the FFT chipset has to do, and an 8k FFT chipset has to perform sixteen times as many calculations as the next lowest option, a 2k FFT chipset.

In the UK, there was a widespread view that DTT should, if possible, launch in late 1997 to match the expected launch date of BSkyB's digital satellite offering. 8k chipsets could not be ready by 1997, but 2k chipsets could. Motorola's UK plant was at that time the only source of FFT chipsets: their technology did not yet stretch to an 8k capability, but they were promising 2k chipsets for the expected launch date. Applying Moore's Law, which states that the capabilities of silicon doubles every two years, allowed the prediction that 2,000 carriers would become possible to process sometime in 1995, and 8,000 sometime in 1997: and then add a year-and-a-half or so for consumer product development. So clearly, 8k was not only going to be more complex and more expensive, but it would take longer to develop. A 2k system would be simpler, cheaper and likely to be available in time for the UK's proposed 1997 launch. Recognising these factors, NTL, with the encouragement of the DTI, pushed hard for 2k.

As the British proponents of 2k argued their case within the DVB, they came up against a blank refusal by many representatives to any idea of having the option. Those who favoured 8k - and most countries apart from Britain did - had genuine cause for concern. They feared that when they came to introduce their own DTT services the silicon vendors would say to them, "What's good enough for the UK is good enough for you", and would point out that 2k chipsets were already in production and were beginning to amortize their development costs, whereas 8k chipsets would require re-investment in foundry costs which the vendors might be reluctant to undertake. So the fear was, allow 2k and 8k dies, and that mattered. To many, the idea of digital television without 8k seemed to lack imagination. Ed Wilson, who minuted many of the meetings, puts it this way:

> With those new, fresh concepts being, in engineering terms, a bit magical, quite wonderful - getting rid of problems we'd suffered from in the

---

[96] In 2k COFDM there are a total of 2,048 carriers, of which 1,705 are used, and of which 1,512 are modulated with 'useful' data and the remainder, 193, carry synchronisation signals. For 8k COFDM the corresponding carrier numbers are 8192, 6817, 6048 and 769

analogue world and the single carrier world all these donkeys years since Marconi - it seemed a bit strange therefore to find that people were already saying, well actually we aren't intending to use single frequency networks, we're going to do this traditional kind of planning of frequencies like we do with analogue.

The atmosphere in DVB meetings began to deteriorate whenever the subject was discussed. Chris Hibbert remembers meetings of the Commercial Module where ...

... you had [what was viewed as] an 'axis of evil' from the UK. It was driven by Motorola and Pace[97] and NTL, severely encouraged by Stephen Temple from the DTI who constantly pushed to ensure that the DVB specification included the two thousand carrier option. There was never any desire [on our part] not to have eight thousand, because in the end that was seen as going to be beneficial. The argument within the DVB was whether to include two thousand as an option.

Recognising the reality of the situation, and now also concerned to ensure a 1997 launch, the BBC in August 1995 had abandoned its insistence on 8k, clearing the way for a unified pro-2k UK position within the DVB. As the anti-2k faction was proving intractable, Ian Dixon, at a DVB meeting on the continent, spent an evening on the phone with his boss at the DTI, Stephen Temple, and they decided to raise their game:

I was the person at the Technical Module who at about ten minutes to midnight told Ulrich Reimers that we were going 2k whatever other countries might do. And I don't think he was happy. There was a lot of pressure to go for 8k and settle on 8k. And we went round saying to everybody, we're going to launch, we have to launch, we would love you to come with us, but if we don't get your investment and backing then there's no way we can go ahead with 8k and we need to get this sorted very quickly and 2k is going to be the only feasible possibility in the timescale. And everybody else made fierce noises about 2k but nobody promised to come with us.

Eventually, David Wood of the EBU, in an attempt to end the deadlock, proposed that both 2k and 8k should be included as options in the specification, a move about which he now has mixed feelings:

I would like to tell you it was inspired by a Damascus-like vision that this was a designed-in useful degree of flexibility for all receivers, but at the time I made the proposal it was with some regret, because we were ratcheting up the complexity of the system. It seemed the only way forward was to include the option for both. With hindsight, flexibility in carriers was a valuable idea, which the Japanese took even further. But at the time, to be

---

[97] Pace Microtechnology: one of the first UK companies to manufacture digital television set-top box receivers.

honest, the main motivation was the belief that the DVB specification would be much less valuable with the UK outside it than with it in.

Faced with a difficult situation, the DVB took the proposal that Wood had made and agreed on having the option, although dissent in some quarters would rumble on. Ulrich Reimers, generously, could see both sides to the argument:

> Personally I was changing opinions during the whole process. There were times when I would have said, who the hell needs 8k? And why the hell do people in Spain push 8k so heavily? So for quite some time I thought the 2k thing was good enough. Possibly with a lack of vision at that time, where we accepted that 1997 would be the launch date in the UK and where I personally thought, well, if this is the launch date, and if technology is as technology is, it may be too early for the 8k and it may not be implementable. What I did not expect at that time myself was that the 8k thing is cheap, easily implementable, and significantly better.

In December 1995, the DVB finally agreed a specification that provided for a dual mode; a choice between 2k and 8k. Later, the UK would begin to speak of 2k as an 'interim solution', envisaging an eventual migration to 8k. And in fact the 8k chips did come sooner, and cheaper, than anticipated, but the row over 2k rumbled on until the very final stages of the DVB's work. One of the first 8k chipsets was produced by LSI Logic using expertise gained from a collaborative agreement with BBC Research and Development. The chip was first demonstrated in May 1998, but too late to be in commercial production for the UK's DTT launch. But only just too late: Sweden, which launched shortly after the UK, could and did adopt 8k. Very soon, however, dual standard 2k/8k chipsets were normal equipment in most receivers on sale in the UK. Gordon Drury notes the paradox that early demand for 2k chipsets actually sped up the production of versions for 8k

> I still believe that without the pressure from the UK 2k lobby the 8k silicon would not have happened anything like as quickly. The UK demand showed the silicon guys that the market could be there and it was a challenge to their pride [to satisfy the demand].

At about the same time as the 2k versus 8k battle broke out, NTL threw another spanner into the workings of the Technical Module. Together with Deutsche Telekom, they came up with alternative modulation variant - DASPK - which, as Bob Ely remembers, was actually a good one, and which in some respects was simpler but was less well tested:

> Its claimed advantages unfortunately didn't extend beyond the lower levels of modulation. At the 4 level - QPSK - 4DAPSK actually looked better, but that wasn't the problem. What we wanted to do was to make 64-QAM and

16-QAM better. At those levels, DAPSK wasn't better. But that of course was an enormous battle [which] Reimers and others had to resolve and I think it could have gone either way.

According to Gordon Drury, NTL had a straightforward commercial motive for co-sponsoring DAPSK: if it was simpler, it should be quicker and cheaper to implement:

> One of the reasons we did it was we wanted the bloody spec out, and if this [DAPSK] was gonna happen, it was either going to be proved to be useless, or proved useful, and we thought it would be better to support that activity and get it done and we'll know what the result is, and it goes in the spec or it doesn't.

In the end, the decision rested not on the technical benefits or disbenefits of DAPSK, but on the matter of patent rights. Bob Ely:

> It would have been neither better nor worse, but from the point of view of actually getting the [DVB-T] system adopted quickly the balance of benefit was to go with the system which had fewer patents, which was more widely supported, and that I believe caused Reimers and others to drive towards the outcome we actually got.

In fact, seeking consensus in his role as the Technical Module's chairman, Ulrich Reimers had decided that DASPK should be dropped as a candidate for inclusion in the DVB-T standard. It was, he said later, not a easy decision but a good one.[98] What was now concerning Reimers was the sheer complexity of the system which was being described by the draft specification that his group was putting together. Most aspects were resolved, but the detail of the modulation system, in particular, was worrying. The row over 2k and 8k had been resolved only to the extent of allowing the option of either. But this increased the level of overall complexity even further, as additional FEC and guard interval rates needed to be introduced to accompany the 2k variant. The first draft of the specification was very bulky and very complex, as Gordon Drury remembers:

> So this big spec, when we'd more or less finished it and it was looking as if more iterations of it weren't going to take us much further, we said, oh my God, look at what we've created!

Reimers decided on radical action, as Bob Ely recalls:

> It was a very courageous decision that, right at the final stage of the DVB's specification, in order to achieve that compromise between NTL and the rest, the specification was torn up, a new specification - which again was the best of both worlds - was put together.

---

[98] Not many people knew at the time that the key patent describing the DAPSK version came from Braunschweig Technical University – from the institute that Ulrich Reimers manages.

For commercial reasons, NTL were still pushing very hard for an early completion of the spec. Gordon Drury explained why:

> What we wanted was cheap silicon by any means possible. You take out of the spec anything that's not proven in tests to be essential to the exploitation of the full potential of this stuff ... That was the NTL position and one that was held more or less throughout, and it was really because of this focus on getting it done quicker.

There was worry that building silicon to cope with the much greater bandwidth of a television channel might be too difficult, and a similar reassessment of each of the DAB features of COFDM to confirm their suitability for television broadcasting. One of those features was a system known as 'time interleaving', strongly supported by IRT in Germany, which provided greater immunity from impulse interference such as is caused by ignition systems. Despite the fact that it was highly desirable to build in whatever protection was available, the impact on processing capability would be considerable, and some had their doubts. Gordon Drury was one:

> [time interleaving] was felt to impact silicon costs as well and in the argument over its impact on performance it was decided ultimately to drop [it]. I think it was a mistake, personally. This was one of the things we were very uneasy about dropping, but given the time pressure, given the silicon cost issues, maybe its got to go, and it was voted out.

At the Commercial Module, to which the technical work was being reported, Henry Price remembers keenly the NTL representative consistently and insistently arguing his case:

> To be frank, he was an absolute pain! He was the one who led every time he wanted the spec to stop going in a particular direction. So he would come to the Commercial Module - he was a Technical Module man - to basically talk the Commercial Module out of a particular topic. And I think their actions did enormous damage to the spec.

In this difficult atmosphere, Gordon Drury credits Reimers with managing the re-write in masterly fashion:

> Reimers did his usual trick - he was very good at this - his coffee break was a solution to all sorts of problems. He would lobby people. He would listen to the major players, the people who had the need to do it quicker, he would understand and deal with the issues of the people who were scientifically oriented and wanted to go away and do some more R&D. He could understand how to get these things in balance, and I think ... he took a gamble and called the major players, with a real interest in getting it done, as opposed to the research institutes, and said, look, what do you think, [is it not] too complicated, too expensive to implement?

Nevertheless, this was a risky course of action. The first draft had a solid basis in the test and measurement of the experimental implementations of a number of projects - like dTTb. The rewritten specification now actually defined, certainly in its detail, a completely different animal. As Bob Ely remembers with some feeling, it described a system ...

> ... which nobody actually knew would work, because it was completely untested, and it had pared to the bone the capacity allowed for synchronisation and equalisation. Nulls had gone. Cazacs had gone - we just had the 'scattered pilots' left to assist channel equalisation. And I would say that people just hoped that it would actually work.

The consensus in the Technical Module was that this was a draft that could be agreed upon. And agreement was sorely needed: Reimers wanted it - allow too long for deliberations and you risk losing the plot, and the UK were hammering the table - we need a specification, we have to launch. But some had mixed feelings, like the BBC's Ian Childs, who was Reimers' deputy chairman:

> The first spec of the DVB standard was in some ways better than the second spec was. Only in some ways, because the first spec was 8k only. But equally it had flaws. The second spec fixed many of the flaws of the first spec, but also removed some features which, in retrospect, might perhaps better have been left intact.

In January 1996, the DVB finally approved and published its DVB-T digital terrestrial television specification. There would follow a period of testing the specification, both by modelling in simulation, and building working systems. Feedback from these activities would allow validation of the specification, which if successful, would allow the DVB to submit it to ETSI - the European Technical Standards Institution - for ratification and adoption. Only then would it become the 'bible' for the broadcasters and manufacturers who were anxious to press ahead with building national DTT networks and a market for receivers.

That would take the best part of another twelve months, much to the frustration of some people in the UK.

13
Pilots and Planning

By the Autumn of 1995, Michael Starks' Digital Broadcasting Project was working towards the launch of a DTT pilot service against a very tight timetable with a programme of demonstration planned for the following Spring. The following six months would be one of the most intense and onerous for the BBC's research and development team at Kingswood Warren. From being a participant, but a 'fast follower' rather than a leader, in the work of the DVB and the contributing European collaborative projects, they were now being asked to build a fully conformant DVB-T chain - the complete system of coder, multiplexer and modulator, together with the receiver's demodulator, demultiplexer and decoder.

The Research team already had partial funding to build coding and multiplexing equipment under the Eureka VADIS programme, and from the ACTS[99] VALIDATE project for the modulator and demodulator.[100] Michael Starks' Digital Broadcasting Project found the balance of the funding, but insisted upon a very tight timetable for completion of the work. Bob Ely puts the challenge graphically:

> Building the transmit end is relatively easy; the receiving end is a hundredfold more difficult, both in terms of sheer volume of hardware and in terms of intellectual requirement. So the 'send' end we had completed in a few weeks, but once you'd completed that then, how are you going to decode it? That is the huge challenge. So that is why there was always focus on getting the receive end working.

[99] ACTS (Advanced Communications Technologies and Services) a programme under the European Community 4th Framework Research &Technology Development programme: it was the successor to the RACE programme.
[100] The purpose of the VADIS project was to complete and test the MPEG-2 specification, and VALIDATE was the project in which a number of participating organisations built working modems to prove the DVB-T specification.

Thinking that it might be constrained into privatising its Research and Development arm - as the IBA had done to its research department - the BBC had reorganised the way the department worked. Bob Ely no longer led a research team, but acted as client liaison officer to Michael Starks and the Digital Broadcasting Project. Ian Childs, too, had moved from Kingswood Warren to the Corporate Centre where, removed from the day-to-day business of managing research, he was now responsible for the strategic direction of the department. He recalls:

> It was quite clear to me that the green light was definitely shining brightly on digital. It was also quite clear to me that it was going to demand a huge work plan shift at R&D, but yet I was no longer fully in control. I was the commissioner, if you like, but I didn't manage it. Made a lot easier for me by the fact that there were a lot of sympathetic voices within R&D, of which Bob Ely was probably the principal - he was definitely a mover and shaker in this context. But by no means the only one. And Bob and I working together succeeded in coming up with a plan for resourcing digital research within R&D. Because Bob was saying it, the plan achieved the support of the management [of R&D]. And because I was saying it within Policy and Planning, the plan was able to get the necessary political consensus.

With teams in place, and building on the knowledge gained from their work in international projects, R&D set about constructing the modem. It was a very tight schedule. Michael Starks had, in true project management style, put a date in his diary for the start of high profile demonstrations, timed to take place at just the right moment during the passage of the Broadcasting Bill through Parliament: March 1996. Ian Childs thinks that this was probably the most intense period in the work of R&D since he joined the BBC in the 70s. Yet, he says:

> I think R&D engineers always have deadlines. The stakes tend not to be quite so high, because they tend to be technical conferences like IBC and Montreux. You know, six months or a year beforehand you tend to say "What are we going to show next IBC? By then we should have got X and Y ready, so let's plan to show X and Y." And that seems really comfortable at the time you take the decision. Three weeks before IBC is due to start and things haven't progressed quite as fast as you had hoped - perhaps there are still bit-errors on the demonstration pictures - you've got a deadline. It feels quite pressing, and you are passionately committed by that stage.

Bob Ely put his feelings more bluntly:

> It meant people were working against a deadline which is always very difficult in research. There's a point which I don't think Michael ever understood: when you're doing a technology project with known technology - something that somebody's done before - you can reasonably say, right, I know its going to take me so many days to actually clear the room; so many days to install the equipment; so many days to connect it up; and so many

166

days to test it. But when you're doing a research project like this you simply don't know how long it's going to take, because there is going to be a moment at which you say, ah yes, I now see how to make it work, and that might come in an hour, a day, a week, a month: it may never come. And that was a very uncomfortable position. It is a tribute to the team that they never lost hope that they could do it.

And Ian Childs had a view about the rationale behind the urgency:

> A lot of the timescales that were being put forward were hopelessly ambitious - I mean, absolutely hopelessly ambitious. We knew they couldn't be achieved: we equally knew that Sky couldn't achieve them either. Everybody was saying Sky were going to launch in '97, and we knew they couldn't launch until '98. But what did we know, we were just engineers, you know. This was Sky; these were supermen. It meant that we were slightly in a cleft stick. We knew when the real deadline, roughly, was going to be, but we also had to stop our bosses from panicking, so we had to do something to meet the other deadline. So how did it feel? It felt quite like hard work, it felt quite exhilarating, but it didn't feel like totally unusual business.

While all this work, under considerable pressure, was going on, there was still no final, agreed, DVB-T specification. The Kingswood team building the BBC modem made a very configurable general purpose device. There were a lot of standard circuit boards, there were two or three types of boards where the algorithm corresponding to any one of a number of possible DVB configurations could be loaded into memory. If the specification changed, the board could be changed.

In January 1996, the DVB specification was finally frozen, but there was still no sign from Kingswood of a working modem. Michael Starks became alarmed.

> I remember being very worried that the DVB had taken so long to finalise the specification that nobody had ever used, and I didn't entirely understand why in the later stages it kept changing from things that had been tried previously, but it did. And when I asked the question, has anybody actually done this, not used a specification that was rather different, but used the actual specification, and the answer was no. And when I asked the question, well can we do it, and the answer was, well we're not sure, it did seem to me that we needed to be pretty sure pretty fast.

Bob Ely too was beginning to worry about the rate of progress in building the modem.

> We hadn't built one before, so we had a double problem of a) working out how to do it and b) to keep track of a very rapidly emerging specification. Michael had promised his demonstration for March '96, and by Christmas it was fairly obvious that we weren't going to have a modem ready in time and in fact we didn't even have a specification - the specification wasn't frozen until January and the demonstration was meant to be in March.

Feeling that he was unable to get Michael Starks to recognise the problem, Bob Ely felt that he had to share his worries with his superiors at the corporate centre, Ian Jenkins and Phil Laven. In an internal memo which he now candidly calls his "not waving but drowning" missive, Bob Ely set out his concerns.

Their modem, he wrote on 15 January 1996, although complete and operating, did not yet yield performance which would be acceptable for field trials and demonstrations. Amongst a number of problems, the most intractable was a difficulty in getting the receiver to synchronise with the transmitter, which Bob Ely attributed to the omission of the null and cazac symbols from the emerging specification (which was essentially a political compromise in order to achieve agreement at the DVB Technical Module). This had removed some of the information within the transmitted signal that the demodulator could have used to acquire synchronisation. Apparently, the SPECTRE project - now in the hands of DMV[101] - was experiencing similar problems, and the French engineers at CCETT were telling anybody who would listen that without the discarded nulls and cazacs the terrestrial system might well be unworkable.

But there was worse to come. The modem which the BBC could not get to work properly was not the one that Michael Starks thought he was getting. The industry, in the form of the UK Digital TV Group, had the working assumption that a 2k/16-QAM system would form the UK implementation, and that is what Michael Starks was expecting for his April demonstrations. But the Kingswood modem was an 8k/64-QAM version. Bob Ely, in his memo, set out the options: should they start to rebuild as a 2k modem and lose three months, or get the 8k modem working (and so be clear about the validity of the DVB specification) but fall short of Michael Starks' requirement? Bob Ely sought guidance. It quickly came.

The issue came into the open in front of very senior BBC figures during a routine Project Review to which Michael Starks reported. After that meeting, the balloon went up, as Michael reacted in the only way he now could: officially. Bob Ely was down in Hampshire visiting the Snell and Wilcox company[102], when he got the phone call:

> I got a phone call at three o'clock in the afternoon saying come straight back up to White City, and Ian and Michael and the Head of Personnel had

---

[101] DMV. DigiMediaVision, a News International company which had acquired NTL's R&D assets.

[102] Bob Ely recollects: 'Roderick Snell, founder, Technical Director and co-owner of S&W, had very kindly arranged a workshop for me in which he and several of his top engineers independently reviewed Kingswood's work to implement DVB-T specification in the presence of a few of the Kingswood modem team. The conclusion of the workshop (after I left for White City) was that we could make the March deadline - but only just'

actually been assembled. Michael sat in full state in the Boardroom and ... it was a court martial! And the consequence of that was it was decided that I must immediately give up the DTG Receiver Group that I was chairing and all other external activities such as DVB and focus entirely on getting this modem working. And a missive went down to Kingswood that it became the absolute first imperative to get that modem working by March, and they [must] put all of their staff on that.

Michael Starks felt that he had no option, that too much was at stake:

I don't recall anything which I would describe as a court martial, but I do recall being very conscious that by then on the back of our earlier demo and all the policy work that we'd done on it we had in effect taken a lead within the UK, and the UK had taken a lead within Europe. We'd said: this is feasible, we're going to do it, and we were at that stage seeing the shape of the regulatory proposals. The commercial companies had a timetable to make up their minds about whether they were going to accept the guaranteed spectrum, and whether they were going to develop new services on the side, and these things were all coming to a head in the middle of that year [1996]. And I think like everyone else I was aware of the history of MAC and the history of the [BSB] satellite failure and so on. It seemed to me that we really could not get ourselves into this situation again, and that therefore we either had to get this spec to work, or we had to own up and say, look, we've been going a bit faster on the policy front than the technology justifies.

There is no doubt that from the outside looking in, as were many of the BBC's policy-makers, the same concerns were being felt. The stakes were now too high for there to be a fumble. Michael Starks had no option:

I certainly put the pressure on at that stage and said to them, look if you've gone along and you've signed up to this DVB spec in your technical fora and you said this is the outcome, then you ought to be able to make it work. And I think that was a form of pressure which I'm sure worried others, I mean it worried me. It was not an easy time but I think it was the right thing to do, to bring it to a head.

Throwing additional resources into a flagging project might, on the face of it, seem to be an advisable course of action. In this case, Bob Ely was not convinced.

Actually, if a research project is in difficulty, the last thing you want to do is to import a number of people who don't know anything about it into the project team, because what you actually do is stop it in its tracks! But nevertheless that was the directive, and fifteen people were transferred overnight to work on the project, and the only thing we could actually do was to keep the fifteen people back from the people who were actually doing the work! And hope that the people actually doing the work can solve the problems.

Finally, on 9th April 1996, the R&D codec - 2k and 16-QAM - was demonstrated. It was, Bob Ely says:

> ... just about working. There was still quite serious problems with the synchronisation - it was taking minutes to lock up at that stage. It was the last problem to be solved, because the designers of the specification had pushed the specification to the very limits and beyond of what was known - correctly so as it now turns out. And that was a very courageous step when that was done. I think had I had more direct influence on the specification it would have been more conservatively engineered and had more synchronising information in it

The BBC claimed that it was the first ever demonstration of a working system which was compliant with the DVB-T specification.

The April demonstration of a working modem was a low key affair, using a research tool and with only one programme service coded into the multiplex. But it was progress, and highly reassuring to Michael Starks, who could now point, with justification, to a working technology based on an agreed specification. It was reassuring also to the team who were working to put in place the full pilot service.

The plan for the pilot service was to generate a complete multiplex of three or four programmes, together with an EPG and some interactive content, to broadcast it from the London transmitter at Crystal Palace and, with regional opt-outs, from the transmitter serving north east England at Pontop Pike. In both locations the digital receiver would be incorporated into a set of display panels, and the venues used for a series of demonstrations. In the event, the London display area was more comprehensive and was used for a much longer period. It used the same boardroom in White City which had been used for previous summer's demonstrations.

The team which put together the pilot was a big one and drew expertise principally from BBC Research and Development but also from a number of other corners of the BBC, the soon to be privatised BBC Transmission, Project Management, Graphic Design, Presentation Department, and at one stage the Television Outside Broadcast Department (Tel OBs). It also drew on the expertise of a small number of companies in outside industry with whom R&D had begun to collaborate. The author was given a coordinating role to establish and run the pilot demonstrations.[103]

The heart of the receiver would consist of the Kingswood modem, but would use a modified satellite receiver from Pace Microtechnology. Pace had developed a commercially available DVB-S set-top box in which, as a result of the DVB concept of a family of standards, all the components of the box other that the satellite demodulator 'front end' were common to the

---

[103] with the rather grand title of Project Director

DVB-T specification, principally the demultiplexer and MPEG decoder stages. Pace modified the box to receive the output of the Kingswood demodulator.

At Television Centre, a tiny playout centre was constructed, in which a set of MPEG coders and a multiplexer were installed, the output from which was sent as a multiple programme transport stream to the two transmitters. The system was originally configured to work at a multiplex capacity of 18 Mbit/s, which at the time was the BBC's preferred mode. This capacity was used to transmit digital versions of BBC-1, BBC-2 and - to represent a putative BBC News 24 - the international service BBC World. A fourth service stream was used to carry video elements associated with a number of early EPG and interactive applications, and which could be selected or modified from the playout centre.

As in the previous year's demonstrations, Michael Starks wanted to use the pilot service not just to receive and display programme services in a multiplex, but to represent both the BBC's service proposition and the whole range of features and services a UK digital terrestrial system would offer. Few of these features were yet fully developed, and had to be simulated, but one feature, the electronic programme guide, was now real. Every day in Television Centre, a brave soul from the Presentation department was deputed to key in to a computer the day's schedule for all the services being carried by the pilot. The information could then be transmitted and received by the pilot and displayed with the press of the handset button on the TV sets.

Real 'red button' interactivity in the end proved impossible to achieve. It was too early for provision to be made for real-time interaction between interactive software and the receiver chip sets. The solution was to create a simulation, which ran on an Apple Mac computer (which also controlled some other functions of the receiver).

Another simulation was provided by BT, and was there to demonstrate the 'back office' functions of subscriber management for pay-TV services and to show the basis of handling transactional services - buying direct using the TV interactive content. Originally, the display was intended to be more extensive, and the hope had been that some elements might be real and not simulated. But BT dragged their feet a little. Later, it became clear to Michael Starks why:

> There was some thought that an alliance between the BBC and BT might be an interesting one, and so some discussions were held along those lines. [But it emerged] that BT's primary interest was talking to BSkyB and satellite.

The assembled equipment for the pilot receiver filled two flight cases, and was certainly the largest 'set-top box' ever seen. But it worked convincingly. The first off-air pictures from Crystal Palace were displayed on the White City screens early in June. But one element was missing: widescreen.

The whole of playout and receiver configuration was intended to represent the BBC's aspiration that digital terrestrial television should be in 16:9 widescreen. But very few BBC programmes were made in widescreen, and none were transmitted in anything other than the square 4:3 format of conventional analogue television. Of course, some sort of widescreen content could have been played out from a videotape machine in the playout centre on the pilot's fourth service, but the author felt strongly that the real thing would be better as a launch event to mark the pilot service's inauguration.

I still had close links with Television Outside Broadcasts from my days as a producer. The BBC OB engineering base at Kendal Avenue in West London had two outside broadcast units which could be switched to operate in digital widescreen (but hardly ever were). Talking over a beer one day with an old colleague, producer Steve Morris, we hatched a scheme to do that summer's BBC-1 coverage of Trooping the Colour in digital widescreen as a simulcast. Simulcasting meant using the finished programme to feed both 16:9 digital and 4:3 analogue services. Morris had some experience of 16:9. A few years before he had been one of the producers who directed experimental HDTV coverage of a number of events which were used in demonstrations of HD-MAC. There followed rapid consultation with the Head of OB Events, Philip Gilbert, and with the channel controller. It was agreed that the analogue picture would be slightly 'letterboxed' to a 14:9 ratio, and that the programme would be made using 'shoot-and-protect' rules in which important action in the scene is kept away from the edges of the widescreen picture.

On Saturday 15th June 1996, the live transmission took place. For the first time anywhere, a complete end-to-end digital widescreen simulcast was being broadcast live as part of a full service multiplex using a fully DVB compliant digital terrestrial television system. In the White City viewing area, a small gathering of BBC Broadcast chiefs watched the digital transmission alongside its analogue equivalent, and at times browsed a live digital interactive component which displayed a quarter-screen widescreen picture surrounded by textual information supplementing the programme. As an old programme maker, I thought the digital widescreen pictures were mouth-watering. The interactive application, although primitive, nevertheless turned out in retrospect to be a reasonable indication of today's ubiquitous 'red button' offerings.

The technical team's view of the transmission was not one of entire satisfaction: the problem was the performance of the MPEG coders. A set of coders and a multiplexer had been ordered from, and delivered by, Thomson but were not yet ready for use: as delivered their software was

172

still suffering some bugs. In their place, equipment which had been developed by Nick Tanton at BBC R&D as part of the VADIS project was used. Bob Ely remembers that a difficult decision had to be made:

> We'd got that very prestigious demonstration of Trooping the Colour - first live DVB compliant broadcast - and Nick and his team understandably were extremely keen that their VADIS codec be used for that because it was their baby: they'd built it and they trusted it. But actually, by that stage, the Thomson codec was probably better. We just, by the skin of our teeth, got through that Trooping the Colour demonstration because the equipment did freeze, it did get coding artefacts. Because the VADIS codec was only a very first generation research tool. Was that the right decision? Don't know. Difficult even now to say.

Not long afterwards, the VADIS equipment was removed and replaced by the Thomson equipment. Over the next five months, the author would conduct over ninety lengthy demonstrations to BBC staff, and to industry professionals from UK industry and abroad, building confidence in the technology. Over 70 companies from Europe and the Far East as well as from the UK, came to see the demonstrations. The pilot was used to understand better the practical detail of interactive programming, electronic programme guide design, and the compatibility issues of widescreen and 4:3. A few months later, in October, the pilot service was reconfigured to run at 24 Mbit/s, following the BBC's agreement with other broadcasters to adopt 64-QAM and benefit from having more services on offer.

Michael is generous in his praise of the work that BBC Research and Development did at that time:

> I thought they were marvellous. I had no reservations at all about the - support's the wrong word - leadership in many ways that came from that quarter. I thought they were terrific.

And the threat of privatisation had finally been lifted: Michael Starks' earlier work had contributed to that:

> I was familiar with the issue from the work we'd done on the Technology Task Force in the work we'd done in the context of Charter Review. We'd concluded that it would be a mistake for the BBC to either lose or even change the location of R&D. I think we thought that Kingswood Warren should be properly looked after. Particularly on anything to do with frequency planning, the strategy of having the right spectrum for the BBC's needs, I think we always felt that R&D was central, and we sold that message upwards. So I wasn't conscious of a question over its future. I was aware that the rest of the place had been through a rather harsh set of economies and, you know, we took a fairly hard view of the cost base.

It came as a relief to many, including Ian Childs who, not long afterwards, would leave the Corporate Centre to return to Kingswood Warren as Head of Research:

BBC retained Coopers & Lybrand as consultants to advise them on what the BBC's position should be over privatisation of transmission and privatisation of R&D. Their recommendation to the BBC was the BBC's best interests was served by having transmission as a wholly-owned subsidiary, but I remember a phrase in their report which said, "With respect to R&D, we are unequivocal..." It was a very strong recomm- endation - it should remain as an in-house operation. And fortunately the government listened to that.

The digital widescreen simulcast of *Trooping the Colour* was the success- ful culmination of a great deal of work and worry by a very large number of highly talented people.[104] But in another way, it was a quiet affair. By June 1996, events were moving on rapidly. The Broadcasting Act was given Royal Assent a month later, and the BBC committed itself to launching its new digital services on satellite. The work of the BBC R&D engineers would now rapidly move towards systems engineering - designing and specifying the installed plant that the BBC would require for the day-to-day business of digital broadcasting on cable, satellite and terrestrial. The set of imperatives of the last few years - to design, build and prove a new digital technology - would quickly be replaced by another equally demanding set of tasks and short deadlines.

On 15 October 1995, SES-Astra launched its first digital broadcasting satellite, Astra 1E, from the Korou in French Guyana, and commercial digital satellite broadcasting in Europe began shortly afterwards. The first services to use the new satellite were provided by Canal Plus to France and Kirch to Germany, but Britain's BSkyB was quick off the mark to reserve transponder space for services to the UK. The general assumption on the part of Sky-watchers was that their services would launch in mid to late 1997.

At the BBC, one of the issues that Michael Starks had examined was the impact that digital satellite broadcasting would have on the BBC's plans for digital services. Already more or less committed to a digital terrestrial future, the question was, what should the BBC's attitude be to the development of alternative delivery platforms? The BBC's disposition was to think of terrestrial transmission as its natural home, and to view the prospect of digital terrestrial as an extension to that. For a while, that was the view shared by the new Director-General, John Birt. But his Director of Policy and Planning, Patricia Hodgson, was according to Michael Starks, of a different mind:

---

[104] In September 1997, Andrew Oliphant, on behalf of the Kingswood Warren team which had worked on the pilot service's modem, received the prestigious Editor's Award for Technological Achievement at the International Broadcasting Convention in Amsterdam.

I think Patricia and colleagues were instinctively inclined to work on a broad front. And while we were spending a lot of time working on terrestrial she had others beavering away producing papers on cable and so on and we were all rather carefully monitoring Sky to find out what was going on in the satellite world.

In the new Labour government, the Secretary of State for Culture Media and Sport, Chris Smith, had also done some fresh thinking on the future broadcasting landscape. At the ITVA, Barry Cox was becoming concerned:

Very interestingly, the Labour government of '97 changed the rules of the game, in this respect. The Tories were very much more pro-DTT and said so, that's my strong memory of it, and then Chris Smith comes out very early on with this platform-neutral stuff, which obviously he and Hodgson cooked up between them. And I thought, God alive, why? They don't like Sky, but why are you doing this? But despite my close connections with them I could never get them to shift on that.

Under the umbrella of his Digital Broadcasting Project, Michael Starks was asked to produce a report on the arguments for and against putting the BBC's licence fee funded digital services on satellite, and hired the consultancy firm of McKinseys to assist. After twelve months of work, the report, completed in August 1995, advised that the BBC should make its services available on all platforms. Bob Ely, who contributed advice to the study, says that the advice ...

... was certainly driven to a large extent by the fact that Kingswood had advised - I advised - that there was no possibility of getting universal terrestrial coverage: the best we could hope for prior to analogue switch-off was going to be in the region of 90 per cent, but with significantly lower coverage in some key rural areas such as Wales, where the coverage might be as low as 60 per cent. And it seemed fairly clear that if, given the BBC's obligation to universality, and given that the plan wasn't just to replicate the existing services but to offer new services, interactivity, widescreen, high definition, that to create a two-tier Britain whereby some people would not have any possibility of access to those new services, could threaten the entire licence fee. McKinseys agreed with that

Michael Starks found the argument that the BBC's digital services had to be universally available completely compelling:

I recall a young guy called Michael Ross, a young McKinsey consultant, who worked with us from the outset, suggesting this pretty early on. I think the answer was coming from the top down and the bottom up simultaneously, and he looked at the commercial risks as well as what was going on in other countries and said if I were you I'd back all platforms.

This aspect of BBC policy did not help the consensus-building efforts that the BBC, led by Michael Starks, had been making around the wider industry. Barry Cox remembers the reaction within ITV to the news that the BBC wanted to put its services on BSkyB's satellite system.

> Quite unnecessarily, I thought, they effectively opted-out of what had originally been the terrestrial united front. But Patricia was of the view, and persuaded John Birt, that they had to be platform neutral and therefore they would do a deal with Sky. That was a blow. A real blow. Up to that point, we'd worked pretty carefully together. I was very disappointed. They of course had perfectly plausible reasons for what they'd done but I just thought they were missing the point. And I still think they missed it.

In his view Michael Starks remains convinced that the BBC got it right and ITV got it wrong:

> I think we got to the right answer quite straightforwardly without too much agonising. I think the fact that ITV chose to put all its eggs in the terrestrial basket was a much more high risk strategy as events proved.

For a time, ITV remained resolutely committed to a terrestrial-only, free-to-air, presence, while the BBC would open negotiations with their arch-rival, BSkyB, to accept carriage of its licence fee funded services.

The BBC's first move was to establish a means of being present on the same satellite as BSkyB. This was an essential first step to ensuring that Sky digital viewers could watch the BBC's services. In April 1996 Michael Starks went to talk to the satellite operators, SES-Astra:

> What I did was I went up to the Director-General of Astra at the end of one of these conferences that were very often on digital television in those days and said, shouldn't we talk? And he said, "Yes. When do you want to come to Luxembourg?" I went over with a colleague from BBC Worldwide and at the time we didn't know that Sky were intending to have a new satellite in a new position in the sky. And we had a fairly commercially confidential discussion with Astra as a result of which we flew back with an offer of two transponders provided we made our minds up in a couple of months.

The Astra satellites for digital broadcasting would occupy a different orbital position to those which had been delivering their analogue services since the early '80s. And to SES-Astra, the international consortium which financed the building, launching and servicing of the satellites, the BBC was another potential customer, just like BSkyB or the many other European broadcasters who were seeking capacity from them. There were, as Michael Starks recalls, the Chinese walls of commercially confidences, but when the contract with Astra was initialled at the end of July 1996, the BBC had secured the first part of its platform-neutral strategy without yet having to talk to BSkyB.

> Astra were very careful about what they could tell us and what they couldn't tell us, and what guarantees they could give us and what

guarantees they couldn't give us, and it was quite an ingenious contract, but it worked. And it meant that we then had the ability to get our services up to - we could form our own uplinking arrangements - up to the satellite, broadcast in our own capacity from it.

Distancing itself from Sky was important for the BBC, and preserving an independence essential, but that could only go so far. The 'gatekeeper' function of the electronic programme guide was already being understood in Broadcasting House. If your service is not listed on the Sky's proprietary EPG, then the viewer cannot tune to the service. To get your service listed, you have to do a deal with Sky. The European Commission's *Television without Frontiers* legislation, so strenuously lobbied for by the BBC and ITV, was by now embodied in UK regulatory practice, and it obliged Sky to make such EPG listings available to third parties like the BBC on 'fair, reasonable and non-discriminatory terms'. The BBC found also that it needed to encrypt its services because much of the programme material had rights clearance only for the UK. But the Astra satellite 'footprint' reached well beyond UK territorial limits - to the Mediterranean coast of France for example, where many expat Brits were - against the rules - using Sky's analogue satellite boxes and could be relied upon to do the same when digital came along. But encrypting the BBC services needed further agreement to the use of BSkyB's own encryption system, to which again the new regulatory regime gave the BBC right of access.

But that did not mean in practice that the process of reaching agreement would be short, simple or anything other than very expensive for the BBC. Negotiations took eighteen months to finalise and the eventual cost to the licence fee payer, although never made public, was said to be considerable.

14
Building Alliances

As the detailed planning for the BBC's DTT pilot began in the summer of 1995, Michael Starks set out to realise another plank of his strategy: building bridges and forming alliances with other major industry players. He did not have to look far to find people with the same idea:

> I do remember a group of us saying, we can't possibly make this work without having some form of collaboration across the industry. I would certainly claim to be responsible for the insight that BBC needed to co-operate with ITV and Channel 4 and make sure there were rival digital terrestrial services if anybody was expected to make digital terrestrial receivers on a commercial basis. But the idea of forming what we [later] called the DTG went wider than that and drew in the manufacturers and I think was built very much on the realisation that having the chips was fundamental and that if we didn't have some collaboration with the people who would be developing and ordering chips then we wouldn't really have a proper grasp of the timetable or of the risks.

While the BBC was tentatively building up its relationship with the other broadcasters, another group had, very quietly behind the scenes, begun to meet. The transmission company NTL, the set-top box manufacturer Pace, chip-maker Motorola and consumer electronics manufacturer Sony, together with BT (who were actively investigating all possible new commercial opportunities in content delivery short of actually being a broadcaster, which at that time it was barred by legislation from becoming) had formed a group which was called the UK Digital Terrestrial Television

Technical Integration Group. In March 1995, BT invited the BBC to join and Bob Ely and Mark Maddocks went along to learn more.

The pair found the UKDTTTIG determined to promote the introduction of digital terrestrial television in the UK. They spent most of the meeting discussing what specific objectives an augmented group might set itself. The five industry players seemed concerned to limit membership to a small number of organisations who were already working on the technology of DTT. Programme providers, like the ITV companies, were to be excluded (the BBC was asked to keep a 'Chinese wall' between its R&D and programme arms). The group would need the DTI's blessing, but nobody wanted a DTI takeover. Bob Ely reported back that the group seemed determined to continue with or without the BBC.

The BBC's Digital Broadcasting Project had already established a limited working relationship with a number of the UKDTTTIG's members, and the opportunity to merge this group with that of the broadcasters must have seemed to the BBC to be an opportunity not to be missed. Very quickly the BBC's senior management agreed that the BBC could join the group, with Michael Starks insisting that they should do so only on condition that ITV and Channel Four could also join. As Chief Engineer of Channel Four, Chris Daubney was approached by Michael Starks:

> I'd known Michael from when we were both at the IBA together, when he was Head of Radio Broadcasting. Michael realised that while the BBC was always going to play a very big part (in it) it wasn't solely the BBC - government wished it to be all the UK broadcasters. Knowing me he approached me and ... I said yes, we'll muck in and join you.

So too did the ITVA. After a number of other meetings in that year under a rotating chairmanship, Michael Starks was elected as the group's first formal chairman. He then set about a re-launch of the group, with a formal Memorandum of Understanding and eight founding members[105], as the Digital Television Group in January 1996. After that, the DTG's membership grew rapidly, as more and more interested companies joined. For the largest meetings, the DTG started to hire the Mayfair Conference Centre near Marble Arch. Gordon Drury, of NTL, attended:

> There was a massive big square table with huge numbers of people round it. The primary task was to form a consensus among the players - a sufficient body of interest to make it workable. The DTI were there observing these things. As it were, visibly present [as if to say] the government is interested in this: you are industry, you will make it happen, we will do what we can to help. So Michael's job was to primarily find that consensus and to get the

---

[105] Eight 'original parties' signed the MoU in January 1996: BT, NTL, Pace, Sony, Motorola, and the broadcasters BBC, C4 and the ITVA, together with eleven 'new parties', the technology companies DMV, Snell & Wilcox, and SGS-Thomson Microelectronics, the broadcasters Teletext and Pearson Television, and the manufacturers Hitachi, Panasonic, Philips, Pioneer, Samsung and Toshiba.

commitment of those players to make it move forward. And all it was at that time was the DTG, there wasn't any structure to it - it was a forum.

In its early days, the DTG provided a useful place to exchange news and information, but it needed to do more than be just a forum. A raft of practical technical matters needed to be settled urgently if a full public service of DTT was to be launched within two or three years. But first, rather as the DVB had found, senior people in the participating organ-isations had to be convinced that there was purpose and value for their staff to participate in the DTG's activities. Michael Starks set about selling the idea of an effective DTG to senior executives:

> To begin with it wasn't the way organisations were used to working. We had to sell the idea upwards and we established it fairly firmly at working level before we took it upwards. I think as ever when it comes to signing a Memorandum of Understanding people want to know what they're committing themselves to, what it means financially, what it means in risk terms, what copyright and patent issues might be involved and all the rest of it. And we did enough work to be able to answer all those questions in a way that we thought would be acceptable before we took it up. And that was the right thing to do.

At working level, the DTG began to form sub-committees and working groups to tackle specific issues. Bob Ely, having handed over chairmanship of the Receiver Group to Terry Hurley of Sony in January 1996, returned to chair the new Systems Integration Group from April 1996. The task of this new group was to identify and agree any elements of the overall UK DTT platform (apart from the receivers and set-top boxes) which needed to be mutually agreed between the various broadcasters and the multiplex op-erators. Bob Ely:

> It was a very interesting and quite difficult task because no-one had ever before designed a digital TV platform for more than one broadcaster: the early digital systems - in the Far East, South Africa and the USA - were all single broadcaster proprietary systems. The people round the table had hugely different views as to what extent the overall UK digital terrestrial television platform should be engineered as one complete system. And some ITV and Channel 4 representatives, very much as you might expect from former IBA people, thought that the whole thing ought to be designed as one complete system: that we ought to agree on [using the] same codec/multiplexer etc.

Others thought that this proposal did not fit with the reality, which was that each broadcaster or multiplex operator would want the maximum flex-ibility to design and implement their own broadcast chain without having to consult others. Clearly they would insist on having the independence to pursue their own ideas on how best to do it, and to choose for themselves which manufacturer to buy equipment from. The BBC's view was that there should be no more to a set of rules than the absolute minimum to make the system work: Bob Ely was briefed to advocate that minimalist approach within the DTG's System Integration Group:

> And I remember using the analogy at the first meeting we held of saying, as an example of the way we are going to work, "You will recollect that we sent out an invitation to this meeting that told you [just] the date, the time, and the place: I did not tell you how to get here, how to leave, when to get up this morning, or what clothes to wear. That's the way it's going to be." And of course it turned out actually what we needed to produce was the 'D' Book.

The 'D' Book is the shorthand name for a lengthy technical handbook which is properly entitled *Digital Terrestrial Television: Requirements for Interoperability*. It was the DTG's first, and possibly still, its greatest achievement.

The DVB-T specification, completed and frozen, but not yet verified as an international standard, was a complex and flexible toolkit. It was always envisaged that countries would select from the toolkit those features, modes and variants most suited to their needs. The essential task that the DTG recognised very early on was that it had to write the UK's implementation guidelines, making a selection of the available DVB-T features which most suited the UK's requirements.

The sheer range of options in the specification was nowhere more true than in the Service Information (SI) sections. Once again, the diversity of opinion within the DVB had resulted in the wholesale adoption of most of its members requirements, which included many features that were rarely to be used. Bob Ely recalls that it was one of the DVB's most difficult drafting tasks:

> The DVB-SI specification, I think anybody would say, was not one of the best parts of the DVB's work, because it had just got too complicated, too diverse, too many different conflicting inputs.

Service Information is the essential 'glue' that holds together a network of digital multiplexes. Some SI content is mandatory: a receiver needs to sort out from the multiplex transport stream which sections of data comprise parts of a particular service so that it can rebuild the content. The receiver needs also to know from the received data what the service name is, whether it is scrambled or not, what channel number it should appear with, what the programme title is, what its beginning and end times are, and the same details about following programmes for anything up to seven days. It needs to know which transmitter the multiplex is being broadcast from and what other multiplexes are also available, and the details of the programmes being carried, and whether or not interactive services are being carried, and where to find them. To do this, sets of service information data are included in each multiplex which describe features of the network, the service and the 'event' or programme. Within each set provision is made for so-called 'private data', which a network can use for any additional purpose. And quite apart from the mandatory SI there are numerous additional specified but optional features.

So the DTG set out to make the detailed selection of features which, besides SI, covered the required characteristics of the transport stream, of transmission parameters, and later for interactive and other data services, conditional access, together with a baseline receiver specification. Much of the detail involved reference to the various national and international technical standards, and reference also to the technical and regulatory specifications issued by the Independent Television Commission. It was a mammoth task, begun during the summer of 1996 but one which could go so far and no further in the absence of the operators of the four commercial multiplexes. The passage of Act, and the selection of multiplex licensees, would not come until early in 1997, at the same time as the DVB-T specification was finally standardised.

The DVB froze the terrestrial specification at the start of 1996, but before it could become a recognised standard it had to be ratified by ETSI - the European Telecommunications Standards Institute. As part of that process, the robustness and validity of the specification had to be clearly demon-strated. The principal vehicle for this verification process was another international project, VALIDATE,[106] which was set up under the European Commission's RACE II programme. It was led by the BBC with nineteen other partners and started work in November 1995.

Verification required the partnership to check that the specification was clear and unambiguous by demonstrating that first simulations, followed by actual hardware implementations, put together in separate laboratories, would all work together and would perform as expected both in the lab and in actual field trials. The work would take until the end of the following year.

Meanwhile, in August 1996, the ITC's SPECTRE modem went on air in the London area. The research team who built it, who once worked for the old IBA, then for NTL after privatisation, now found themselves working for DMV, a subsidiary of the News Corporation company NDS. They, too, rushed to build a compliant system as soon as the DVB had frozen the specification. Gordon Drury:

> We knew what we had to build. And in order to demonstrate that the spec is
> sound clearly we had to build the thing to the spec. So we had to modify our

---

[106] VALIDATE: Verification and Launch of Integrated Digital Advanced Television in Europe. Partners included the BBC, TDF-C2R, CCETT, IRT, RAI, Retevision, the EBU and others.

model of the modem to comply with the spec, independently. Read the spec, look at the model, do what you have to do to make it compliant, as far as you think it's compliant.

At the BBC, inquisitive researchers tried to pick up the NTL transmission carrying the DMV signal but found that, although they could synchronise to it, they could not decode it. After several months of embarrassment it was clear that the BBC and DMV could not receive each others broadcasts. DMV insisted that theirs was DVB-compliant and, what's more, that it had demonstrated the first end-to-end compliant system before the BBC's April demonstration. Their claim remains today. As part of the VALIDATE programme however, the BBC and the DMV systems had to be demonstrated working in tandem. Eventually, in November 1996, DMV took their modem to the BBC labs at Kingswood Warren. Gordon Drury went along with his colleagues:

> It was easier for us to go to Kingswood than to anywhere else in the world, so we just took our modem up to the lab at Kingswood, connected them together, and it didn't work! But we quickly found out, thanks to the diagnostic features in the BBC modem, what it was, and we [went back to our lab and] fixed it, went back [the next day] and it was fine. Then we went through a range of tests: we go through all the modulation options, all the FEC options, whatever parameter options you've got, and play around with everything in sight that's possible in the spec, and prove that it's compliant.

The source of the problem was tracked down to a setting on the DMV modem: all the modulation options, QPSK, 16-QAM and 64-QAM are built by adding two components - an in-phase component and a quadrature component - together.

> We had the Q phase of carriers upside down. Of course at labs our two modems worked together because they were both, as it were, upside down. So they worked, each to the other, but our compliant version and the BBC's compliant version were different, so they couldn't demodulate our transmission and we couldn't demodulate their transmission. Trivial thing to get wrong, and a relatively trivial thing to put right.

The BBC never said publicly that their competitor's modem was non-compliant, fearing that there might be damage to the specification, and was at pains to reach an amicable and satisfactory outcome.[107] As for DMV, Gordon Drury says,

> We were not interested at this time, unlike perhaps other times in our history with Kingswood, in proving points of virility. We also wanted the spec to be proven and also had the ready market for commercial product to think about so we had an incentive not to get too upset about who was right

---

[107] I am indebted to Andrew Oliphant of BBC R&D, who led the VALIDATE work, for background information to this account.

and who was wrong. When you think of all the DVB-T parameters and all the things that could have been wrong, this one relatively easy thing to fix showed that the failure of the modems to match was almost trivial.

There were times in the history of digital television, and this was one, when diplomacy was as important as the engineering.

There was scope too for some further diplomacy in Europe: the row in DVB between the British, who advocated the 2k modulation option, and the rest of the membership, who wanted to wait for 8k, was rumbling on, despite the finalisation of the DVB specification which allowed the option. Some of the principal 8k protagonists - still fearful that 8k would not survive given the existence of 2k - formed a lobby.

Spain in particular was very keen to be able to use 8k. At the top end of the UHF frequency band there were five channels, 65-69, which Spain, in common with some other European countries, had used for military purposes. With the departure of the Franco government, these channels were now vacant and available for television broadcasting. Spain's plan was to use all five for national single frequency networks, a very efficient way of bringing twenty or more digital TV services to the whole country. Without 8k, that couldn't be done. The government ministry responsible for broadcasting - the Dirección General de Radiodiffusión y Televisión - together with the national transmission utility Retevision, started signing up like-minded countries to what became known as the '8k Interest Group'. Sweden was one of the first to join, and two men, Per Mellberg of Terracom and Jose-Luis Tejerina of Retevision, started to make the running.

In the UK, some of the principal members of the DTG saw in the 8k-IG a potentially powerful lobby that might risk the rapid agreement needed to allow an early start to digital terrestrial television, based on the 2k system, in the UK. Michael Starks discussed the situation with like-minded individuals in the DTG Council:

> We decided we needed some kind of forum in which better working relations and a degree of mutual understanding about the different circumstances in the different countries and why one could help one another, were required. And I think it began forming in my mind as a solution to the problem of what are we going to do about these semi-public technical policy clashes between the UK and Spain. The answer was: be more mature - take a broader view of it. Which was absolutely right, and worked rather well.

The diplomatic moves began. Ed Wilson, at the EBU in Geneva, recalls being on the receiving end:

> Peter Marchant from the UK, who was at the time with NTL, kept phoning me up and saying, "Look I think we need to do something a bit like the

185

DTG but in Europe." That was certainly an early start of that. Now you could see [the] thinking: we need economies of scale for what we're going to be doing that will go beyond Britain, whereas the 8k-IG was not doing that. It was thinking well the UK's kind of a competitor trying to establish something we don't want - a 2k-only environment. So they were, in a sense, strange bedfellows to bring together into DigiTAG, and DigiTAG of course was spawned from the EBU, the Digital Television Group and the 8k-IG.

On 13 June 1996, the first meeting of what was originally called 'the Digital Television Initiation Group' took place in Geneva. It was effectively a tripartite meeting between the DTG, the 8k-IG and the EBU, the latter presumably playing the honest broker. The chairman was Herman van Wijk of the Dutch broadcaster NOS, but wearing an EBU hat, and therefore neutral. The two principal protagonists of the 8k Interest Group, Jose-Luis Tejerina of Spain's Retevison and Per Mellberg of Sweden's Teracom, attended together with Chris Daubney, then secretary of the DTG, with Ed Wilson and David Wood of the EBU. Agreement was reached to set up three main task groups to discuss services and equipment, legal and regulatory issues, and to conduct marketing and promotion, and to seek a wider membership. At IBC in Amsterdam that September, remembers Ed Wilson ...

> ... we held a launch meeting in September 1996 in the Onyx Room of the RAI Centre. We had a number of speakers, Herman, Chris Daubney and others, and we had invited lots of people. About 80 took part, and after a few weeks we'd signed up 42 organisations to be members, and we had our first really proper kick-off meeting in the December of that year with the first General Assembly and the first elections of the Steering Board and the Presidency and so on.

With the statutes written - they were based on the DVB's statutes - and with its name now the Digital Terrestrial Television Action Group - DigiTAG - regular meetings began. Ed Wilson, who has been Project Manager to DigiTAG since its inception, believes that the most valuable thing that DigiTAG did in its early years was, "to demystify the technology":

> What we discovered from the very beginning was we were dealing with a very diverse Europe. The diversity meant that it was very difficult to take a model from a particular country and apply it universally. We were very good at networking, bringing people together who could talk to each other about why they'd done things. And coffee breaks and lunches were great for networking as well. Formally speaking, the seminar structures were used for examining a topic or looking in detail at a particular country, and informally putting people in touch with each other.

And DigiTAG soon established a presence at the European parliament and at the Commission. Never a lobbying group - it couldn't be because of the natural diversity of view within its membership - DigiTAG developed a valuable and respected role, as Ed Wilson recalls:

> Right from the start we made a special approach to Europe, we would go and actually find some time with the European Commission staff, go to Brussels, meet them in their offices, or we would take a room in an hotel near to the Commission, and we would invite them to come to a seminar that was very much targeted at the European administrators. And we did do that from the very beginning. We were never formally focused on lobbying, but we were quite useful in going and explaining [things] to the Commission, and there were times when we went there and got a very good positive response, and other small groups of people were going and getting a very bad response.

The role of DigiTAG has changed very little since its inception, but its membership has. As the countries of the old East Europe developed their thinking and began to explore digital terrestrial broadcasting, new faces appeared round the meeting tables at the EBU in Geneva, and in seminars now held from time to time in other cities across Europe. There is no doubt that the organisation did, and still does, play a vital role in bringing people together to share ideas the better to understand both the technology and each other. And there is no doubt either that it succeeded to a large extent in defusing the 2k-8k row.

As detailed work on the new digital services began in Britain, concern began to be felt about interoperability between the three proposed platforms, satellite, terrestrial and cable. Providing a receiver which can receive digital television from all three is technically possible. The receiver would need separate front ends for the demodulation of the received signal from each of the three delivery systems, but significant downstream stages of the receiver - notably the MPEG-2 decoder - are, because of the commonality deliberately built in to the DVB family of systems, the same. To begin with, a combined receiver was seen as a means to encourage the use of open standards on all platforms, and essential in terms of achieving volume production - and therefore relatively low initial retail prices.

The practical problems in having a single receiver arose principally from commercial interests. Pay operators could choose from a growing range of proprietary conditional access systems, among them Canal Plus's Mediaguard, Irdeto and a system devised by NDS, a News Corporation company. Similarly, there was a choice to be made of an Application Programme Interface - the API - a system which also resided in a receiver and which formed the engine which powered the interactive elements of digital television. The decisions were clearly going to be made on the basis of cost and whether the features on offer fitted with an individual operator's business plan. Of the two systems, the most significant obstacle to interoperability lay in the prospect of different conditional access systems being adopted for each platform.

CA scrambles the signal usually at the MPEG-2 transport stream level. Descrambling requires the receiver to be in possession of the appropriate 'keys' which are generated by decrypting control words, called Entitlement Control Messages (ECM). The latter are transmitted as 'private data' within the multiplex. The keys needed for descrambling change every few seconds which means that a continuous stream of ECMs is needed.

To control access to programmes by each individual subscriber's set-top box, a second set of data, called Entitlement Management Messages (EMMs) is needed. These enable (or disable) the ability of an individual subscriber's box to decrypt the ECM.

EMMs are themselves transmitted in encrypted form. To decrypt them a 'secret key' is used, which is unique to the subscriber/set-top box/smart card combination and is made up partly of information securely held in the set-top box and smart card and partly delivered over-air. The stored and over-air components of the EMMs are cryptographically combined in such a way that the secret key is never revealed outside the secure device in which it is 'buried'. The most straightforward way to incorporate CA in a set-top box - and the natural course to follow in a vertically integrated pay-TV service - is to embed it, usually as part of the demultiplexer chipset. But of course that means the receiver can only unscramble the pay-TV services of one operator, the operator who has provided the set-top box. The DVB had looked at potential technologies to allow a receiver to unscramble pay-TV services using different CA systems and had come up with two different solutions each of which is appropriate for different circumstances.

The first is called 'simulcrypt' - or more correctly, 'head-end simul-crypt' since all the processing involved goes on at the head (i.e. trans-mission) end of the system. Simulcrypt is suitable for use where it is desired to make broadcasts accessible via two or more populations of set-top boxes each with its own, different, CA system embedded. For example, Canal Plus acquired the Italian satellite broadcaster Tele+ in 1996 and used simulcrypt to enable its services to be decoded by both its own set-top boxes in France and by former Tele+ set-top boxes in Italy. Another use is during change-over of SMART cards - this cannot happen overnight so during the transition period operators such as BSkyB use 'internal-simulcrypt' to enable their services to be decoded with both the old and the new issue of cards. Simulcrypt is analogous to having two doors to a house, each with a different lock and key. Whilst this allows independent access it can only be used between, or within, organisations which trust each other since compromise of either CA system (or any if there are more than two CA systems involved in the simulcrypt arrangement) could result in mass piracy of the service(s) being simulcrypt. Simulcrypt, cannot, however, solve the problem of making one set-top box capable of accessing two or more services each of which uses a different CA system.

For the latter circumstances, the DVB adopted another pre-existing concept, 'multicrypt'. In contrast to simulcrypt, multicrypt requires no co-operation or trust between the broadcasters and no changes at the head-end. It does, however, require that the set-top box or receiver is able to 'plug-in' the different kinds of CA decoder/descrambler needed for each CA system it is to receive and decode. An important specification for multicrypt is the European Common Interface Specification which had been developed and standardised in the 1997 under the auspices of CENELEC[108]. The 'Common Interface' allows different conditional access modules to be plugged into a set-top box/receiver via a standard 'PC-card'/PCMCIA[109] socket. Pay-TV operators who had subsidised the development and deployment of set-top boxes, were understandably opposed to giving other operators a 'free ride' by allowing them to use a Common Interface socket to plug in their own CA system into an existing populations of set-top boxes. There were also allegations that the Common Interface created increased security risks though these seem not to have been substantiated[110]. Although the Common Interface/multicrypt has taken many years to be adopted its take-up is increasing, especially in integrated digital TV receivers (IDTVs)[111].

In the Spring of 1997, while the ITC was still considering bids for the multiplex licences, and while much of the technical detail of the DTT platform was still undecided, the Digital TV Group issued a briefing document entitled *Does the UK want a common digital TV receiver?* which

---

[108] CENELEC: Comité Européen de Normalisation Electrotehnique - European Committee for Electrotechnical Standardization

[109] PCMCIA (Personal Computer Memory Card International Association) is an international standards body and trade association which is based in California, USA and which has over 100 member companies; it was founded in 1989 to establish standards for integrated circuit cards and to promote interchangeability among mobile computer devices.

[110] Owners and licensees of high-value rights in programmes such as movies have a particular concern that a duly authorised Common Interface Module delivers the digital transport stream in the clear across the interface back into the set-top box; this in-the-clear transport stream could in principle be recorded or redistributed via the Internet. It is not clear, however, whether this is a real threat or only a theoretical one: the DVB is considering changes to the Common Interface Specification to eliminate this potential weakness.

[111] Regulation 7 of the Advanced Television Services Regulations 2003 of Directive 2002/19/EC of the European Parliament and of the Council (Access to, and interconnection of electronic communications networks and associated facilities) requires that:
'All television sets [placed in the market after 25 July 2003] with an integrated decoder of digital television signals and an integral viewing screen of visible diagonal greater than 30 cm shall possess at least one open interface socket (conforming to an industry wide specification) e.g. the DVB common interface connector permitting both the simple connection of peripherals and able to pass all the elements of a digital television signal, including information relating to interactive and conditionally accessed services.'

tackled head on the thorny issues of interoperability between the platforms. This was an issue close to Michael Starks' heart. Why, the thinking went, should a licence-fee payer not wish to receive programmes from each of two, or all three, digital platforms? Digital, after all, was about greater choice, and having to have three set-top boxes in order to exercise that choice looked like a disincentive. And surely the manufacturers would reap the benefit of the larger combined market that would be on offer to a single receiver capable of receiving all platforms.

In the real world, of course, such altruistic thinking had no impact, and the manufacturers started talking to the proposed pay-TV operators about big contracts for production runs of hundreds of thousands of proprietary boxes, all with the operator's specified - and embedded - conditional access, API and EPG implementation. For a while, a compromise appeared possible - the concept of a 'sidecar'. This envisaged a module which contained the demodulator and conditional access for one platform being built on to a common interface module which could then be plugged in to a receiver produced for another platform. BSkyB told the National Heritage Select Committee that it would provide a port on their boxes for a DTT sidecar, and the two bidders for the terrestrial multiplexes, BDB and DTN, envisaged providing sockets for any satellite sidecar that might one day be forthcoming. For the BBC, the lack of concrete progress in getting any of these agreements to stick was of great concern, and an early digital satellite launch was considered essential. Bob Ely found himself in the middle of the discussions:

> And quite late in the day there was still quite a lot of talk about simulcrypt or trying to get mandation of the Common Interface on the Sky box, so we could have a separate conditional access system. And that was very, very difficult [to achieve]. So given the first priority was to launch on satellite - because Patricia [Hodgson] and John [Birt] had said, we have to launch at the same time as Sky, we can't be a year later because if we are by that time once it's a successful platform we won't be able to afford it. And we will also be in danger of being marginalised into a terrestrial ghetto. Therefore, the BBC would use Sky's encryption system.

For some time to come, BSkyB would hold the gatekeeper's keys to the satellite services of Britain's licence-fee funded public service broadcaster.

With the passing of the Broadcasting Act in July 1996, the Independent Television Commission now began the process of advertising the licences for the non-'gifted' terrestrial multiplexes, setting a deadline of the end of January 1997 for all bids to be submitted. Carlton Television, one of the big ITV companies, was very keen to bid and had been working on a business plan for DTT for some months. Granada, the other major ITV company had pursued a different strategy, forming Granada Sky Broadcasting, a joint venture with BSkyB, to supply subscription-funded digital satellite channels. Barry Cox remembers that Granada's boss, Gerry Robinson, took a very poor view of the prospects for DTT:

> I can remember an occasion where I went to one of their awaydays where Gerry Robinson effectively said, we're not interested in this, we can get on with Sky, we're perfectly happy with our deal and I don't think DTT's going to happen or it's not going to be worth it. So they kind of lost interest.

Robinson's view echoed that of quite a number of people in the industry, that digital satellite was a sure-fire winner and its terrestrial equivalent was unlikely to succeed. Which made the approach in December 1996 by BSkyB to Carlton, asking to join their bid for the DTT licences, all the more surprising. Carlton agreed: BSkyB was bringing to the table the offer to provide a Carlton-BSkyB consortium with premium sport and movie channels. Barry Cox still finds amusement in remembering what happened next:

> I can remember [with] great amusement when it emerged that Carlton and Sky were going to bid for the multiplexes, and Granada moved heaven and earth to get themselves in. You know, whatever happened to Gerry Robinson's "We don't need DTT - it's going to be satellite"? They panicked at that point. A complete about face, and they wanted in on it.

So the consortium, now called British Digital Broadcasting, agreed to take in Granada as an equal partner. As the deadline for bids came at the end of January, BDB looked a strong candidate but there was one other bidder in the form of the Digital Television Network, headed by International CableTel which now owned the transmission company NTL. Both consortia were bidding for the three multiplexes, B, C and D. The BBC, ITV and Channel 4 had earlier agreed to take up their guaranteed multiplexes, but only at the very last minute did a bid come forward for multiplex A. This hybrid public service/commercial multiplex was to carry Channel Five and, in Wales, S4C, but had vacant space for new services. Late in the day, S4C attracted the interest of NTL and United News and Media (the third big ITV company) who together formed S4C Digital Networks (later SDN). Barry Cox recalls the heroic efforts of a S4C executive in putting together their last-minute bid:

> United suddenly found themselves the odd person out, and I think it was brilliant the way Emyr Bryn Hughes did it, he put together inside four days the S4C/United/NTL bid. And all credit to him it was quite extraordinary. But United were well pissed off being left out.

The ITC spend the best part of six months considering the bids, so it was not until June 1997 that they dropped a bombshell: they wrote to BDB to say that BSkyB's presence in the consortium would ensure that they were not allocated a licence. Worried by the growing influence of News

Corporation, which was BSkyB's major shareholder, it had sought legal advice, and advice from the Office of Fair Trading, and - unusually - from the Competition Commissioner in Brussels. The ITC found it had no option but to stipulate the exclusion of BSkyB. This came as a blow to Granada and Carlton, who were relying on the satellite operator's accumulated experience in conditional access and the whole complex business of subscription management. It sought to retain BSkyB's premium programme supply arrangement. Intensive negotiations against the ITC's tight deadline produced a deal which Chris Hibbert remembers:

> A very hasty divorce was arranged - very quick. I wasn't involved in the detail, but I what I observed was there were some deals done where a large amount of money was handed over to Sky just to take their name off the headed paper. But the contra-deal was that Sky said they would continue to offer first preference on the lease of the Marco Polo building - they owned that, and it was a possible multiplex centre - and agreed to supply a number of channels for a number of years at a reasonable rate. There were certain people in Granada who were saying that at that stage we should have pulled out. Michael Green was still keen to do it and Granada went along with it.

The ITC announced the multiplex awards on 24 June. BDB had won the three multiplexes, B, C and D. Emyr Bryn Hughes consortium, SDN, was awarded the licence for Multiplex A. Together with the 'gifted' multiplexes - multiplex 1 for the BBC and multiplex 2 shared between ITV and Channel Four - the future shape of digital terrestrial television in Britain was determined.

There would follow seventeen months of intense activity as the existing analogue broadcasters and the new digital licensees put together their technical infrastructures and finalised their service proposition and marketing strategy. It proved a far from straightforward process, and led to some surprises along the way.

15
Shaping the Platform

When the ITC announced the multiplex licence awards in June 1997, the work within the Digital TV Group to agree the details of the terrestrial platform moved up a gear. Until that point, in the absence of a confirmed holder of the licence for multiplexes B, C and D, many decisions had to be shelved until the decision was known. Now that it was, the BDB people - later to be known by their brand name, ONdigital - could now talk specifics. The BBC's Bob Ely, who at that time was Chairman of the DTG's System's Integration Group (which was, at this stage, still responsible for the 'D-Book') remembers how the absence of a confirmed licence holder had frustrated progress:

> The DTG had been working for round about two years by the time that ONdigital were awarded their multiplexes and had stalled. The D-Book was going very slowly indeed, there was not consensus about some very important issues, and no particular view as to how we were going to agree a receiver specification.

On the eve of the ITC's announcement, the Digital TV Group had published a second version of the D-Book. It was by then already a substantial document, and the new edition benefited from a substantial amount of feedback from the industry to the first edition. But it was far from complete. Much of its content was aspirational rather than definitive. It sorely needed the detail, and only the new licence holder, BDB, which was bound to subsidise the first generation of receivers, could make the necessary decisions. Bob Ely remembers:

BDB, once they'd got their franchise, faced a sudden project deadline and had to shift gear very markedly in order to get anywhere near the launch date. BDB were paying for the receiver so paid for the specification. It completely changed the pace of working from what had happened before, when in a rather abstract way without it being clear who was paying there had been strong debate at useful but perhaps rather abstracted levels.

Chris Hibbert was a supporter of the DTG. He had represented ITV there from its early days, and represented BDB on the DTG Council. He remembers the awkwardness of the new relationship.

> We got accused of trying to hijack the DTG, and we weren't going to do this and we weren't going to do that and we were saying, look, if DTT doesn't work, you are not going to go into liquidation. So you've got to let us push this along. We'll let go more and more and more the more confident we feel that other people are going to start taking risks and other people are going to start to help to drive the platform. So that was the balance we were playing all the time. I was getting berated from within BDB by some people for spending so much time helping the DTG. And I'm saying, yes but in the long term this is going to help us. But other people were moaning about ONdigital - keeping their cards close to their chest, not telling us anything, not releasing the receiver spec. But we managed through that process and I think we proved over time that we were supportive. But we were a start-up business with a major investment.

At senior levels within ITV and BDB certainly, there was a view that the DTG was too large and unfocussed an organisation to take the strategic decisions, which were regarded as the prerogative of the broadcasters alone. Barry Cox:

> The DTG did not feature in our brains as a place to do it. I was only very vaguely aware of the DTG - in my view it was an engineering group. That was fine, but the engineers representing ITV in there never suggested that DTG was anything like the vehicle for anything. And I think they were probably right. It does a great job, it just couldn't have run the multiplexes, it just couldn't have done that. It did prove very difficult to manage this platform effectively.

So the broadcasters formed their own exclusive 'club', the DMux Group. The Group had been formed by Michael Starks of the BBC and Barry Cox of ITVA, and had met in embryonic form before the licences were awarded and before the final shape of the legislation became clear. At one point the various bidders were invited to attend in an effort to form a consensus. Now, with the licences awarded, it had an exclusive membership of the four multiplex operators, BBC, D3&4, SDN and BDB. It became the place where most of the critical decisions were made, where the broadcasters decided between themselves what the shape of the terrestrial platform would be. It was quickly clear to Peter Marshall, then with Channel Four, that this was the place where the important decisions would be made, and that BDB was making most of them:

> I remember going up from Channel Four at one stage for a meeting of that group and we went to Carlton's premises just near Hyde Park Corner, and I remember it quite clearly because it was when I realised that the cosy co-operation that we'd been doing up to that point was not the name of the game any more. BDB were pulling all the strings - for good reason, I'm not knocking it, but in order to get launched as quickly as possible they had to be working with a relatively closed group.

From then on, much of the crucial and unfinished D-Book work was done by the BDB on behalf of the DMux Group, work which was largely funded by BDB, with decisions largely taken by BDB and then agreed by the other multiplex operators in the DMux Group, and passed to the DTG for inclusion in the next edition of the D-Book. Work had to proceed with great speed: ITC licence conditions required launch to be before the end of 1998. With a similar view of the need to launch the terrestrial platform as soon as possible, the BBC gave its support almost unreservedly to BDB.

There was a lot of unfinished D-Book work to complete, and one of the most important tasks was to complete the set of rules for using Service Information (SI), the codes embedded in each multiplex which in receivers are the key to navigating around the content and decoding it. As part of this work, there needed to be a view on how the SI would find its way into the multiplexes in the first place. Each of the four multiplex operators had their own unique network architectures. While BDB's services would be the same everywhere in the country, those of the BBC, ITV, and Channel Four and SDN were regionalised, but regionalised to differing extents. ITV was a highly regionalised and federated organisation which was made up of 15 regional companies with quite separate programme schedules outside peak. It further sub-opted some regions to provide local news. Meridian, the contractor for the South of England, covered an area which stretched all the way from the tip of Kent, along the south coast to Bournemouth, and as far north as Oxford. It provided separate local news from Maidstone, Southampton and Abingdon. Other ITV companies did the same. In the early weekday evening, there were no fewer than 29 separate programmes across the network. This would be replicated in the ITV digital simulcast. The BBC at various times of the day broadcast 14 separate opt-outs on BBC-1, and planned not only to replicate this in its digital simulcast, but opt the national regions on the new digital-only service, BBC Choice. Channel Four provided the same programmes across the whole UK, but ran separate bundles of commercials in six 'macro-regions'. SDN's digital services would differ inside and outside Wales.

The patterns of region and sub-region differed between the BBC and ITV, and that meant that no fewer than thirty different versions of service information would be needed at different groups of transmitters across the UK. The solution to this challenge came from a team led by Andrew Glasspool (an independent consultant contracted by BDB) working with Richard Cooper, Judy Nunn and others from BBC Research and Development. They took the pragmatic view that the way to achieve this was to combine all the sets of service information constructed by each broadcaster by gathering them together at a central SI collator, which BDB offered to host. From there, the SI data would be fed to 30 transmitter sites which were designated 'service insertion points'. Each of the 30 transmitters was a 'parent' transmitter servicing in turn 'daughter' relay stations which carried the same regional content for all the broadcasters and would therefore carry the same service information. The feeds to the 30 SIPs (SI insertion Points) from the central collator progressively filtered out the unwanted SI leaving only the relevant content to be reinserted into the six multiplexes at the each SIP. Richard Cooper, looking back on the decision the UK made, says:

> I think the decision to go for a central collator model was the only way the business could have gone, doing it another way is simply not one that I would try to do, and we've seen that on networks elsewhere, there really isn't another model.

It is worth underlining just how novel and difficult a task it was to devise and specify a workable SI implementation of this nature. Bob Ely pays tribute to Richard Cooper's ground-breaking work:

> When I handed over the first draft of the D-Book to him I was reminded of the task of re-assembling one of Harrison's sea clocks at the Greenwich Museum - a box of bits: some missing; some broken. It took Richard's genius (ably assisted by Judy Nunn) and persistence to make SI into a workable system for DTT. I doubt if anyone else could have done that.

This elegant solution to a complex problem was viewed with some amazement by European broadcasting engineers when it was first described to them. All would later face the same SI challenge when their own turn came to go digital, but at the time their thinking on the subject was rather less advanced.

The next most important set of decisions that had to be made by BDB and agreed by the DMux Group centred on the specification for the receiver. Manufacturers would need a lengthy lead-time to develop, test and supply receivers, and the timescale was critical if launch were to be in the late summer of 1998, now just fourteen months away. Three choices had to be made: the choice of middleware, conditional access and API.

Middleware is the receiver's operating system - roughly the equivalent of Windows in a personal computer - on which run applications which, in the case of a digital television receiver, include the conditional access system and the engine which enables interactive features, the Applications Programme Interface or API. But there was a choice of architectures, open or closed. In a closed, proprietary receiver, the conditional access system and the API are closely integrated - embedded - with the middleware; in an open system, the API stands independently of the middleware, allowing different manufacturers to adopt different middleware but still run the same API. And in an open box, the conditional access system can be physically separate, and carried on a module which slots into the DVB Common Interface socket. This allows for choice and competition in the selection of the CA provider. In these early days, a handful of commercial digital satellite services had started in America, in the Far East, South Africa and on continental Europe. All were owned and operated by a single broadcaster which specified closed receiver systems. Nobody had yet tried to design a platform around an open receiver. The former typically could be closely defined and securely controlled by the broadcaster, the latter would be less easy to agree and to control, and potentially less secure. Peter Marshall:

> BDB was very sceptical about the collaborative approach. And for good reason, because the only digital platform that existed at that time was a vertical market, so its a natural consequence that to secure their future they had to produce their own vertical market box. So I think the attitude always was, if there is a horizontal market it'll do it anyway but we have to secure our future with a vertical market box.

Faced with these pressing decisions, BDB again hired Andrew Glasspool, who had experience of putting together a digital satellite platform in Thailand, where he had worked with the set-top box manufacturer Pace. Bob Ely says that:

> Andrew very sensibly decided to treat BDB's terrestrial broadcasts as if it was a satellite broadcasting system, and did exactly what he had done for those which was what everybody did: you choose your conditional access system which gives you the heart of the receiver, and that predicates a lot of decisions because, in effect, its like designing a computer: if you've chosen Windows everything then follows from that.

After surveying potential candidates, BDB settled for the software suite being offered by the French company Canal Plus, the Mediahighway middleware and Mediaguard embedded conditional access, which the company had developed for its own domestic satellite direct-to-home service. Chris Hibbert recalls:

> The more we got to know the Canal Plus people, the more we liked them. We liked their technology, and we also like their naivety about price,

because they'd never sold to anybody outside the Canal Plus group, and they had aspirations to go out and be a CA vendor in the market place. So they were very keen to get in. We ended up accepting their offer and completely annoying NDS.

Until shortly before the deadline for multiplex bids in early 1997, BSkyB had been a partner in BDB, but had been forced to withdraw by the ITC. News Corporation, which owned BSkyB, had established a subsidiary company based in Israel, News Data Communications (NDC: later, with DMV, part of News Digital Systems), which marketed a proprietary middleware/conditional access system called Videocrypt. For a long time, even after BSkyB withdrew from the BDB bid, the assumption had been made that BDB would use the NDS technology, and that included their audio and video coders. But John Egan and Andrew Glasspool much preferred the Canal Plus offering, as Chris Hibbert remembers:

> We liked what they could offer - video on demand in the future - we liked the whole construction of their system - it was less complicated and it was newer because, you know, things move on, and their pricing was good. They had integrated their systems with Divicom, my preferred compression system supplier, and they had the software to put in the box to manage downloads. It was all very nice. So there was going to be a big stand-off between the staff and the board

The engineering decision to adopt the Canal Plus alternative annoyed Michael Green, who summoned Chris Hibbert:

> I got to his office, and he's walking up and down with his shoes off which is always a frightening thing: if he takes his shoes off it means he's serious! I got to the door threshold. He's looking out of the window. And he said, "What have the fucking French got the fucking Israelis haven't got?" So I explained to him we just thought it was a better system, the price was better and we would be independent of our competitor. For me, from the technology point of view, it was a no-brainer. I discovered later that Michael had asked all of the technical management team the same question, picking us off one at a time.

But Chris Hibbert got his Divicom coders.

BDB's next choice was to select a suitable API. The choice of API would to a great extent define the scope and character of the interactive services that were planned. Interactivity was regarded as one of the great attractions that would entice viewers to digital television in the first place, ranking alongside the other perceived 'must-haves' of more services, better sound and picture quality, and widescreen. There were a handful of proprietary systems available on the market, and most had been adopted by one or other of the early satellite services in various parts of the world. During 1996, a year before BDB was awarded its multiplex licences, the DTG had carried out an assessment of the systems then available. Richard Cooper of BBC Research and Development was (and still is) an expert in this area of digital technology, and had been the brains behind the interactive demonstrator of the BBC's pilot service. He participated in the DTG evaluation process:

> A little group of us in the DTG scurried around and did an evaluation of the various APIs that there were around, and getting it down to the final three was not a very difficult activity. We went and looked at an awful lot more, but in actual practice at that time there were only three that were up and running. Mediahighway, Open TV and MHEG-5. MHEG-5 at that time was almost a completed ISO specification. Open TV was already in use, and Mediahighway was already in use. We could go so far in our evaluation, and on the outcome of our evaluation we said if we're going to go with open standards there is only one choice. If we're going to go with proprietary standards, there are two choices.

Much of the early work on MHEG-5 had been carried out in France by CCETT, and was based on the work of an international body, DAVIC[112]. The later development of MHEG-5, much of which was done in the UK, moved away from DAVIC's initial approach, which had more of a network focus with internet usage in mind. MHEG-5 had been optimised for television broadcast use. It was the only open system then available. Richard Cooper recognised that:

> MHEG-5 was actually quite well designed in terms of controlling presentation on the screen, the relationship between objects, and most of the basic functions that you need to do interactive applications were already built into it. MHEG[-5] has loads of drawbacks, [but]it does have the benefits that it's [an] open standard. We did the work, it's there, it's deployable, we demonstrated that it's deployable, and its memory footprint is very small which means it operates very effectively in cheap receivers, and also its application life cycle is very efficient in that it can operate very effectively within very low bit-rate channels. You can still get a good response with a low bit-rate channel.

These last considerations were important. 1997 was early days for serious digital processing in consumer devices, and the cost of memory chips was very high, and the available bandwidth on the digital terrestrial platform was severely limited, at least in part by the stipulations of the Broadcasting Act, which limited to ten per cent the proportion of capacity in any multiplex which could be used for interactive, or 'additional', service. Even so, as Richard Cooper puts it:

---

[112] DAVIC - the Digital Audio Visual Council, a non-profit Association based in Switzerland which ran from 1994 to 1999 and produced a family of specifications of open interfaces and protocols that maximise interoperability of applications and services across all audio-visual delivery technologies

> There was still a big decision to be taken: was it going to be MHEG-5 where the benefits of an open standard and multiple suppliers - all that kind of stuff? Drawback: you just can't go and buy it, you can't place a contract on somebody to supply it and off-load the risk. So you take on board a lot more risk. And within the DMux group, and specifically ONdigital who've got to make their boxes work and so on, that was a big decision for them.

The DTG team could not, of course, make a final choice. Besides the differing capabilities of the candidate systems, and their potential for future evolution, there other considerations of a purely business nature. Richard Cooper:

> The next decision beyond that requires the commercial input on behalf of the network operators because there are investments to be made on the closed ones, there are commercial negotiations to be had, and while we've gone part way down the line to that in terms of understanding the framework around costs of network operators, around costs of receivers, and all that sort of stuff, we can't go all the way and place a contract because the DTG was not a contract-placing body, it needed BDB to be formed which was the company that actually placed the contracts.

When BDB did get its feet under the DMux Group's table, they encountered an undoubted predisposition amongst a number of leading players to favour an open standard API. The BBC was for it, and the ITV representative on the evaluation group also favoured it. Some important manufacturers also supported an open API. A receiver could be a set-top box or a completely new television set with a built-in ability to receive digital signals. But to complicate matters, they could be made in two flavours. In one, the digital receiver was effectively a copy of the set-top box specified and subsidised by BDB, and built in to a modified analogue television set. In the alternative flavour, much supported from very early on by Sony UK, the integrated television set had middleware chosen by the manufacturer running the MHEG-5 API. As one manufacturer's representative put it at a DTG meeting, OpenTV was proprietary, requiring a licence fee and perhaps a royalty, whereas MHEG-5 is in the public domain. Manufacturers wanted to see a pan-European market for integrated receivers, and regarded the existence of proprietary systems as a barrier to achieving that. There was no problem in accepting subsidised set-top boxes with embedded solutions, he said, but integrated TV receivers must be future proof

BDB looked again at the candidate systems, and eventually settled on MHEG-5, but not, as Peter Marshall was aware, before a lot of infighting inside both the DMux Group and BDB itself:

> There was behind closed doors a very powerful and very strong argument between a proprietary API and MHEG, the most wondrous thing was that MHEG was ever adopted, I suspect. But it was always a delicate compromise.

The specification of MHEG-5 was an absolute minimum in order to limit the risk that late availability of the API could delay the launch. Specifically, the return path and dial-up modem was left out to reduce complexity and cost. Peter Marshall was one of the cynics who read into the decision a Machiavellian approach by BDB:

> I have a suspicion that John Egan who made the decision was forced by the others to accept the MHEG API, and one of the reasons the return path was left out - there was an upfront reason and a hidden reason - the upfront reason was that he argued that it would prejudice the launch, it would delay the launch date. But the hidden reason was that I think he wanted it to fail so that he could plug in a proper proprietary API.

Together with DigiTAG, the Digital TV Group began work to define a more advanced version of MHEG-5 which would incorporate a return path. It was dubbed EuroMHEG because it was regarded as a candidate system for adoption by the DVB. The DVB was starting work on its Multimedia Home Platform (MHP) API, an ambitious programme to develop a more advanced design. As originally conceived, it would adopt the DAVIS proposal for an MHEG-5 presentation engine with an optional Java virtual machine. But it was not to be. The DVB has always favoured a cutting edge approach to its standards and MHEG-5 was regarded by many DVB members as old and peculiarly French. So when agreement was finally reached in a vote at the Steering Board of the DVB, in July 1998, it was for an API totally based on Java.

In the event, it took the DVB sixteen months to agree on the essential aspects of MAP, a further seventeen months to finalise the legal agreements, and until 2004 before the very first receivers with MAP appeared. It was, to be sure, a highly future-proofed specification, which took in all manner of possible applications in a future world of converged communication. While receiver manufacturing costs, particularly the cost of chips for data storage, remained high, MHP with its heavy processing demands was late in becoming a consumer product. The decision by the DVB not to countenance MHEG-5 - not even as a cut-down version of MHP (the two systems shared some common features) - disappointed many British engineers who had contributed to putting together EuroMHEG, but had the satisfaction of knowing that many of their ideas were picked up and used in the MHP specification.

Many countries in Europe delayed launching their terrestrial platforms until they could be certain that the MHP API could be present in receivers. But by the time that happened, MHEG-5 interactive services were being viewed in several million British homes and the number was growing fast, while the broadcasters' expertise in authoring content, and managing the tricky business of having numerous independent service providers, was coming on in leaps and bounds.

In retrospect, the DVB's approach to the API was flawed in that it was based on the premise that rich interactive content presented through the API would become a major driver of new television services and a source of significant income. Neither has really happened. Some income is derived from transactional services on satellite and cable (which do have a return path), and some broadcast interactive content is popular, particularly when associated with major sporting events. But by and large, broadcasters have learnt that interactivity can easily detract from the main purpose of watching television. The PC is streets ahead in providing internet based content and services.

In early 1998, with the open standard MHEG-5 agreed by BDB, a receiver specification could be drawn up. It would meet the obligation on the broadcaster set by the Commission Directive and the ITC's licence conditions that the platform should use open standards. Chris Hibbert sums up the view that BDB came to hold:

> We knew the government were looking for a common platform which would replace analogue terrestrial, which would provide free-to-air services, and the opportunity to implement pay. And it had to be offered as a harmonious service to the consumer. So that is how we ended up with a specification for the receiver which was based totally on DVB, including the CA. There's a European Directive which says, if you provide a pay-TV box, you must not disable the ability to watch free-to-air television. So we couldn't leverage against the free-to-air stuff at all, we'd be in breach of our licence. On the other hand, the government knew that we were the people who were going to seed the market, because we were going to be subsidising the boxes. They were going to be BDB boxes - subsidised at the point of sale by some means - which happened to do free-to-air as well. So we knew the ground we were on. Rather than fight it, we embraced it.

For the longer term, there was a widespread view that the reliance on the new terrestrial pay operator to subsidise receivers would be short lived. Quickly, it was thought, a buoyant market in open standard integrated digital television sets would be created as consumers swapped out their old analogue receivers. The option of adding pay services from BDB would be easily accommodated by plugging in a conditional access module to the TV set's common interface slot. Within a few short years, a horizontal market would be established in digital terrestrial television, similar to the market that had always existed for analogue television, and BDB would be relieved of the onus to subsidise receivers: paying for the CA module would be very much less costly. As it turned out, by the time that happened, the company that began life as BDB would have gone out of business.

In the spring of 1998, enough work on the D-Book and the receiver specification had been completed to allow BDB to order set-top boxes. The company had earlier sent an invitation to tender to twelve companies, and selected six. One of them was the set-top box division of the multinational company Philips, based near Paris. Philips appointed a marketing man, David Johnston, to look at new business opportunities generally in the UK, and specifically whether Philips could make boxes for BDB. Johnston started to attend DTG meetings on a regular basis, and there established contacts with the BDB. He remembers how important to Philips the prospect was of having them as a customer:

> Philips held the global number one position in set-top boxes, and terrestrial was seen as one to go for. Also remember that around that time other countries were talking about digital terrestrial. France specifically was talking about terrestrial services. And so was Spain. Spain was a little bit more ahead in its thinking than France was, but we could see that within twelve months we would start the same process with France and Spain. We could have gone into there with all the knowledge we could have gained in the UK, into much more important markets for Philips. The French market is very, very important for Philips.

Not everything about the market prospects in the UK made an immediate appeal to Philips, according to Johnston, including the complexities of the contract:

> We ended up with an extremely complicated three-way relationship between BDB's requirements to Canal Plus, and then Philips had to enter a formal relationship with Canal Plus for the software provision for us, and we had a formal relationship with BDB. So you had this extremely independent but interdependent three-way relationship.

And there was the financial aspect of the deal:

> Initially it was pretty fraught because it looked like Philips was taking a phenomenal amount of the risk involved. BDB were going to Dixons and saying this is our new service, this is what's going to happen. At that point a number of manufacturers were commissioned to make boxes. Although we had an underwrite, we had to make a huge effort to make sure we could actually sell the quantity we were going to build. We were having to do the selling.

These complexities were ones that all the six manufacturers who eventually provided BDB boxes would have to contend with. Even so, given large enough quantities in the order, this was a business opportunity not to be missed. Not all the selected manufacturers said that they could deliver product by the November launch, but by the summer, BDB were confident that at launch there would be receivers in the market: set-top boxes from

Philips and Pace[113], and an open standard integrated set from Sony. They were however, much less sure that the MHEG-5 software would be completed in time. It looked inevitable that digital terrestrial television would launch with no interactive content apart from a minimalist electronic programme guide which used data already present in service information, and which could run on the proprietary software of Mediaguard in the Philips and Pace boxes, and Sony's own version in its iDTVs.

Emboldened by this progress, and the publication in June 1998 of the third, vastly expanded and much more definitive, edition of the D-Book, BDB unveiled its consumer branding. Called from now on ONdigital, it unveiled its consumer proposition, claiming that it would become the most successful digital platform within a short time of launch, which it promised for September that year.

As the time to launch began to be measured in months, not years, it became clear that there was no hope whatsoever of all three digital television platforms adopting a common API. BSkyB had already committed to using Open TV, and the cable operators were said to be casting about for their own option. The BBC, which was then alone amongst the main broadcasters in planning to broadcast on all platforms from launch, began to work out how it could author each interactive application in three different forms. Like BSkyB, they recognised the importance of having interactive content available as an added attraction of the new digital service offering.

By that time also, Simulcrypt was dead, and so was cross-carriage of SI between platforms. A sidecar spec was issued in the course of 1998 but none was ever made. There were no multi-platform receivers. Neither ONdigital nor Sky wanted them. Nor did the retailers. As one senior executive from a major retailer was fond of saying, "Interoperability is a SCART connector."

---

[113] The contrast between the two companies could not have been more marked. Philips, the vast corporate entity,. multinational, bureaucratic, sometimes slow to make decisions, with several divisions in different countries all with a sector of the receiver market. Pace, the small start-up, based in a converted textile mill in West Yorkshire, innovative, fleet of foot, and already making inroads into the world market. Pace was already lined up to supply boxes for BSkyB.

Part Four

Triumph and Tribulation

16
The Race to Launch

By the summer of 1998, the broadcasters were well into the process of building the infrastructure to provide the new digital television services. Yet again, there were pioneering aspects to this, not the least of which was that digital terrestrial, as an open platform, would see each multiplex operator prepare its content for distribution to transmitting stations quite independently, yet for the viewer, the complete range of services had to appear and behave as a coherent whole. This had never been done before. All digital television systems so far built - and there were only a handful of satellite services across the world - had been unitary systems, vertically integrated, tightly specified and put together by a single powerful pay operator. By contrast, what was being proposed for the world's first open standard terrestrial platform looked to many like complete anarchy. For the systems engineers who were building the playout centres, the coding and multiplexing installations, the distribution networks and building the new transmitters, it significantly increased the complexity of their tasks and made huge demands on the co-ordinating mechanisms within the DMux Group and the DTG.

In some senses, the man with the most straightforward job was Chris Hibbert, whose principal responsibility was the commissioning of the ONdigital multiplexing centre, which would gather together all the constituent services in the ONdigital offering, and code them in MPEG-2 and combine them into their three multiplexes. He was starting from scratch.

> I got involved about six hours after the licences were announced, Nigel Walmsley who had been my boss at Carlton saying, "Would you like to come over and be Chief Engineer?" And I was working with my old friend John Egan again. He was project director at Carlton, and he'd been leading - effectively - the BDB consortium: he'd been doing all the work. My job was to come in and get the infrastructure built on the broadcasting side, which is the multiplex centre, and sign up the transmission contract.

ONdigital's new headquarters was the Marco Polo building in Battersea, another bequest from the frustrated bid partnership with BSkyB.[114]

> When we took possession of the building I had pretty much a free run, because there were no staff. I mean, it was a start-up company and there were about six people in the company. We had the top floor and the one underneath it, in one half of the Marco Polo building. So I worked out what I needed to cram in there. One of the biggest problems was - people who are not engineers don't understand the amount of mechanical and electrical plant that you need to cope with lots of electronic equipment producing lots of heat, and I had little space. We had chillers and fans and pipes and all this stuff. If we'd put them in on the floors, there wouldn't have been anywhere to put staff - the office staff - later. But there was room on the roof. I was working with the architect and the Mechanical and Electrical contractor and challenged them to get everything on the roof. They worked out they could do that, so my next obvious thing was, well, that's got the M&E kit in, where is the actual broadcast equipment going to go? As close as possible to the M&E plant. To keep the pipes short, to keep the cables short, to keep the airflow-ducts short.

His immediate boss, John Egan, was quite happy for Hibbert to use the top floor, and both agreed that the security of the equipment area, which included the highly sensitive conditional access equipment, and which was of prime importance, would be enhanced in that location. The top floor was, of course, designed as a corporate boardroom, and Hibbert remembers that when Stephen Grabiner was appointed as ONdigital's first Chief Executive:

> He was a bit concerned that he couldn't have his office on the top floor - overlooking the park - because we'd put all this kit up there! He said, what would it involve? I said, about nine million pounds and drilling holes through your office to get the pipes through. Too late. It's done.

---

[114] BSkyB had inherited the building from the merger of Sky with BSB. The doomsayers noted that the building had been the home of an earlier enterprise which had promised a broadcasting revolution, but which had failed within a year of launch, and pronounced it an unsuitable place to be the home of another!

Hibbert's next task was to select his suppliers, and the difficult choices lay in the selection of a manufacturer to supply coding and multiplexing equipment - the new technology part of his technical architecture. There was a very limited choice. Like his colleagues in the BBC, Hibbert had looked at the early products from Philips and Thomson, and also from NDS. He began by deciding not to go automatically for the latter, despite the complication that during the erstwhile relationship with BSkyB it was assumed that the equipment would come from the fellow News Corporation company. Naturally there was a practical reason in his decision:

> The only reason I was able to choose my own multiplexing equipment was because the company had crossed the Rubicon in terms of NDS and BSkyB. If the call centre and the conditional access had had to stay with NDS then we'd have had NDS compression equipment as well. No disrespect to NDS at all, they're a highly competent technology company and I have great respect for them. But, then, all those years ago, you could not buy plug and play broadcast equipment. It was very early days. Satellite had driven digital television, satellite was Pay, compression systems were (then) an integral part of one big system which included the conditional access. You couldn't tear them apart - there were no standard interfaces. It was only when the Canal Plus Technologies people had integrated their CA with another completely different manufacturer's broadcast multiplexing system, then we knew it could be done. The company's decision to go with Canal Plus for the CA released me from - de facto - having to [have] an NDS compression system. As always in life, there are leapfrogs going on in the technology, so we had the beginnings of choice, and broadcast engineers like to be able to choose whose cameras they buy, whose tape machines they buy, whose monitors they buy. You know, turnkey doesn't mean everything from one equipment vendor any more. So that was just one of those turning points at a time when I needed to make some decisions.

Freed to make a choice, Hibbert was on the verge of buying from one of the large European manufacturers when a contact suggested that it would be better for ONdigital's purposes to look at the product being developed by DiviCom, a small Californian start-up now owned by C-Cube. Hibbert followed up that advice.

> They had a representative in the UK and they had one coder they could show. So I said I'm going to look at this, and I took Meirion Hughes along - who was working for us - an old colleague from Carlton days. He's got golden eyes. We went to Charles de Gaulle Airport, to a tiny office where DiviCom had two people and they had a couple of coders set up, and we took our MPEG 'cracker' tape with us - the tape with all the nasty pictures in them - took it to Paris and eventually forced their coders to break. But we were incredibly impressed by the improvement of picture quality with high compression compared to the rest of the systems available at the time.

The challenge that ONdigital faced was to find the coder technology that would allow them to carry as many services as possible in each multiplex.

The more services the better the consumer proposition. But the more services there are in a multiplex the lower the bandwidth available for each, and quality - particularly picture quality - suffers. Too many services and the quality is so bad that it breaches the ITC licence provisions. The BBC and ITV, who had picture quality issues as a prime concern, were choosing coding rates of over 5 Mbit/sec for each service, which allowed only four services in each multiplex. The choice for them was coders which produced good results at those bit-rates. The coders that did that were much less impressive at the lower bit-rates which would result from ONdigital's proposed five or six services per multiplex.

The DiviCom coders not only coded much better at lower bit-rates than anybody else at the time, but they also offered statistical multiplexing. With 'statmux', the bitrate at which a service is coded constantly varies, and at any instant is decided automatically on the complexity of the picture and the demands being made by the other services in the same multiplex at the same time. By having a careful mix of high demand (e.g. sport) and low demand (e.g. a movie channel) services in a given multiplex, more services can be carried. The DiviCom product looked good.

At John Egan's insistence, Hibbert next went to the DiviCom plant in Silicon Valley along with a financial expert hired from PA Consulting. Could the company deliver product to quality, on time and on budget? The answers were positive. Not only that, but they were willing to tackle the special requirements of the UK terrestrial platform:

> I negotiated a price out of them which was significantly less expensive than the large European manufacturer. Got commitments to do things they'd never head of. Yes we'll give you AFDs[115] whatever they are; yes we'll do simulcrypt; yes, we'll do audio description. We don't know what it is, but we'll do it for you. And I got all this signed up in the contract. And I said, I'll need you to set up a maintenance base in the UK. And they said, yes when we get more customers in the UK. I said, no, I want a maintenance base in the UK - I need service engineers. So they said, do you mind if we recruit one or two service engineers to work to our business but when they start working for us they're based at your building. I said, "Fabulous! I'll give them a desk and a bench." Divicom were keen to achieve their first significant European sale and I knew I had a negotiating advantage. I shook hands with their Sales Director, got back to London, went to the lawyers and said, we need to write to this other manufacturer saying we're not going to take up the option in the letter of intent, and I need a letter of intent faxed tonight to Silicon Valley. Six weeks later the equipment arrived!

---

[115] Active Format Descriptors. A code to ensure that different shaped pictures (4:3 or widescreen 16:9) are displayed in the optimum form on both 4:3 and widescreen receivers. Chris Hibbert thought them up; the author chaired the DTG committee which wrote the implementation guidelines.

So confident was Chris Hibbert of the performance of the DiviCom coders that, knowing that compression technology was bound to improve by leaps and bounds in a short time, provided space in his equipment bays for no fewer than eight services per multiplex.

The equipment was delivered in early August, and Hibbert had his multiplexes on air in early September over the handful of transmitters so far commissioned. But there were no consumer receivers. David Johnston of Philips remembers a stormy meeting that summer at which ONdigital executives were thumping the table and demanding to know when receivers would be available. The September launch date could now not be met, and Philips, one of only two manufacturers remotely likely to provide receivers before the end of the year, were still rewriting the receiver software. David Johnston:

> After that meeting we said, no more changes. We were going to launch with software pretty bloody flaky, but we'll make that version of the software as robust as we can even though we were working on an upgrade pretty damn fast. But we were continually changing it up to the point where we said enough is enough: you have to launch with something. That's when the line was drawn in the sand.

Philips were the only manufacturer to supply boxes for ONdigital's delayed November launch, although Pace began deliveries only a few weeks later. Other manufacturers began to deliveries in the Spring of 1999. Besides the problems of writing robust software, Chris Hibbert thinks there was another reason why deliveries from some manufacturers were so late:

> I think some manufacturers were just taken aback by the fact that it was actually going to happen and they hadn't allocated factory time. Manufacturers plan twelve, eighteen months ahead, and I think a lot of them although they'd signed a contract and said, yes, we'll supply boxes, yes we understand the spec, yes we'll do this, but they hadn't actually within their organisations taken us seriously and they'd allocated their factory time to make microwaves or whatever else. It was only when we got closer and closer to launch that they actually thought, oh my god, they actually want these things. They were too late, basically.

And Hibbert gives all credit to Philips for being first:

> They got the boxes out and all credit to them, and they bore the brunt of some criticism because they were brave enough to release their boxes and of course it's first generation. And, yes, there were some glitches.

Glitches or no, eight years later, a few of those first generation boxes are still in use.

While Chris Hibbert was building a single multiplexing centre, from where three multiplexes would be fed directly to the transmitter network, the BBC was facing a set of challenges of a much greater order. The decision made back in Spring of 1996 that the BBC would make its digital services available on all three platforms, satellite, cable and terrestrial, made the BBC's systems engineering a highly complex task. At the point at which the BBC's Digital Broadcasting Project was wound up - its mission completed - the hard-pressed teams of engineers at Research and Development overnight became the System Design Authority, with the task of designing and specifying the technical architecture that would be required. Bob Ely:

> Engineers tend to go rather misty-eyed when you talk about systems engineering. It's kind of regarded as the pinnacle of the profession. And basically what it implies is delivering - in modern-speak - the business benefit. So a systems engineer is basically somebody who can work with the end customer for the system, and say, right, you want to achieve 'X', I will design it for you - like an architect designs a building - an end-to-end system which actually produces what's required. The modern term is 'technical architect' because it is so like being a building architect. You are obviously choosing all the elements of the system and the various components and integrating them together.

And as Bob Ely explains, the big challenge for the engineer is systems integration - making it all work once everything is connected:

> Systems integration: that's the mortar that glues the bricks together. Using that analogy, if the system is well designed, it doesn't need much mortar: because the bricks go together and they interlock nicely and they all fit together beautifully. If it's badly designed you end up with a lot of mortar - a very messy design, which won't be that robust. So elegance in systems engineering is regarded as essential. It is also very closely related to cost-benefit: if you over-engineer one part of the system, it's never going to be stronger than its weakest link, so you've wasted money on that part.

To make a complex task yet more difficult nobody in the BBC could be sure when each of the three platforms would launch. The timing of the satellite launch was dependent on BSkyB's decision to put receivers on the market, which was expected to be in mid 1998. The ONdigital launch was hoped for in September, but was expected to slip. Cable launches were even less predictable. So the decision was made quite early on that the BBC's services would be available on each platform before the operator's official launch. Ian Childs, now back at Kingswood Warren as Head of Research, realised the daunting scale of the work being planned:

> The thing that worried me wasn't the standards - the compression standard, the broadcast standard - the thing that worried me was the sheer amount of installation that was going to have to go on in the BBC as a business in order to play these channels out, in order to acquire the programmes and so on. R&D were technical architects, so we were designing the system and helping iron out all of the bugs, but we were not really in the critical path in

terms of actually installing the kit and training the people who had to run it day in and day out.

The launch bouquet of BBC digital services would be simulcasts of BBC-1 and BBC-2, together with BBC Choice, BBC Knowledge, and BBC News24. A Parliament Channel would also feature, but on terrestrial would, at least to begin with, be audio only. Programme chiefs decided that the national regional opts of BBC-1 would be replicated in digital, but the English regional opts would have to wait until after launch. BBC-2 opts would not be carried in digital, but BBC Choice would come in four versions, one for England, and one for each of the national regions, Scotland, Wales and Northern Ireland.

From this followed some of the major decisions about the technical architecture. Coding and multiplexing equipment would be built at four sites, the main studio centres in London, Glasgow, Cardiff and Belfast. This required a sustaining feed of the London services to be distributed to the nations. From there, the regionalised services would be fed to the regional transmitters for terrestrial broadcasting, but sent back to London for remultiplexing and uplinking to the satellite transponders. This required a whole new inter-studio network of circuits to be acquired and commissioned. In the four centres, new playout suites were built, and the rate at which digital equipment was replacing PAL in studios, outside broadcasts, editing and graphics suites was accelerated.

A series of regular meetings brought together representatives of all the technical teams from every area of the BBC to review progress of the many detailed issues in the presence of the R&D design and systems integration specialists, and representatives of the implementation teams from BBC Broadcast and the Corporate Centre.[116]

The devil, as always, was in the detail. Progress on the coding and multiplexing installations; tracking the integration testing with Sky, which was perpetually slipping; progress on the Sky conditional access installation at Television Centre, and the progress on building terrestrial transmitters and the international frequency clearance work. Work was in hand to implement widescreen switching - the codes transmitted with the picture to describe its shape, DOGs - the digital on-screen graphics which showed the service name in the corner of the screen, digital text, digital subtitling, and to commission SID - the BBC's service information generator, the output from which would need to accompany feeds to all three platforms. Progress on these and many other matters was compared to the critical path plan, and woe betide anybody whose project was slipping behind schedule.

The schedule itself was forever changing. As the BBC and other broadcasters designed their facilities and specified, ordered and began install-

---

[116] The author was a member of the BBC Broadcast Digital Implementation Group.

ation of equipment, and as the decisions were taken on the detail of service propositions - how many interactive text pages, or how many hours of programmes to be subtitled, for example - there arose much frustration at the delays which were creeping in to the development of essential pieces of equipment. The dates which the receiver manufacturers were quoting for delivery of the first set-top boxes and integrated sets began to slip, as they struggled to get the software right. Professional equipment manufacturers faced the same difficulty, and it became clear that launch might have to go ahead without some of the promised features.

And contracts and budgets: always budgets. The BBC had secured DCMS permission to allocate ten per cent of its licence fee income to introducing digital television to which it was allowed to add the proceeds of the sale of BBC Transmission. The overall implementation project was costed at £600 million, and led by Charles Evans of PA Consulting. Evans was a hugely likeable and capable man whose previous assignment had been the procurement of locomotives for Eurotunnel. His grasp of technical matters was impressive, and amongst other activities, he co-chaired the DMux Group and attended DTG meetings on the BBC's behalf.

While work on the multitude of installations went on, the old pilot service continued to operate. By June, with the first handful of terrestrial transmitters now operational, and with uplinking to the interim Astra 1D digital satellite also working, the BBC could broadcast four services, BBC-1, BBC-2 News24 and a special Widescreen Preview Channel both terrestrially and on satellite. Designed as a foretaste of one of the great benefits of digital television, and intended to have a major public relations impact, the widescreen channel was less than successful, but from it came many valuable technical and operational lessons.

The BBC had long wished to introduce widescreen broadcasts, and saw the advent of digital broadcasting as the opportunity to do so. So too did ITV and Channel Four, the latter building on its experience with PALplus. This earlier analogue system employed by Channel Four[117] had condemned the viewer with a conventional 4:3 television receiver to viewing what became known as a 'deep letterbox', whereby the whole widescreen picture was accommodated on the screen, but leaving black bands at top and bottom. The BBC knew intuitively that wholesale introduction of PALplus wide-screen transmissions in its analogue service would produce an un-sustainable level of complaint. British viewers were already known to be, unlike their continental counterparts, inherently conservative, prone to complaining, as they did when from time to time when on rare occasions an analogue channel broadcast a cinema movie in letterbox format, that they were being deprived of a full picture to which their licence fee entitled

---

[117] And to a more limited extent by Granada TV

them. But for digital broadcasting, the DVB specification and the D-Book interpretation of it, described a way of doing it. The big question was, in a simulcast, as was intended for BBC-1 and BBC-2 after digital broadcasting began, how best could a widescreen broadcast be delivered on the analogue service? At the time, there was no question that the analogue services could in any way be disadvantaged: for years to come, it was keenly felt, the analogue viewers - licence-fee payers all - would predominate, and there could be no compromise to the quality of service they received.

The author had undertaken some studies in late 1994 which, based on earlier work by Brendan Slamin[118], had pointed out that a compromise letterbox, with an aspect ratio of 14:9, would present the analogue viewer with much less noticeable black bands top and bottom of screen, while at the same time would not compromise to any great extent the exploitation of the wider aspect by programme makers. This became the BBC's policy, and was readily accepted by ITV and Channel Four.

The BBC tested the reaction of its analogue viewers in early 1998 by broadcasting an entire weekend peak-hour BBC-1 schedule in letterbox. There was a reaction, and complaints came in, but they were few in number, and the policy was felt to be sustainable. So the drive to increase production of widescreen programmes became intense, and the author spent much of his time in the year or so leading up to launch selling the idea of moving to widescreen production to programme makers inside the BBC. By the middle of 1998, the policy was well established.

In June 1998, with the BBC's digital multiplex on the Astra satellite and also being carried by the Crystal Palace transmitter in London, but with digital satellite and terrestrial platforms not yet launched, the BBC decided that demonstrations of digital widescreen broadcasting would take place in public venues. Anticipating a much earlier launch of the platforms, the BBC had acquired a second set of rights to coverage of the 1998 World Cup football games being played in France. Besides the conventional coverage, there was secondary coverage in high definition, provided by a consortium of European and Japanese broadcasters. High definition was widescreen, and many in the BBC believed these pictures, downconverted to standard definition, would form an impressive trailer for the soon-to-be launched digital offering. For the duration, many of the matches were shown to the few people who cared to pause in railway stations and country fairs where special receivers were situated.

The quality of the pictures, however, was disappointing, and at first it was not obvious why. After a thorough investigation, the reasons emerged, and a number of important things which had been only half understood by

---

[118] *High Definition for Programme-Makers: Understanding Widescreen*, by Brendan Slamin, published by BBC Training and Development, 1993

operational engineers became quantified and codified. It was finally demonstrated that, in the new digital broadcasting environment, where there was pressure to accommodate as many channels as possible in a multiplex, great care would have to be taken about the nature of the signal presented to the MPEG-2 coders. Every stage of the production process, from cameras, through editing and special effects equipment, to recording and editing, and to transmission over contribution circuits, had to avoid unnecessary or inappropriate digital processing.

Other broadcasters, too, were beginning to notice that digital broadcasting did not always ensure better quality. The mixture of analogue and digital source material, and the way in which conversions were made from PAL to serial digital, and how often, had to be carefully controlled. The effects of 'concatenation' - the accumulation in a programme chain of too many stages of digital processing - could, it was finally realised, have a devastating effect on picture quality which would then be made worse by the final MPEG coding for transmission.

The resulting operational codes of practice, and the wider discussions in the DTG and elsewhere, together with a programme of education for programme-making teams, brought the potential problems under control. The episode also served to increase the pressure by broadcasters on coder and receiver manufacturers to take these factors into account as they began to work on improved algorithms for their next generation of product.

By the summer of 1998, the first of the new digital transmitters were coming into operation. The intention was to have twenty-two of the eighty planned sites functioning by launch, an ambitious schedule which made great demands on the two transmission companies, NTL and Crown Castle[119], who between them operated all the television transmitting stations in the UK. All the new digital transmitters shared sites with existing analogue services, adapting the existing infrastructure, the buildings which housed the equipment and the masts. Even so, the process of equipping them was not straightforward.

To accommodate six multiplexes at all 80 transmitter sites, the frequency planners had in many instances allocated for digital use channels which were adjacent to those used by analogue, either the next channel above or the one below - the so-called 'taboo' channels. The planners had also decided that, wherever possible, the existing analogue antennas at the transmitters would also be used for digital, to try to ensure that digital coverage was similar to analogue. This in turn required the use of combining units which enabled both analogue and digital signals to use the

---

[119] The IBA transmitter network had been privatised in 1990 and bought by NTL: in 1997 the BBC sold its transmission interests to Castle Transmission Services, later Crown Castle International.

same feeder, the conduit which ran from the transmitting equipment, up the mast, to the antennas, and which resembles a thick water pipe. To avoid interference between analogue and digital signals in adjacent channels, sophisticated frequency filters had to be included, and to make the process easier, the decision was taken that the digital signal could be offset from its nominal value by 0.16 MHz.

But adopting these frequency offsets had a critical effect of receiver performance and for Andrew Bolton, who was ONdigital's man responsible for the procurement of receivers, it meant yet another battle with the manufacturers. Peter Marshall was present at one of the meetings:

> The noise figure the manufacturers could achieve in terms of the ONdigital set-top box was a critical matter. I remember I was at a meeting where he tried to goad them into saying they would achieve a noise figure of 5dB and they wouldn't go for that and I think they settled for 7dB in the end, which I suppose at the time proved right.

Shoehorning new digital channels into the already crowded spectrum had raised other difficulties. At many sites, coverage of some of the digital services had to be reduced in certain directions to avoid interference with other analogue or digital broadcasts either in the UK or on the continent, and that required a different transmitting antenna, and at some sites as many as four had to installed. At a few sites, the masts were not strong enough to carry the extra weight, and at some (Sudbury in Suffolk is an example) a second mast had to be built.

The consequential inequality of coverage by the six multiplexes meant that many homes could receive some but not others, which gave ONdigital considerable marketing and consumer support problems. Their principal solution was to make use of the coverage predictions which had come out of the joint BBC/NTL frequency planning work to produce a database which mapped coverage against postcode. The predictions were just that, of course, theoretical and approximate: nevertheless the postcode database was an important tool. Printed tables were distributed to every retailer who, in theory at least, would ensure the customer knew whether digital reception was possible at his postcode, and how many multiplexes he should expect to receive, before buying a box..

The DTG wanted to make the same information available on an internet site, and on CD-ROMs, but ran into resistance to the idea from ONdigital. Peter Marshall decided to force the issue, and approached the BBC planning team direct for access to the data:

> We published and be damned, so to speak, to establish the precedent by doing it and there were a fair old number of ructions. Then it was agreed it was better to work with co-operation. There was great concern at one stage that the DTG information came from the BBC whereas the ONdigital information had been modified by ONdigital - from a BBC source - so the ultimate decision was that in order that the two databases should be seen to

be singing from the same hymn sheet, they [ONdigital] would provide us with the information and accept our presence as part of what we were doing. It was a fairly delicate matter.

ONdigital's modification of the raw data had a sensible purpose: they recognised that nothing would be worse for their business than for a customer to install a receiver, only to find that reception was unsatisfactory, incomplete, or even non-existent. ONdigital therefore used a more pessimistic set of coverage predictions in an attempt to minimise such experiences.

While work to construct the digital transmitters progressed, two more programmes of work were under way. In many transmitter areas, the frequencies chosen for the digital multiplexes were also in use at some of the small analogue relay stations in the area. An intensive programme to re-engineer these relays to use other channels was set up, which involved a major effort to ensure that viewers understood the need for retuning their TV sets, and ensuring that they succeeded in doing so. By October, this retuning work was complete at 21 of the 22 stations. Alongside this work, an intensive programme of bilateral negotiations with other European countries was under way to gain final frequency clearance for the new digital transmissions. One issue raised by the French was the interference likely to be caused in Normandy by digital transmissions from the high power London station at Crystal Palace. A novel solution was found which involved tilting the southern beam from the mast so that its signal did not extend beyond the South Downs. By April, negotiations with the Dutch were completed, and the planners were reporting that while there were "issues" with the Belgians, they were "optimistic" about the Norwegians and "relaxed" about the Irish.

By early November, twenty-one transmitters were operational and Philips were supplying ONdigital with initial stockpiles of receivers. (10,000 were available at launch and in the weeks immediately following, the company were manufacturing 2,500 a day.) The BBC had begun to broadcast its services over each transmitter as soon as it was commissioned, and had had its services on the Astra satellite since late September. Services from other broadcasters were appearing over the terrestrial transmitters. ONdigital went ahead with its consumer launch on 15 November 1998 in a blaze of publicity, offering "digital television through your aerial", and with a range of services which included two sport channels and a movie channel from BSkyB.[120]

---

[120] At launch, the terrestrial platform offered nine free-to-air services from the public service broadcasters, including their analogue simulcasts, together with 17 primary pay and five premium pay services from ONdigital.

It was a world first, and a remarkable technical achievement. It was also an impressive demonstration of how close collaboration between the whole range of industry players could harness an infant technology and deploy it successfully in an open, horizontal market. The British example was closely followed elsewhere in Europe, and largely emulated in the service launches in Sweden, Finland and Spain over the following two years. Britain had won the international race to be first with digital terrestrial television, but its broadcasters lost the domestic race to launch the terrestrial platform before satellite. BSkyB's commercial launch came on 1 October, six weeks before ONdigital. The stage was then set for a fierce battle for subscribers as the two platforms went head-to-head in the market place. And in the final outcome, the technology each employed would play a crucial part.

17
Battle of the Boxes

The curiosity is why BSkyB delayed their launch for quite so long. They were using a DVB standard which pre-dated the terrestrial equivalent by almost exactly two years. They sourced their coder and conditional access technology from sister companies within the News Corporation network, and had a thriving analogue satellite business from which to build. Nor were they by any means the first company to launch a digital satellite pay-TV service. But when Sky Digital did launch it rapidly became the most successful such venture anywhere, and trumped its terrestrial rival in the market place.

Although BSkyB's system was ready in the Autumn of 1997, they were faced with the same market imperative as ONdigital: the need to subsidise their set-top boxes to an acceptable consumer price. BSkyB's boxes cost getting on for £500 apiece, and like ONdigital, they saw a retail price of £199 as the highest the market could bear, and had to find the difference. Their answer was to create a complex joint venture with BT in a business called British Interactive Broadcasting - BIB - which planned to use the proprietary Open TV API as the vehicle to launch a transactional service to satellite viewers. Eventually dubbed *Open...* (the three dots were part of the branding), it was hoped that receipts from interactive sales and betting would provide the profits to fund the box subsidy.

BT had been running a trial broadband service in the Colchester and Ipswich area, and had some early experience of designing and administering an interactive television transaction service. It looked like a winning partnership, but it took a long time to sort out the design and functionality of the service and the underlying operation of the business. The result was that BSkyB - and BIB - missed their proposed Spring 1998 target date, finally launching six weeks ahead of ONdigital at the beginning of October 1998, but still without *Open...* which launched at the end of March 1999, rolling out home shopping, banking, information, games and email services over the following six months.

The quality of the Sky Digital product was unquestionably good. It launched with many more channels than ONdigital could accommodate, and its marketing was highly effective. But the technology helped too. BSkyB retained a much greater degree of control over the suppliers of receivers than did ONdigital. The broadcaster took immense pains to ensure a common and satisfactory performance of the boxes which were eventually sourced from six manufacturers. Sky carried out its own conformance testing on each product ensuring, as one BSkyB engineer put it, "You test, test again, and then test again, and you keep doing that until you are sure this thing is not going to fall over." BSkyB understood that the receivers must function flawlessly, and that if the customer pays the money, it should do what it says on the packet. One crucial insight was to insist that all manufacturers used a common design of remote control handset, a design into which BSkyB put a very great deal of thought and which resulted in a device much easier and more intuitive to use than anybody else's handset, including those for ONdigital where every manufacturer had their own design. And if every Sky box had the same handset, no matter who had manufactured it, then the Sky call centre could so much more easily talk a confused customer through troubleshooting a fault. It was a well-judged decision.

The same meticulous care went into the specification, design and implementation of the new digital systems required at the broadcasting end. While Sky took full responsibility for the overall systems integration the News subsidiary NDS, as a supplier of equipment and specialist advice, played a crucial role. Gordon Drury, working for NDS, found himself drawn deeply into the process:

> We had long periods of intense consultation about what the system has to look like from a technical perspective: what we would have to do to build it, and what they would have to do to work it, and implement it. So there was lots of to-ing and fro-ing going on and lots of arguments about this and that, but it came to a consensus because we were both part of the same organisation. We were told what we were required to provide in the way of transmission equipment and functionality so that the receiver did what it was supposed to do. There was always control by Sky.

But necessary control for good reason:

> People to this day think of them as being control freaks, but that misses the big picture. What they're doing is protecting the business in every way they know how. And they will test and test and test again. To my mind, if you're looking to meet commercial demands, and to make sure you hit your targets, to be predictable to your shareholders and all that sort of stuff, you've got to take control. And you've got to go to the ultimate degree of testing: I can't see how you can launch a new technology of such a magnitude as this is, and with its uncertainties, using that traditional model.

But in ONdigital's equivalent terrestrial world the manufacturers retained much of the independence of that traditional model. That presented considerable challenges.

Conformance testing of receivers for terrestrial was largely in the hands of ONdigital, but the DTG's new chairman, David Youlton, saw a future role for the DTG. When Michael Starks stepped down as the DTG's chairman in the summer of 1997, Youlton - who was then chairman of the specialist equipment manufacturer Snell & Wilcox - gave a new direction to the Group. Youlton shared the view, increasingly held by many in the DTG, that with the appointment of the multiplex operators and the formation of their club, the DMux Group, the DTG's role needed to change. One of his early moves was to recruit Peter Marshall from Channel Four to become the DTG's first Technical Director. Marshall recalls that some expressed to him their surprise that he should leave a good post for an organisation whose day, they thought, was passing.

> Certainly when I was recruited that view was expressed that I was joining something whose job was finished. I hoped it wasn't true and David Youlton certainly took the view that that wasn't true. DY was strongly of the opinion that the horizontal market needed to be kept. It was DYs view that there was still work for the DTG to do in two particular areas. One was in developing the horizontal market. The horizontal market at the time was very strongly seen as receivers - TVs rather than set-top boxes. And the second was that developing the horizontal market meant there had to be a testing regime.

The idea of a testing regime had been doing the rounds within the DTG long before Youlton's appointment (and indeed even before the launch of the DTT service), but as no more than a general recognition that, somehow, the horizontal market needed to find a way to emulate the vertical market's quality control over the growing number of manufacturers who, one day, would want to market unsubsidised receivers. To which there could only be one answer: not regulation or diktat from broadcasters, but an industry-led initiative.

To begin with, support within the DTG for such an initiative came from Chris Hibbert of ONdigital, who saw the benefit to be had by the devolution of testing responsibility - and it costs - to industry. Industry, too, was inclined towards a regime over which they could exert some influence. But, says Peter Marshall, few could see the importance of the horizontal market or had a clear view of how a testing centre might be established or financed. It took the determination of the DTG's new chairman to bring it about. Youlton was heard to postulate a future in which a testing subsidiary would become the DTG's principal concern, and to moot the possibility of an eventual 'reverse takeover' of the parent group's activities by the growing sibling.[121]

To look at how a possible testing regime might work in a horizontal market, the DTG formed a Conformance Group and by late September, its chairman, Gordon Drury, was able to outline the scope of a possible DTG facility. ONdigital were testing their own subsidised receivers: they had neither the resource nor any obligation to test every unsubsidised receiver, in particular integrated sets. They insisted that, for the time being at least, they would continue to vet the product they were responsible for, but both they and the TDN (the new name for the DMux Group) supported the idea of an independent, industry-led conformance centre which might test all receivers entering the market. So too did the DTI, which produced support funding which, along with financial backing from four manufacturers, allowed the formation, in mid 2000, of DTG Testing Limited.

Meanwhile, out in the market place, things were about to change.

The most effective arm of the Sky strategy was in its arrangements with retailers. Backed by a highly effective advertising campaign, retailers were offered an extensive investment in in-store promotion. Very quickly, huge displays promoting the Sky brand appeared in the major chains, together with an ample supply of set-top boxes. Salesmen were given incentives to promote the Sky route into digital television which had an immediate appeal not only for existing subscribers to the Sky analogue service - who quickly recognised that the digital version of the subscription service would be much more of the mix they already enjoyed and appreciated - but also to customers new to the notion of subscription television. In the Spring of 1999, Sky reported in its half-yearly accounts that it had 350,000 subscribers, of whom 130,000 were new to pay-TV. A few weeks later ONdigital announced first quarter results reporting 110,000 subscribers. By 5 May, Sky claimed 550,000 while ONdigital had not yet reached 200,000.

That spring also saw a development that nobody had expected. David Johnston of Philips was trying to cultivate a relationship with Sky so that

---

[121] An outcome yet to materialise.

his company could become a supplier of boxes to them, as well as to ONdigital:

> The terrestrial and the Sky set-top boxes were using the same processor at the time. Suddenly the supply started drying up. And there were other indicators, because Philips was also supplying the remote control to Sky. And I started hearing whispers that Sky had started building a massive inventory. My gut conclusion was that Sky was going to go free. And I started to see whether ONdigital was going to go free.

Both rivals had made the decision, virtually simultaneously, to subsidise the full cost of the receiver, effectively giving them away in a bid to attract new subscribers. Johnston, on a visit to Thorn Rentals, got confirmation of his hunch:

> I went there on a Friday morning. And they said that they had received a phone call from ONdigital that morning saying that the following Tuesday they were going to go free. You can imagine that was a bit of a bombshell. As soon as the meeting was finished - the meeting finished rather quickly at that point - I phoned them [ONdigital] and asked them, "What are you playing at?" They hadn't told Philips at all, and more important they hadn't built any surplus over the inventory they were already sitting on. Sky had built a phenomenal stockpile and within five days of ONdigital going free all the Philips stock of set-top boxes had vanished.

The effect of the free box offer on subscription uptake for both satellite and terrestrial services was marked and by the summer, Sky's subscriber numbers passed the one million mark. For ONdigital, the results were not at first sight so impressive, but for a period, and discounting conversion of Sky analogue subscribers to digital, both companies were signing up roughly equal numbers of subscribers new to pay-TV. To the analysts of the City, however, it was the absolute numbers which mattered. BSkyB looked like a success story, while ONdigital looked very much the poor relation. At the BBC, the Corporate Centre's own analysts took the same view, as Henry Price remembers:

> The Policy & Planning take-up projections had terrestrial at the bottom, and cable and satellite vying for the top slots, and they really believed that. John Birt took papers from Policy & Planning: they said this platform is unlikely to go anywhere, it's got limited coverage, it's got a pay operator that's struggling, the best it's ever going to do is less than a third of the market.

Henry Price also remembers how quickly his Head of Policy and Planning, Patricia Hodgson, began to doubt openly the viability of digital terrestrial:

> ONdigital had been on the air for, I think, only a few months, and Patricia said to us at the end of a technical demo we'd given somebody, "How long do you think ONdigital's going to last? Do you think it will be gone by the end of the year? What are we going to do if it goes bust?" So I think from the word go they thought this was a really uncertain proposition.

225

At that time, few shared this pessimistic view. There was broad agreement amongst most of the industry - supported by the Digital TV Group - that a fully horizontal market was going to develop in digital terrestrial, which it was widely believed would be good for business and good for the consumer. The view was that a strong pay-TV operator was necessary to kick-start the market with subsidised boxes, but the future lay in receivers as unsubsidised commodities, as it always had been with analogue television sets. Confidence in the future of digital terrestrial was reinforced as the platform speedily consolidated: by September, more than fifty terrestrial transmitters were operational, and most of the remaining 30 would come on-air over the following nine months. ONdigital's subscriber numbers rose until at the end of the year it stood at over half a million. More manufacturers began to supply receivers. Following Philips and Pace, who had been first into the market, Nokia, Toshiba, Panasonic and others began deliveries of set-top boxes, while Sony and some other manufacturers put integrated sets on to the market. In the run-up to Christmas ONdigital launched a pre-paid scheme, making set-top boxes available on supermarket shelves with a year's subscription included for the price of £119. This innovative marketing ploy had the desired effect, and by March 2000, ONdigital could report 673,000 subscribers.

The market for integrated sets took off very much more slowly. With free boxes on offer from both Sky and ONdigital, few had an incentive to buy a new television set specifically for digital TV. Sales of the much cheaper analogue sets - particularly widescreen sets - remained buoyant. David Johnston of Philips thought that the free set-top box offer "killed the market for iDTVs stone dead." And Arjon Verdonkschot of JVC told a DigiTAG meeting in Geneva that iDTVs were a "prerequisite" for a migration to digital, but warned that, "Manufacturers will continue to make analogue TV sets, particularly if set-top boxes are given away."

Customer confusion was beginning to set in. In the summer of 1999, the cable companies began to introduce digital television over their networks: now digital television came in three flavours: satellite, terrestrial and cable. Or four, if you separated the pay element of ONdigital's terrestrial offering from the free-to-air content of the same platform. People were no longer sure what getting digital TV involved. To make matters worse, manufacturers had started to use the word 'digital' to market some of the features of analogue TV sets - like 'digital sound' (Dolby) or 'digital image processing' (100 Hz display features). Many customers bought new analogue widescreen sets quite convinced that they had 'gone digital' and marvelled at the 'widescreen pictures' which, because there were no widescreen programmes being broadcast in analogue, were actually 4:3 pictures stretched to fill the screen. Many of the independent retailers went to great trouble to explain the differences to a potential customer and to ensure they bought the right product, but in the major retail chains - which accounted for by far the greater part of consumer sales - some salesmen seemed to have little understanding and even less inclination to spend time in education. These major chains relied heavily on the in-store displays and the marketing provided by ONdigital and Sky, and Sky was much better at it. And as more and more ONdigital subscribers found that they were having problems with reception, the reaction of the big retail chains was to concentrate even more on marketing the largely foolproof and profitable Sky Digital package and to sideline the displays of ONdigital receivers. For many customers, the salesman's advice was not to bother with ONdigital "because you can't get it in this area", and sell a Sky subscription package instead.

Through all this confusion, the Sky marketing message came through by far the strongest. Very quickly, 'Sky' became synonymous in the public mind with 'digital television'. But the fault lay not only with the relative weakness of ONdigital's marketing: the shortcomings in the terrestrial technology were beginning to show.

It wasn't long after launch that evidence began to accumulate suggesting that all was not quite right with the way that the digital terrestrial television technology was functioning. Britain was about to pay the price for an over-hasty launch in which, as it later turned out, some important technical corners had been cut, and some wrong choices made. It wasn't that the DVB-T specification was faulty, it was the choice of parameters allowed within it that the UK had chosen.

The first problem to become obvious was the most unexpected. Dissatisfied viewers were complaining that their digital picture would freeze momentarily, or disintegrate into blocks. The more seriously affected customers were returning their boxes and signing up to Sky instead. The problem was quickly recognised as impulsive interference, caused by domestic thermostats in refrigerators and central heating systems. As the thermostat switched on or off, a short burst of radio energy was emitted which would be picked up by the TV receiver's aerial lead, or passed through the house mains electricity system. Passing road traffic could cause similar problems in areas of marginal reception. The early COFDM chipsets had very poor immunity to this impulsive interference. The truth dawned that a very high proportion of households had aerials that were only just good enough for analogue and nowhere near good enough for digital. Reception problems became the root cause of ONdigital's biggest customer service headache

Back in 1995, under pressure from British representatives who wanted an early launch and were pressing for an early completion of the specification, the DVB had agreed to drop time interleaving. The technique would have spread the disturbance to the picture over several frames, much reducing the effect on each, and rendering the interference much less noticeable. Without it, the effect was devastating. Now, four years later, many engineers regretted that decision. It was now seen as one of the biggest drawbacks to the UK's implementation of DVB-T. Later designs of chipsets were an improvement, as manufacturers like Philips Semiconductors employed ingenious design solutions to minimise the problem. But at the time, for the affected householder, although an improved aerial system could sometimes help, what was really required, and could not yet be offered, was a stronger signal from higher transmitter powers.

Even with all 80 transmitters now operational, coverage was nowhere near universal. But the original coverage predictions themselves now proved over-optimistic. Constrained by the need to limit interference to existing analogue services, the coverage achieved for the six multiplexes was not equal, ranging from a predicted 90 per cent for the best - BBC - multiplex, to as low as 60 per cent for the least good ONdigital multiplex D. But these prediction had been calculated on the basis that a good quality aerial was being used, situated on a rooftop at a minimum height of ten metres. The true state of the nation's aerials, it rapidly became clear, left a lot to be desired.

Many rooftop aerials dated from the introduction of UHF analogue services in the late sixties and seventies, and many were in a poor state, rusted or blown out of alignment by wind, and with equal deterioration to the downlead, and the flylead which connects the receiver to the wall socket. It was discovered too that a surprisingly large minority of homes used 'rabbit ears' aerials on top of their TV sets for second and third sets, and some for the main living room itself. Using these, reception of analogue was tolerable, but reception of digital rarely satisfactory. And there was another problem. In many areas, frequencies for digital channels could only be found by going 'out of band', using frequencies from a different part of the UHF spectrum from the analogue services, and outside the frequency range for which aerials were designed. Coverage of out-of-band transmission was, in the absence of a new aerial installation, much below the actual prediction. Replacement of a domestic aerial system was an additional expense to the householder wanting to 'go digital', and fraught with pitfalls.

From early in 1998, well before launch, the DTG had been putting together working groups to look at best practice in aerial design and installation, working with some aerial manufacturers and the Confederation of Aerial Industries. Out of the work came a number of publications and training initiatives for aerial installers. Unfortunately, the CAI was largely powerless to influence the dodgy end of the trade, the cowboy outfits and the bloke in the pub, who used inadequate equipment, often badly installed, to do a cheap job. Too many such new installations were as poor as the old aerials they replaced.

Taken together, all these factors effectively reduced coverage by about a third[122], which was bad news for ONdigital, whose three multiplexes were already the least good. By the Spring of 2000, the Independent Television Commission had the first results from the joint frequency planning group[123] which had been asked to look at ways of improving coverage from the existing transmitters. The first aim was to increase 'core coverage', which meant coverage areas where all six multiplexes could be received. The first proposal was so-called 'equalisation': to increase the coverage of the three ONdigital multiplexes to bring them closer to the coverage achieved by the three public service multiplexes. The study showed that in the south east of England, adjustments to the six transmitters at Crystal Palace, Sandy Heath, Hannington, Oxford and Hemel Hempsted, could benefit up to two million people, bringing them within range of all ONdigital's services for the first time. Similar studies were undertaken for groups of transmitters in the Midlands and the North West which showed similar potential benefits. Work started to implement the equalisation programme. Peter Marshall:

> The equalisation plan, if it had been fully carried out, could have got the ONdigital multiplexes up to the mid-to high 70s - something like 78 per cent, I think, without to any significant degree reducing the coverage of the BBC and ITV muxes. But of course the plan was only partially carried out. There was an agreement in the DMux group that the broadcasters who benefited from the change would be the ones that paid for it, and the early part of the equalisation work quite clearly ONdigital benefited all the way and paid for it, until they came to that bit of work around Sutton Coldfield where by a quirk of fate the company that benefited most - everybody benefited, but the one by the financial calculation ended up paying for it - would have been SDN and they had no money, and they said, we're not doing it, and that's where it all ground to a halt.

The decision not to proceed was a blow to ONdigital, who were left with core coverage on only 73 per cent. The frustration felt by many, including Peter Marshall, was considerable: an opportunity lost, or at least delayed:

> There were some years when I was pushing for some further work on equalisation to be done until such a point that it was quite clear that the broadcasters were not interested in spending a penny more until they spent the big money on switchover.

Next, the planners found another potential way of increasing the coverage, and doing so at modest cost. It had become clear that the original plan which had digital transmitters operating at -20 dB (one hundredth of the power of the analogue) was over-cautious - a decision made, of course, in

---

[122] from a prediction of 73.5 per cent coverage to an actual figure nearer 50 per cent.
[123] The Group now consisted of the ITC, the BBC, and the two privatised transmission companies, Crown Castle and NTL.

the early planning process on the best available understanding but in the absence of any real operational experience with digital broadcasting. The expected levels of interference of digital-to-analogue failed to materialise and it became obvious that higher powers at the digital transmitters could and should have been used. To find out by how much the digital power could be increased without causing noticeable interference, trials began in January 2002 using one of the six transmitters at Larkstone in the Cotswolds, later followed by others, including one at Heathfield, a main station in the south of England. Peter Marshall remembers the results:

> The high power trials showed that they could have been increased by 5 maybe 6 dB, of which 3 dB was carried out as an expedient by putting the two transmitters - the main and the standby - into parallel, but another 2 or 3 dB was there to be had but was never implemented of course.

Installing other, more powerful, digital transmitters to achieve the full 6 dB advantage was financially out of the question: not only would the new transmitters be costly, but the perfectly serviceable digital transmitters recently installed would have to be taken out with nowhere else to go. Then the planning engineers came up with their idea. When the digital transmitters were installed, each multiplex had a main and a standby transmitter. Both were powered up and running, but only the main one fed the aerial, the standby transmitter instead fed a dummy load. By combining the output of the two transmitters, main and standby, the transmitter power would be doubled - increased by 3 dB. The failure of one transmitter would temporarily reduce the service area, of course, but this was felt to be a risk worth taking.

The high power trials were part of a much more extensive programme to take a thorough look at the whole UK frequency plan with an eye to maximising DTT coverage in the run-up to switchover. In mid 2001, the power of all six multiplexes was doubled on a trial basis at the Bilsdale transmitter (serving North Yorkshire) and at Black Hill (serving Central Scotland). A more extensive programme was planned, but before the work was complete, the ITV Digital was in its death throes, and the power doubling programme was halted.

When ONdigital launched in November 1998, the technical make-up of its receivers was incomplete. Many features which were intended for inclusion, and which taken together would have helped to differentiate in the public mind digital television from its analogue predecessor, were still under development. So features like a full electronic programme guide, subtitles, audio description, and interactive applications were not present, although promised later. Not only were the software developments for the receivers still incomplete, but the equivalent work to build the playout infrastructure within the broadcasting centres was often delayed. Of these, the most immediately obvious missing feature was interactivity.

Richard Cooper, who became Head of Technology for BBC Interactive, defends the decision to launch without interactivity:

> It's not just about the technology, there's a whole lot of business rules you need to put in place, with quite complex head-end equipment that's not nearly as mature as the stuff that's just playing out the bog standard video and audio and SI and so on. And there's also an argument that says, why wait? Because actually if you've got the rest of the platform ready to go so you're ready to do your digital channels and your widescreen and all the rest of it why wait for interactivity? You can layer it on top [later]. I think we trod the same path that everybody else did but there was definitely an underestimation of the amount of time and the amount of work that would be necessary to really complete all of the work.

The decision by the broadcasters to use the open standard MHEG-5 API was taken before the final shape of the MHEG specification was known. By now it was accepted that the API would have to be introduced after launch, and receivers were designed to allow the necessary software codes to be downloaded over the air to receivers. In fact, the BBC was able to transmit from launch a basic MHEG-5 service - mainly intended to assist manufacturers to test their prototypes - which consisted of pages of text with similar content to the analogue Ceefax service, but of course there were no receivers capable of receiving it outside the development laboratories.

The key missing receiver component was the 'content decoder', the MHEG-5 software device which processed the interactive content datastream passed to it from the MPEG-2 decoder, determined how it should be displayed on the screen, and acted on commands received from the viewer via the remote control to navigate through the content. The exact design of the software, however, was a matter for the designers of receivers, and with the growing diversity of interested manufacturer, by late 1999 there were no fewer than four independent implementations under development for receivers, and three for broadcast systems.

By November 1999, the first batch of ONdigital set-top boxes - the type supplied by Philips - were offered an over-the-air download of an operational content decoder, and interactivity was publicly launched. But it would take a long time for the other manufacturers to be able to do the same thing. Because ONdigital boxes used Canal Plus Mediahighway middleware, on which the MHEG-5 content decoder ran, each supplier once they had acquired their version had to send it off to Canal Plus for integration testing. Canal Plus proved to be very slow at this task, so much so that one unfortunate supplier to ONdigital, Nokia, had not been able to complete the process by the time ITV Digital failed. The manufacturers of free-to-air integrated sets had a much more straightforward integration task, having made their own choice of middleware. Eventually, the majority of terrestrial viewers could enjoy interactivity, which featured amongst other things a quarter-screen moving image of the broadcast channel surrounded by text rendered in the much clearer 'Tiresius' font, developed in collaboration with the RNIB.

In September 2000, the DTG magazine, *Digital News*, carried a survey of integrated television sets. Products from nine manufacturers were listed, the majority of which were free-to-view only. Those from Toshiba and Bush contained embedded conditional access - they were effectively TV sets built around an ONdigital set-top box. The LG receiver was unique at the time: it was built around a Sky Digital set-top box, but also featured a free-to-air receiver for digital terrestrial. All the others - from Grundig, Hitachi, Philips, Samsung, Panasonic, and the pioneering manufacturer, Sony - were free-to-air only. However, all featured a Common Interface socket and into this socket a module could be inserted which carried the conditional access needed to receive pay-TV services from ONdigital. But few modules were available.

UK regulator responsible for such matters, the ITC, had noted the complete absence of CA modules back in the autumn of 1999, and had had to remind ONdigital that supplying them was a condition of their licence. They set a deadline of May 2000, by which prototypes were available. But few were ever issued. Consumers continued to go for free boxes and analogue widescreen sets. Sales of iDTVs trundled along at tiny volumes that left the manufacturers dismayed.

Some expected features took years to appear. One was the full electronic programme guide, able to display programme schedules for a week or more ahead. All that was being transmitted was the mandatory details of the programme on air and the programme to follow - the 'now and next' data carried in DVB-SI. The D-Book had included a specification for using additional data fields in service information to carry the full week's schedules. The broadcasters had even reserved the data space in their multiplexes. Henry Price, who attended the TDN[124] meetings, more than once attempted to persuade the other broadcasters that introducing a full 7-day schedule would be in the interests of all: the Sky platform had a sophisticated EPG, which was regarded as highly desirable feature in consumer terms. The terrestrial platform rather obviously lacked any equivalent. Henry Price was unable to make an impression on the TDN.

> I presented TDN with a BBC proposal for putting the full schedule data on the platform, which we thought would be useful in the development of recording systems. It was completely opposed by ONdigital who didn't

---

[124] The D-Mux Group had renamed itself The Digital Network (Group) (TDN) in early 1998.

want it at all, and if ONdigital decided they didn't want it then it wasn't done.

By then, ONdigital were trying hard to enhance their own subscription offer, and had introduced a box that enabled the viewer to access the internet, together with pay-per-view capability and other features. There were clearly other financial priorities, and a seven day EPG was not one of them.

By the summer of 2001, ONdigital's two shareholders, Carlton and Granada, now also owned all the ITV franchises in England and Wales. The two companies confidently expected that within eighteen months, the government would agree to their merger. In anticipation of this, the network was radically restructured and centralised, and as part of the process ONdigital was rebranded as ITV Digital, and a new digital terrestrial subscription channel created, ITV Sport. The companies were putting the weight of the ITV brand behind their joint digital venture.

To some observers, this looked like a desperate move. Uptake of terrestrial subscriptions was beginning to lag seriously behind that of BSkyB, and the cable companies were also beginning to pick up a useful number of pay-TV customers. In August 2001, the DTG's magazine *Digital News* reported subscription numbers for the three digital platforms, BSkyB, cable and ITV Digital, as 5.3 million, 1.6 million and 1.1 million[125] respectively. BSkyB announced that it would close its analogue service that autumn, having migrated to digital the remaining small number of subscribers still using it. The City had no doubts about where an investor should buy his shares, and it was not with ITV.

Worries about ITV Digital's finances reached the box manufacturer, Philips. David Johnston remembers that:

> When ONdigital became ITV Digital, there was another invitation to tender. By this time the price of the boxes had been driven down dramatically. I was advising Philips, and after a while I said to myself hold on a second, I don't like this. Every indicator I was getting I didn't like. I started getting very, very uneasy. And a decision was made not to go for it.

Doubts about the future of ITV Digital were compounded by an earlier decision by Carlton and Granada to pay the huge sum of £315 million for rights to broadcast Football League games on its ITV Sport channel. Bidding by rival broadcasters had forced the prices of all football rights to record heights: but Sky had proved that sport, particularly football, pulled in the subscriptions and ITV Digital sought to emulate their success. A year

---

[125] The terrestrial figure counted only ITV Digital subscribers. Adding the numbers of set-top boxes and integrated sets used only for free-to-view, the total uptake of the platform was estimated to be around 1.5 million.

later, when the expected flood of new subscribers had failed to materialise, and with a sharp downturn in advertising revenues becoming apparent, the writing was on the wall. By the autumn of 2001 it was clear that ITV Digital was in trouble. Michael Starks remembers the atmosphere:

> Undoubtedly one of the concerns was whether or not this would lead to such a serious weakening of the digital terrestrial platform that it would never recover, that it would lose all commercial credibility, and I think there were undoubtedly associated with that instincts to see what if anything the BBC could do about to help obviously short of subsidising receivers. Which we never did or ever intended to do.

With the departure of John Birt from the BBC and the appointment of Greg Dyke as the new Director-General, the BBC's attitude to free-to-view digital television in general, and to the digital terrestrial platform in particular, took a significant change of direction. Dyke regarded the growing dominance of BSkyB as a potentially serious threat to the future of the BBC, and concluded that marketing the Corporation's digital services - together with those of the other public service broadcasters - as a free offering would attract substantial numbers of viewers who did not want pay TV. Michael Starks, who had ploughed other furrows in the BBC's domains after the Digital Broadcasting Project was wound up in 1997, was brought into the Strategy Department with a brief to promote free-to-view digital television:

> There were quite extensive negotiations about whether a free-to-view strand could be developed alongside the ITV pay proposition and whether or not ITV could get itself out of such a wholehearted subsidy of receivers for ever and a day. They hit various difficulties most obviously to do with conditional access and proprietary technology. And I think there were all sorts of attempts to see whether or not any form of commercial collaboration between the BBC and receiver manufacturers could play a role and there were various studies done in that area.

Dyke and his Director of Strategy, Carolyn Fairbairn, went to see Carlton and Granada and offered to help turn ITV Digital into a platform largely for free-to-air broadcasters. Discussions were making some progress when serious doubts began to energe about the company's financial health.

The doubts turned out to be justified. In late March 2002, ITV Digital called in administrators, and on 30th April pulled its remaining channels off the air and closed down its operations. Stuart Prebble promptly resigned as Chief Executive, and wrote a passionate article for *The Sunday Telegraph*, in which he blamed not only himself for his company's demise, but the regulators (for giving Sky a free rein), the government (for over-regulation and bureaucratic delay), and the technology: he claimed that ITV Digital's conditional access system had been cracked and that the company had lost over £100 million in subscription revenue; he blamed poor coverage and the slow response of the authorities in agreeing to improvements; and Sky, for charging ITV Digital a higher wholesale price for the Sky movies and sport carried terrestrially than Sky charged retail on their own platform.

Chris Hibbert had been ITV Digital's Chief Engineer, closely involved with the company since the first day, and a constant supporter of the DTG and the concept of digital terrestrial television. For him and for his engineering colleagues, the failure of the company was a black day:

> What I felt really bad about was my staff - all under twenty-five. All had just come out of college or university, and we built a fantastically highly motivated bright and enthusiastic team. There was a hands-off management style. We didn't have a password on a single PC anywhere. These young-sters were running a national pay-TV operation. At weekends there would be three of them in the building, on their own, with a microwave and a coffee machine. They had a sense of loyalty to the company, they were very committed to making a success of it - and they all got chucked on the scrap-heap. And I was really sad about that because they didn't deserve it. But from a broadcast operations point of view, I'm incredibly proud of what we did.

In just under three and a half years, the world's first digital terrestrial tele-vision service had built an audience of approaching one and a half million homes, and had captured roughly fifteen per cent of the digital market. It was a remarkable pioneering achievement, driven hard by ITV Digital in an atmosphere of unprecedented collaboration with the free-to-air broad-casters, and in the most highly competitive market in the world. The company's approach, its collaboration within the TDN and with the DTG, was followed widely in other countries, and copied in some. It left as a legacy a basically sound technological base from which, over the next year, a vibrant new business model for digital terrestrial would rise from the ashes of the brave experiment that ultimately failed.

18
Freeview

There were two views about the collapse of ITV Digital. One, which was confidently held by the City analysts and the markets, and shared by most of the press (including some commentators who should have known better) had it that digital terrestrial television in Britain was dead, that it was based on a deficient technology and a flawed business plan, and should never have been embarked upon in the first place. The other view, held by many members of the industry represented in the Digital Television Group - particularly the manufacturers - held that ITV Digital's demise was a failure of business and management and not a failure of the technology. This view, shared crucially by the BBC's new director-general and his senior staff, was that there was still a platform with enormous potential, and that here was a golden opportunity to fix the technical shortcomings and start again with a better consumer proposition.

There were, after all, two-and-a-half multiplexes still on the air, carrying a broad range of free-to-view programmes from the public service broadcasters - a dozen or more services including widescreen simulcasts of the five analogue services BBC-1, BBC-2, ITV, Channel Four and Five, the new digital-only services from these broadcasters, together with interactive content. Over one million homes still had a working ITV Digital receiver capable of receiving these broadcasts, although the number in use was expected to fall as viewers deprived of their pay TV favourites signed up to one of the Sky Digital packages.[126] The regulator, the Independent

---

[126] In its end of year report, issued in the summer of 2002, BSkyB posted an increase in subscription numbers of 214,000, taking its total to over six million. The increase was higher

Television Commission, moved with commendable speed. The day after ITV Digital came off the air, the ITC announced that it planned to re-advertise the licences for the three now vacant multiplexes, and indicated that the process would be a speedy one.

At the BBC, Greg Dyke and his team surveyed a terrestrial playing field shorn of its major pay-TV operator, and proposed a free-to-air only platform, calculating that the market for pay-TV was approaching saturation, and that future growth in the uptake of digital TV would come from consumers who wanted more quality channels, but not the hundreds offered by satellite and cable, and who were unwilling to become sub-scribers. He had other motives too: a successful free-to-air digital platform would ensure the BBC's longer term future by speeding digital uptake and bringing closer the eventual switching off of analogue services. This in turn would ensure that everybody received the BBC's full programme range which their licence fee pays for. And with shrewd political calculation, the BBC saw that, by establishing a free-to-air platform with a new range of receivers without conditional access, it would be that much harder for any future government to move the BBC's funding away from the licence fee and towards a form of subscription. A free platform would provide a strong counterbalance to the dominance of Sky without being in direct competition for subscription revenues, which would please government and regulators.

After just six weeks, the ITC formally invited applications for the three multiplex licences, and the BBC had its bid ready. It had formed a partnership with the transmission company Crown Castle who had their own reasons to support a bid. Crown Castle held a contract to provide transmission services for the BBC multiplex and had provided the same service for the three ITV Digital multiplexes as well. Now there was a gaping hole in their income stream which needed an urgent solution. So the transmission company decided to apply itself for licences. In joint bids, the BBC applied for Multiplex B, and Crown Castle for Multiplexes C and D. Then, to the surprise of many, BSkyB asked to join, offering to supply some Sky channels: so was born the Freeview consortium.[127] And there was a key proposal in the Freeview application: to alter the technical parameters of the DTT system to improve reception.

In the mid-nineties, in the planning phase of the terrestrial platform, arguments had raged between those who wanted to maximise capacity at the expense of coverage, and those who wanted the priority the other way

than expected, confirming the view of observers that former ITV Digital subscribers were signing up in some numbers.
[127] A second bidder, Digital Television Broadcasting, also proposed a free-to-air package. A joint ITV/Channel Four bid offered a mix of free-to-air and "low-cost" pay TV, and a fourth bid came from United Business Media backed by NTL which offered a subscription service.

round. The BBC, who wanted the latter, were prepared to accept the lower data capacity of the 16-QAM modulation mode which theory said would result in more robust transmissions. They lost the argument in the face of a fairly united lobby from all the other broadcasters, with Carlton and Granada particularly vocal. For commercial reasons, they wanted to have as many channels as possible at launch, and insisted on the 64-QAM mode. The decision had contributed to ITV Digital's technical difficulties. Now, with the BBC leading the push to rejuvenate the platform, there was talk of reverting to 16-QAM. But the potential benefits of doing so were understood only from the theory: nobody had tested it in practice, and nobody had thought of doing so - until the Technical Director of the DTG, Peter Marshall, saw the opportunity:

> I recognised that when ITV Digital had gone we had some blank transmitters that were ready-made for the task. In terms of persuading people, the BBC were persuaded immediately because they'd always wanted to be 16-QAM in the first place, and Crown Castle and NTL came on board easily because it was something to do with the transmitters which were dead at the time, the only difficulty was ITV.

With only a short window of opportunity to set the project up, Peter Marshall moved quickly to secure the agreement of ITV, and then to meet the ex-Chief Engineer of ITV Digital:

> I'd earmarked Chris Hibbert - who was out of a job of course - to lead the trials, phoned him at eleven o'clock and I had lunch with him and it was all signed and sealed and Chris in place in the afternoon.

Hibbert and his team rapidly devised a plan to use the three vacant multiplexes at a suitable transmitter to test not only the 16 and 64-QAM modes, but a number of different code rates - 1/2. 2/3 and 3/4, as well as the differences between 2k and 8k. The Crystal Palace transmitter, which serves the Greater London area, was finally chosen. Peter Marshall remembers the discussions:

> There was a bit of a debate about where to do these trials because Kingswood were looking for a place where the frequencies were reasonably close together so the results were not polluted by separation between the channels. There were other options but London was chosen because [the frequencies] were close enough - and because it was London, you know, everybody found it easy to get to, and it had all the right elements.

Within six weeks the test transmissions began. Survey vehicles from BBC Research, NTL and Crown Castle toured the coverage area taking measurements; tests were carried out in homes which were known to be experiencing reception problems; viewer questionnaires were distributed; and the BBC undertook a series of laboratory tests to compare the performance of a representative sample of set-top boxes when operating at the different parameters of the test transmissions.

When the final report was published in June, the benefits in terms of increased robustness of reception that would result from adopting 16-QAM were clearly demonstrated. This was a welcome, if not totally unexpected result: the aim was to provide more reliable reception to homes within the existing coverage area, rather than to extend that coverage. Most set-top boxes - including the old ITV Digital boxes still in widespread use - worked perfectly well, provided the 2k modulation system was retained. The surprise was in the results for the 8k tests. Theoretically, the longer symbol rate of 8k should have given even greater immunity to impulsive interference, but the tests at 8k were inconclusive. In any case, too many set-top boxes did not work with an 8k signal.

The drawback of changing to 16-QAM was that the useable data rate in a multiplex would be reduced - from 24 Mbit/s to 18 Mbit/s - which would result in a reduction in the number of services that could be carried at the same quality. For the BBC and for Crown Castle, the benefits of greater robustness outweighed the disadvantages of reduced capacity. A proposal to adopt 16-QAM at code rate 2/3 formed part of their joint licence bid, together with a commitment to complete the equalisation and power-doubling programmes. Two weeks after the award of the licences, the ITC approved the use of 16-QAM, which both BBC multiplexes, and the two operated by Crown Castle, had adopted, but it allowed D3&4 and SDN to continue to use 64-QAM. Both still put capacity ahead of coverage, and indeed their business plans depended on that - as the ITC had to recognise. After much head-scratching, the ITC agreed to tolerate the situation, at least until switchover came along.

In a consumer market place which for four years had been conditioned to the idea that set-top boxes for digital television would be subsidised by the broadcasters, there were real doubts that anybody would want to build a new generation of receivers. There was no question of subsidies this time round, none of the bidders proposed it and there would be no obligation to do so in the new licences. Some months before ITV Digital failed, and as Greg Dyke and his team at the BBC were talking to other broadcasters about the future of the platform, Michael Starks was asked to begin a dialogue with the manufacturers:

> My main role was on the receiver side and being able to show that if we launched Freeview, the receiver side would work. And the work earlier to get in all the different demos by people who were interested in entering the market with prototypes. By the time the bid was put together there were about half a dozen manufacturers who would in effect kick-start a free-to-view market by May-June of that year, 2002, so I played quite a significant role putting that side together. And in trying to keep their confidence

through that period: I remember standing up at some gathering shortly after ITV Digital had collapsed and pledging that the BBC would see the industry through.

Central to this pledge of support was a commitment by the BBC to a substantial marketing spend - later masterminded by the BBC's new Director of Marketing, Andy Duncan - which would include BBC on-air promotions for its digital services.[128] The manufacturers responded positively, and by April, a few weeks before ITV Digital closed, the first new receivers - they were called 'adapters' - appeared in the market from Pace and Nokia. As other manufacturers came up with similar products, the Digital TV Group set out to bolster confidence in digital terrestrial amongst the retailers and aerial installers. There was very good reason for doing so. Few doubted that a rejuvenated platform would succeed, but there was a nagging worry that in the six months or so that would elapse before it could launch, the negative publicity surrounding the ITV Digital collapse and the lack of a full channel line-up would cause a steady haemorrhaging of existing viewers.

With financial support from the BBC and other DTG members, a modest 'Free-to-View' exhibition toured that summer's trade shows, publicity material went to every retailer, and a dedicated website was set up.[129] Even so by August, when the ITC announced that the Freeview consortium had been awarded the licences, the number of homes still watching digital terrestrial was thought to have dropped to 800,000.

The Freeview launch, on 30 September, came almost exactly six months after the demise of ITV Digital. It was a low-key affair, but in the two-month run-up to Christmas 300,000 Freeview adapters were sold. The BBC's Andy Duncan told *Digital News*, "It's still early days, but these figures show that there's undoubtedly a major opportunity out there for the idea of simple, free, digital television." Duncan's marketing message was simple and effective: up to thirty channels for a one-off payment (to buy the box). By Christmas, thirteen manufacturers had boxes on the market, most priced at under £100, and Freeview was well on its way to becoming a household term.

Behind the marketing lay a much more sound technology. The second generation of receivers had improved performance and better reliability, benefiting from better chipsets and more reliable software. With four of the six multiplexes operating in the more robust 16-QAM mode, and with completion of the equalisation and power doubling programmes, coverage was much more reliable and in some cases extended. Core coverage, the

---

[128] The promotional pitch was carefully platform-neutral, but effective in raising awareness of the Freeview proposition:

[129] The DTG too had to take a platform-neutral stance: by now Sky and the cable companies were members, but again the terrestrial message stood out. (The author was then the DTG's Director of Communications.)

homes served by all multiplexes, had risen substantially. A new post-code database was available to the public and to retailers which was much more accurate than before. New mathematical models gave improved resolution to the coverage predictions, and for the first time differentiated postcodes where a new aerial might be required to ensure reception of the out-of-band channels. It was a much more solid consumer proposition, and manufacturers found that return rates - because of reception difficulties - were lower than they expected.

In the early months of 2003, Freeview boxes continued to sell in large numbers, and terrestrial take-up grew faster than at any time during ITV Digital's days. The BBC relaunched and rebranded two of its digital channels, and began cross-promoting BBC 3 and BBC 4 to analogue viewers of BBC 1 and BBC 2. The Iraq war brought viewers to the platform's three rolling news channels, BBC News24, Sky News and the ITN News Channel. Other service launches followed, including two childrens' channels from the BBC. Freeview had begun its steady growth.

Behind the scenes, the engineers still had plenty to do, and the most urgent was to replace the central Service Information collator. Shortly before launch in 1998, the then ONdigital had agreed to install the central SI collator at its headquarters at Marco Polo House. With co-operation from the administrators of ITV Digital, the equipment continued to function as Freeview launched, but the arrangement was a temporary one. The administrator's task was to realise the residual value of the failed company's assets, and a replacement was needed. The BBC proposed to site and operate the replacement at Television Centre on behalf of all the broadcasters.

The wish to transmit seven days of schedule data in SI remained, manufacturers were pressing for it, and many of the new boxes were equipped to display it. There was general agreement amongst the broadcasters that this was now a necessary feature of the platform which had for too long been without any real electronic programme guide. But long debates ensued about whether the data capacity could or should be made available and if so how much, and whether means could be found to make its data demands more modest. Already, the DVB-SI specification was looking its age: more sophisticated methods of carrying schedule data (and other information) in much less bandwidth were being developed inside the TV Anytime project.[130] But a complete TVAnytime specification was

---

[130] The TV Anytime project was devising a means of delivering a complex tier of 'metadata' - information about programme content designed for use in a future generation of advanced recorders. By using the DSMCC carousel method, already in use for MHEG-5 and MHP data delivery, considerable savings in bandwidth could be achieved.

thought still to be some years away, and it was agreed to implement the full schedule in SI.

When work eventually began on implementation, Crown Castle, who led the work, found itself facing a number of problems, mostly in the functioning of the equipment at the SIPs - the SI insertion points dotted around the country. It took some considerable time and much effort to make the system work, and along the way involved the SIPs manufacturer doing a complete rewrite of the operating software. Then a series of trial transmissions took a transmitter off the air, and work ceased while a forensic examination was carried out. It was eventually traced to a minute software error which was easily remedied, and the way cleared for full introduction of what became an eight-day schedule. The introduction came at a crucial point, as the first open standard digital terrestrial hard disc recorders were beginning to appear in the showrooms. Personal Video Recorders - PVRs - can use SI schedule data to start and stop recording automatically: without it, they were much less easy to use. Now that the data was being broadcast, more manufacturers had the confidence to bring PVRs to the market, and retailers more confidence in offering them for sale. PVRs appeared with two tuners and DVD recorders followed - although not all had Freeview tuners built in, at least to begin with. The process of product diversification had begun, as the open market encouraged the development of innovative products with a choice of features and at a variety of prices.

The free and open market which now developed did, however, present some concerns. Freeview's marketing efforts concentrated on the services available on the platform, which consumers would naturally expect to be able to receive if they bought a box. The consortium was therefore anxious to ensure a degree of consistency in the functionality of receivers. This required certain features - like interactivity, or the connections for a video recorder - to be present in every receiver on the market. But Freeview was not subsidising the receivers, and could exert little influence over the manufacturers, whose products were not all fully featured and so could give rise to consumer confusion or dissatisfaction. Some early Freeview boxes had no MHEG-5 interactive engine, others did not provide the right plugs and sockets for connection to older TV sets without a SCART socket. And there was concern that boxes, even with the full set of features, might not all operate appropriately.

The situation, it was feared, might get worse. New manufacturers were expressing interest in entering the UK market. Increasingly, both the hardware and the software was being sourced from the thriving industries of the Far East. There clearly needed to be a new look at two things: a new set of recommendations for manufacturers to replace the old D-Book chapter which had set out ONdigital's receiver requirements, and the

243

establishment and acceptance by manufacturers of an industry testing regime to ensure conformance. Both measures were eventually agreed and put in place, but not without delay and disagreements along the way.

Putting together a new functional specification for receivers was led by TDN - the broadcasters' 'club' which now had Crown Castle as members alongside the BBC, D3&4 and SDN. Their draft proposals were refined by a group formed jointly with the DTG and which included representatives from five manufacturers. The process took many months, and at the time Peter Marshall admitted that the group was, "Dealing with widely divergent views, but persevering to establish an industry consensus in what is a very sensitive area for many members." Some manufacturers who were on the outside looking in were deeply suspicious, and as the months dragged on some elements in the trade press made much mischief out of the 'secrecy' surrounding the discussions.

Perhaps this concern had a justification. Consumer electronics manufacturers appreciate good technical specifications, because they make it a straightforward task to design an appliance that works. What they are less keen on is the kind of document that the TDN-DTG group were working on, a functional specification which sought to stipulate the features that must be included in the product. So, for example, when the functional specification made the inclusion of an MHEG-5 engine a requirement, it followed that the manufacturer was then precluded from building a cheap box without interactive capability, even if he saw a market for it. And some did. Against that it was realised that, as the chipsets dropped in price, and as volume production reduced unit costs, the commercial burden of including the extra features that the broadcasters were insisting on became much less significant. Notwithstanding these concerns, when publication of the specification came in the autumn of 2003, there was no fuss - if anything, relief that there was finally a reference document. It quickly gained general acceptance.

There remained one issue of fundamental importance: the testing and conformance verification of receivers. In ONdigital/ITV Digital days, there was no single authority which did this, and test and conformance activity went on in several places. Because they were subsidising set-top boxes and those integrated sets which had embedded conditional access, ITV Digital established its own receiver 'zoo' where it checked the functioning of each type. Another zoo was put together at Kingswood Warren by BBC Research and Development, and the ITV Network Centre had a similar collection at their South Bank Centre. With ITV Digital gone, the BBC bought their old collection from the administrators and, as new Freeview boxes entered the market, acquired samples of each.

One incident in particular highlighted the need for a more systematic and centralised testing regime. One day an MHEG-5 interactive application, broadcast in the Midlands by the ITV company Carlton, caused integrated sets from one manufacturer to crash. Arguments about whether the fault lay with the data making up the broadcast application, or with the software in that particular model of receiver, caused argument and a certain amount of ill-feeling between the parties and was never fully resolved. But it was now startlingly clear that such an occurrence could not be allowed to happen again. There needed to be a central facility where both broadcast applications and receiver functionality could be properly and independently tested. Fortunately, just such a facility was already in existence.

Back in July 2000, the Digital TV Group, with support from the DTI and encouragement from the BBC and ONdigital, had set up an Inter-operability Test Centre. It occupied a small portacabin in the grounds of the BBC Research base at Kingswood Warren, and was being run by David Bradshaw, a senior BBC R&D engineer with many years of experience in international standardisation work. DTG Testing had been set up as a wholly owned subsidiary of the DTG, and had spent some time developing guidelines on the interpretation of specifications, and preparing test scripts and streams. For a time, it shared the BBC's receiver zoo. By the summer of 2002 the Test Centre had available a growing range of test suites, and was providing its services to eight manufacturers, as the first rush of free-to-view set-top boxes was being readied for the market.

A manufacturer would, for his fee, receive from the Test Centre a confidential report. Alternatively a manufacturer could buy copies of the test suites and carry out their own validation, self-certifying compliance. As the capabilities of the Centre increased, and as its reputation in the industry rose, virtually every manufacturer would submit for testing new product under development for the UK market. There was no compulsion for them to do so, but two rather important incentives.

Manufacturers are always pleased when somebody else is helping to market their products, and the increasing frequency and effectiveness of the BBC's on-screen promotion for digital services - with the Freeview message prominent - was very welcome. What manufacturers now wanted to use was the Freeview logo. In a shrewd move, the Freeview consortium agreed to the use of their branding in advertising and point-of-sale material (but not on the product itself) with two very important provisos: that the receiver conformed to the DTG's receiver profile and either had a DTG Testing certificate to say so, or that the manufacturer had self-certified conformance. The major retailers, too, sought to safeguard their businesses by requiring similar conformance confirmation from the manufacturers before ordering stock. In this way, DTG Testing became the de facto national test and conformance centre, and as similar markets opened in Europe, David Bradshaw and his team began to receive requests for testing on product for other countries, and for advice on how to set up a test centre.

The Test Centre's key role was further enhanced in May 2003 when it took over from the BBC responsibility for the management of the system which allowed over-the-air upgrades to a receiver's software. For a number of years, the BBC had made available a 50 kbit/s slice of its public service multiplex for this use. It is called the Engineering Channel. Manufacturers booked a time slot - typically two or three days - during which their data-stream would be broadcast. Now DTG Testing took on the task of administering and scheduling of the service. It also took over responsibility for pre-transmission validation, providing a centralised service to manu-facturers who until then had each to conduct validation tests themselves to ensure that the downloads did not affect the product of another manu-facturer.

The Engineering Channel proved to be an essential facility. Although from the start over-the-air downloads were always envisaged and catered for in the receiver software, the original view was that downloads would consist largely of what engineers call 'bug fixes': small amounts of data designed to replace existing code which had proved faulty or inadequate. But the view was gaining ground that such a facility could and should be used to download the much larger quantities of data that might allow a complete upgrade of all or some of a receiver's functionality. One such was already envisaged. An improved profile of the MHEG interactive content decoder was completed in 2003 together with conformance testing suites. The new profile added useful features which broadcasters wanted to use to enhance their interactive content. But it was no use confining the new profile to new receiver models. A broadcaster might be faced with insuperable compatibility issues if the by now millions of receivers in use could not cope with the new functions. Downloading the upgraded soft-ware directly into the installed base of domestic receivers looked essential.

To a large extent the manufacturers went along with this, and the down-loads went ahead. But they were beginning to worry that a situation was developing where they might be obliged to continue to support, with software upgrades, a growing number of receivers including those no longer in production. Such an open-ended commitment was unthinkable, a commercial liability, and certainly unprecedented in the consumer elec-tronics industry. The manufacturers said rather loudly that there wouldn't be many cases where they would agree to make available the resources to upgrade those legacy boxes.

The principle was then established that future upgrades would generally be limited to making sure that the receiver continued to receive and correctly display the services which it was designed for, and advertised as supporting. The broadcaster would therefore introduce new features at their own risk, and it would be up to them to manage the problems of legacy boxes which could not receive at all, or receive only unsatisfactorily, broadcast features introduced later. The matter did not entirely rest there, for as the industry began to think through the complexities of what might be involved in switching off all analogue transmissions and migrating to an all-digital future, the issue would again be raised.

In the short space of two or three years, a transformation had taken place in both the business and technology of Britain's digital terrestrial television. Most of the technical problems that had contributed in part to the failure of ITV Digital had been remedied; great strides had been taken in the design and implementation of receiver software, and a thriving market had developed for receivers which quickly produced the product differentiation in price and feature sets so essential to and beloved of the consumer electronics industry and the retail market. The broadcasters were assured that receivers would work properly, and continued to market hard their digital services, increasing programme-making budgets and launching new channels. Freeview's success caused one broadcaster, Channel Four, to begin a process of moving its digital services from a pay-TV basis to free-to-air, funded by advertising income.

The response in the market place reflected this new confidence in the platform. The number of Freeview homes increased spectacularly. By the end of 2005, just over two years since the launch of Freeview, ten million Freeview receivers - set-top boxes, integrated sets, and tuner-equipped hard disc and DVD recorders - had been sold. Nearly six and a half million households relied on Freeview for their digital television, and the number of homes using Freeview boxes for second and third receivers was growing, even in homes which also subscribed to Sky Digital.

Britain's digital terrestrial television platform, providing subscription-free services in an open, horizontal, market, was now incontrovertibly mass market and mainstream.[131]

There is an intriguing postscript to the story of the reinvention of the UK's digital terrestrial platform as the non-subscription Freeview. In 2003 two ex-BSkyB executives, David Chance and Ian West, looked at the way Freeview was developing and noted two things: that there was spare spectrum available and that there were still several hundred thousand old ITV Digital set-top boxes in use with embedded conditional access. The following year they launched Top Up TV, which put eleven pay-TV services back on the air, promising to break even with 200,000 subscribers within two years. They provided subscribers with conditional access plug-in modules for integrated sets, and began talking to manufacturers about

---

[131] In July 2003, the BBC moved its satellite broadcasts to a new satellite with a tighter 'footprint' over the UK. With overspill much reduced, and having mollified programme rights owners, the BBC began a process to replicate the open market in satellite television by starting to broadcast their services unencrypted. ITV, Channel Four and Five eventually followed.

again producing set-top boxes with conditional access. The BBC were horrified, fearing a dilution of the platform's free-to-air stance into which so much marketing effort had been invested, and initially tried to strangle the upstart infant at birth, later relenting - as rumour had it at the time - under pressure from the regulators.

Top Up's very limited pay offering was certainly not a reversion to the days of ITV Digital, when the pay operator effectively ruled the platform and the free-to-air services maintained a low profile. Almost the direct opposite is the case. Freeview is a strong free-to-air service with a high profile amongst consumers; Top Up TV's package of pay services is an add-on option.[132]

Many of the engineers who worked over the years to create a digital terrestrial service based on open and internationally agreed standards share the view, expressed by the DTG's Peter Marshall, that what now exists as Freeview exhibits all the technical and business facets that predicated the long years of engineering research and the arguments and hard choices made in agreeing the specification and putting together the platform:

> In many ways what has turned out was I think how I imagined it - it's easy to say these things - but we should have known that the strength of digital terrestrial was something different to hard pay-TV. We should have known that the strength of it was in free-to-air channels and that the Freeview package - with the Top-Up add-on - is going to be about the right model.

---

[132] Following the purchase in 2005 by the broadcaster Five of a stake in Top Up TV, the business was migrated from a pay-TV service to a pay-to-download service using PVRs.

19
Other ways; other challenges

Britain was not alone in its digital adventure. When the UK's digital terrestrial service launched in November 1998, a number of other countries - in Europe and further afield - were in various stages of planning their own platforms, and pilot transmissions were on the air in many of them. But Britain was undeniably the first country to launch a substantial service with a majority of its capacity filled with programme channels, broadcast to a majority of the country's population, and with receivers widely available within weeks of launch. Britain's launch was the first full-scale implementation of the DVB-T standard anywhere in the world. It was watched closely in other countries, and in some its channel line-up and business structure was later emulated. Within the next three years, there were service launches in Sweden, Spain and Finland in Europe, and in Australia and Singapore.[133] In Europe, the three early launches shared some of the characteristics of the British model, but in each country there were substantial differences.

---

[133] In the US, the claim was made to be first with digital terrestrial television. A fortnight before ONdigital launched in the UK, forty-one of the 1,600 American stations began digital transmissions, broadcasting in high definition: but it wasn't a nationwide launch, and they used not DVB-T but the FCC's ATSC standard.

Without doubt, the details of the way the UK had implemented its service provided useful guidance to other countries, but not in the sense of being a role model. Work in other countries was proceeding in parallel with work in Britain, and what was happening here provided a useful comparator rather than an example to be copied. Perhaps the one area in which the UK practice was most closely emulated was in the emergence of two documents which used the DTG's D-Book as a starting point. The first, put together by representatives of the five Nordic[134] countries, was the Nordig Specification, and the second was the later EACEM Specification - actually called the 'E' Book. Both drew heavily on the approach of the D-Book, and indeed the E-Book included much D-Book material, and the principal author was the same Nick Birch. Both the Nordig Specification and the E-Book set out to do the same job as the D-Book, to provide a clear and comprehensive set of implementation rules, but the actual scope of each was rather different to that of the original UK document. The Nordig Specification included rules of operation for open standard satellite and cable platforms as well as DTT, setting out more fully the means by which service information should be cross carried between platforms. The E Book - which like the D-Book largely confined itself to digital terrestrial - set out to be applicable to the whole of Europe, which inevitably resulted in a more wide-ranging and more generalised document. But there is no doubt, as Peter Marshall says, that both owed much to the UK's pioneering work on the D-Book:

> As you go wider for a European-wide book it becomes to some extent more dilute. The D-Book led the way, and in some ways it still maintains its lead because although its only a single country document it represents a singularity which the manufacturers can work to, whereas the E-Book represents a general aspiration but applies nowhere to anybody. If the E-Book was to apply in its entirety in a single territory - which I guess it increasingly will - then we have led the way, but that then becomes the greater standard. In terms of the D-Book's reputation, and the DTG's reputation for collaborative working in an open market, it's internationally renowned.

Demodulator chipsets capable of handling the 8k system became available much earlier than the British had feared during the battles over the DVB standard just three years earlier. All European systems opted for 8k from the start. Otherwise, technical implementation followed a roughly parallel course to that of the UK, and the substantial differences were most obvious in the business structure of the platforms - often dictated by national legislation. Like the UK, digital terrestrial television in Sweden, Spain and Finland launched in a market where there was strong competition from

---

[134] Finland, Sweden, Norway, Denmark and Iceland.

pay-TV operators on other platforms. And like the UK, a combination of factors led to early difficulties.

Anticipating strong competition from BSkyB's digital service, the legislation that laid the basis for the UK services was carefully structured: it ensured that the free-to-air analogue broadcasters would all be present at launch with an enhanced channel line-up; that there would be sufficient finance available to do the job properly through the early loss-making years, and that a strong commercial player was present to subsidise receivers and to bring in new programme providers and with them heightened competition. In the early launches elsewhere one or more of these elements, crucial to success, was missing.

In Sweden, the April 1999 launch was of only three of the eventual six multiplexes, and despite early enthusiasm by prospective programme suppliers, not all who were awarded licences provided their promised services for broadcasting at launch. Emulating the BBC, the public service broadcaster SVT provided simulcasts of SVT-1 and SVT-2 together with the first of its new digital-only channels, SVT News24. But receivers were in short supply and there was poor take-up by the public even when that was remedied. Eventually, the platform had to be revised and relaunched.

Spain's plans for digital terrestrial were highly ambitious: the country had spectrum available for no fewer than eleven multiplexes, many more than most other countries in Europe, and intended to use them for a three-tiered service, reflecting the nation's cultural and political make-up, to provide national, regional and local networks. When launch came in the Spring of 2000, however, only three and a half multiplexes went on air nationally carrying 14 pay-TV services. The operator was Quiero, a company loosely modelled on the UK's ONdigital, and indeed with the UK broadcaster Carlton as a minor shareholder. The public service broadcaster TVE and the other analogue free-to-air broadcasters were absent. The legislation permitted them only to simulcast their existing analogue services: they were not allowed new digital services, as in the UK and Sweden. With little incentive to go digital, they dragged their feet, beginning digital transmission only two years later, just three weeks before Quiero - in a striking parallel with ITV Digital in the UK - failed as a business and ceased operation. It had faced strong competition from two separate but strong satellite pay-TV operators, Canal Satellite Digitale and Telefonica's Via Digital.

Finland launched later than originally planned, having waited in the expectation that MHP-capable receivers would be available. The 2001 launch was, like that of Sweden, over only three of the available six multiplexes, with a strong presence from the public broadcaster YLE, (Again emulating the BBC, with simulcasts of YLE 1 and YLE 2, a YLE News24 and even a YLE Choice channel) but with limited content from new providers. The early uptake of receivers was slow.

Outside Europe the two early DVB-T launches - in Australia and Singapore, both in 2001 - for different reasons bucked the trend that was present in Europe. Australian legislation insisted on digital channels being broadcast in high definition, at least in peak hours. One high definition service was all that any one multiplex could carry, so there was no multi-casting: no new channels and no new service providers. The decision had as much to do with preventing the emergence of competition to the incumbent terrestrial broadcasters as it had to do with a quantum leap forward in the quality of consumer experience. Singapore, by contrast, exploited the ability of DVB-T to provide mobile reception by launching a service to the city's buses, and later taxis. It was a success both technically and with the public, and a notable first.

Just as the launch of the UK's digital terrestrial platform had been followed closely around the world, the collapse of ITV Digital and the platform's reincarnation as Freeview similarly raised enormous interest. In Spain, following the failure of Quiero, the transmission company Rete-vision, now sitting on an unused digital broadcasting infrastructure, led a broad coalition of industry players which eventually prodded the government into a platform relaunch which, this time, was a predominately free platform with the public service broadcasters playing an enhanced role. In some other European countries, plans for terrestrial launches were modified to bolster free-to-air content and reduce reliance for success on a pay-TV operator: indeed, initially both France and Italy launched largely free-to-view platforms.

By 2005, consumer uptake of DTT was strong in all of western Europe's major markets. In the UK, Spain, Germany, France and Italy, and in the smaller markets of Finland and Sweden digital terrestrial was now firmly established, although progress was still slow in Belgium, the Netherlands and Switzerland.

The short history of DTT roll-outs in Europe saw perhaps its most symbolic moment in August 2003, when the German region of Berlin-Brandenburg became the first place on earth to switch off all analogue terrestrial television transmissions. The process had begun nine months earlier, with the first digital multiplex going on air. Four months later some of the analogue services were closed to allow more digital channels to open. The whole transition was successfully completed in a remarkably short time, made much easier because most German homes received their television by cable and satellite: only 150,000 homes out of the 1.5 million in Berlin-Brandenburg relied solely on terrestrial reception. The same rapid launch and switchover strategy was then applied progressively to other German *Lander.*

There is a striking similarity in the way in which, across Europe, digital terrestrial television has become such a popular consumer buy. After some false starts, the platform is perceived and marketed in most countries as a predominately free-to-air service, with or without an optional pay-TV add-on[135]. The role of the public service broadcasters is broadly similar, leading the field in service provision and promotion, in some instances creating effective brand images like Britain's Freeview, backed of course by the BBC. In Germany, for example, there is 'Easy Everywhere Television' (*Das ÜberallFernsehen*) with backing from ARD and ZDF amongst others; In France, 'Digital TV for All' (*Groupement Television Numerique pour Tous*) backed by France Television. In Italy RAI and in Spain TVE play pivotal roles, as do the public service broadcasters in Scandinavia.

And behind their involvement lie national governments, encouraged by the European Commission, anxious to migrate their nation's terrestrial television to an all-digital future, and to reclaim the vacated analogue spectrum. Some countries, like Germany and Sweden had, by 2005, started the process. Planning and preparation for switchover was going on in most others. Thinking about switchover began very early on, often considered at the same time as planning for DTT launch. Some very ambitious targets were set by a few governments, only to be substituted later on for more realistic dates.

In Britain, the government's approach has been determined but cautious, seeming at times in its public pronouncements to be approaching the issue crabwise. The reasons were not hard to identify. With analogue television in use in most UK homes, appearing too keen to switch it off would be a sure-fire vote loser. The UK had no place for the kind of campaigns that Berlin-Brandenburg unleashed on an unsuspecting public: advertisements in the press showing a blank TV screen under the copy line: *Kein Decoder - kein Bild!* (No box, no picture!).

The UK government's first concrete comments on the subject of switching off analogue transmissions came in September 1999, just ten months after the launch of DTT. At the Royal Television Society's annual convention in Cambridge, the then Culture Secretary, Chris Smith, gave a speech which expressed an aspiration to begin a switchover process in 2006, and which set out some tough preconditions. Before switchover could begin, said Smith, the main five analogue channels must be available digitally to 99.4 per cent of homes by one means or another; that the cost of going digital should be "affordable" and that 95 per cent of homes had actually started to use digital TV receivers. In 1999, with terrestrial viewership of only a few hundred thousand, and even the market leader Sky Digital reporting just over one million subscribers, less than six per cent of the UK had gone digital. The Minister's targets looked impossible.

---

[135] Notable exceptions are Belgium and the Netherlands. Both countries have almost universal analogue cable penetration and DTT, to compete, is marketed as an alternative pay-TV package.

At the Digital TV Group, Peter Marshall found himself commissioned by the DTI to write a report assessing the technical obstacles which might lie along the path to switchover: Published in July 2000, *A Study on the Technical Impediments to Switchover* was a wide ranging study which identified a number of difficult issues which required further study. They included the limitations of the existing coverage and the need to find solutions to the challenge of receiving digital TV on sets which used set-top aerials, the difficulties encountered by consumers wishing to record digital TV programmes on VCRs, the prospects - then seemingly remote - for a low-cost converter box, and disincentive then felt by ONdigital and the other broadcasters to do anything about extending coverage without a clear indication from government about their intentions for spectrum use after switchover. Peter Marshall recalls the reaction to his report:

> That's the one that started people thinking about switchover and what had to be solved. I went round and talked to a lot of people and got pulled in several directions at once. The thing with DTI studies is that's there's actually nobody really to act on them. You produce them, if the DTI are happy with them, they publish them, and throw them back at the industry for the industry to react to them as they see fit. And the reaction often takes quite a long while to show. But in terms of the report from which other things flowed - that was the one.

The government set up a Digital Action Plan the following October. Driven jointly by the DTI and the DCMS, and with broad industry and consumer representation, its remit was to provide Ministers with a workable route-map to a possible switchover. It looked in detail at a host of issues - including those raised by Peter Marshall's report - and recommending ways of dealing with them. Working Groups were set up to deal, amongst other things, with spectrum planning, the management of some switchover pilot projects, and a technology and equipment group (TEG) was formed. Henry Price, now retired from the BBC, became the TEG chairman:

> The civil servants thought they ought to be doing something and I think [the Action Plan] was born out of the feeling of frustration - particularly when ONdigital was there - that really the thing wasn't moving towards switchoff. So it was born out of the idea of getting all the parties to work together to focus on the idea of switchover. It started in January-February of 2002 and then within a matter of months ITV Digital collapsed. From that point onwards people did start to co-operate, at least on the terrestrial side, in a really meaningful way.

Peter Marshall remembers a resentment felt by some that the Action Plan had to some extent usurped the Digital TV Group's role:

> There were problems in certain areas of the DTG when [it was] argued that if the DTG had done it properly there was no need for the Action Plan. But the Action Plan was the DTI and the DCMS - the government. It was

spending money, it was focussing ministerial attention. It was doing all sorts of things the DTG could never have done. And I think one of the failings of the DTG these days is that they don't realise that they are only a small cog in a wheel.

Nevertheless, the DTG was an important cog and over the next three years produced a string of detailed reports on a number of issues which informed the debate inside TEG and the wider councils of the Action Plan. Commissioned by the DTI and administered by Peter Marshall (who wrote a number of them himself) the DTG studied subjects as diverse as access to digital TV for the deaf and the partially sighted, recorder technology, the technical performance of receiving aerials, the prospects for in-home distribution networks, product interoperability and testing, and advanced receiver techniques.

The Action Plan was wound up at the close of 2004. Its final report[136] outlined the practical measures which needed to be taken to achieve switchover, and looked at how best to manage the potential impact on the various sectors of industry and the consumer. It contained a risk analysis, recommended further actions, and looked at timing options. Ministers now knew how they could take Britain to switchover, who would be responsible for doing what, and what the costs and benefits of it would be.

In October 2005, again at an RTS Cambridge Convention, the DCMS Minister, Tessa Jowell, finally came off the fence and announced that the switchover process in the UK would begin in 2008 and be complete by 2012, a timetable that happily fitted with the European Commission's attempts to set a Europe-wide switchover target.

As the DVB celebrated its tenth anniversary in 2003, it could with justification point to a series of remarkable achievements. Digital television delivery over satellite, terrestrial and cable systems using DVB standards had been in existence for up to five years; DVB standards were in use on all continents; a growing number of nations outside the US and Canada were confirming their choice of DVB-T for their terrestrial platforms.

In recent years, the DVB has put considerable resources into the promotion of its standards, particularly in those countries which have yet to decide on what technical system to adopt for terrestrial use. Many of these countries lie within what might be regarded as the American sphere of economic interest: Taiwan and South Korea in Asia, and in South America. While Taiwan eventually settled on DVB-T, Korea remains committed to ATSC. In Japan, a home grown variant of DVB-T has been adopted. Called ISDB-T, it adds a number of technical features including the time interleaving that were left out of DVB-T. China is evaluating the Japanese,

---

[136] The final report was written by Michael Starks. Having retired from the BBC, he became the Action Plan's Project Manager.

European and American systems alongside a number of home-grown systems, and in South America, neither Brazil nor Argentina, the two biggest markets, have yet made any choice. The satellite standard, DVB-S, has gained an almost universal acceptance. Now the DVB was on the verge of publishing a group of new standards as ground-breaking in their way as the original satellite, cable and terrestrial specifications had been a few years earlier.

The first of the DVB's second generation of standards was a much improved satellite standard, DVB-S2. It used an extended toolkit of modulation and error correction modes which gave the system a much greater flexibility of use and ruggedness, and a remarkable bit-rate capacity gain of up to 35 per cent. With these advantages over the earlier system, commercial uptake was rapid. DVB-S2 is highly efficient, and works very close to the theoretical limit of performance - the so-called Shannon Limit. DVB insiders, notably Ulrich Reimers and Alberto Morello of RAI, who chaired the group that developed DVB-S2, are fond of pointing out that it is so good that nobody will need to design another satellite broadcasting technology for at least a generation - if ever. Work later started on a similarly improved DVB-T2.

The one new standard which will undoubtedly revolutionise television broadcasting came a little later. DVB-H is designed for the transmission of low-bit-rate images and audio to hand-held and mobile receivers. The system, which can coexist with conventional DVB-T in the same multiplex, or can equally well be applied to cellular networks similar to those used for mobile phones, is already showing healthy signs that it will rapidly become a commercial success. During 2005, DVB-H service trials were carried out in many countries, notably Norway, Germany, Britain and the US. Even in those countries where alternative technologies to DVB-T have been chosen - like the United States - DVB-H services are being planned.

2004, too, was the year when high definition television became a commercial reality in Europe. On New Year's Day that year, the European satellite broadcaster Euro1080 began a regular public service. Other services followed, including one in the UK from BSkyB which launched in May 2006.

Two major technology developments finally made possible commercially feasible high definition services in Europe. The cost of manufacturing high quality, reliable, flat screen television displays - using plasma or LCD technologies - finally fell to levels at which a mass market could develop. At the same time, a new family of compression standards was produced by the Moving Pictures Expert Group. MPEG-4 gave a step change in compression efficiency, which made it possible to compress the 1 Gigabit datastream of a full high definition picture into 18 Mbit/s. This changed the economics of broadcasting high definition, whatever the platform. With the expected improvements in coder performance, data rate reductions below 10 Mbit/s should be possible within a few years. For terrestrial use this would hold out the prospect of accommodating at least two high definition services in a single multiplex.

The result of these developments was to give an even greater impetus for plans to switch off analogue television services in Europe. There was virtually no space left in the spectrum - now being used in most countries for both legacy analogue television transmissions and new DVB-T services. Only after switchover would there be sufficient spectrum for high definition and DVB-H mobile services with anything approaching widespread coverage.[137] These developments, coming so rapidly, have concentrated minds wonderfully.

Nowadays, ten years can be a long time in terms of the onward march of technology. Nevertheless, it is still a matter of some wonder that it has taken only a decade from the day that the DVB-T specification was frozen to a point where digital terrestrial services are running, or being piloted, in many countries right across the world. In Britain, a third of households watch DTT, and 70 per cent have digital television of one form or another. The numbers continue to grow rapidly

Technology does not stand still, and the continuing achievements of the DVB bear testimony to that. Another ten years and the whole world of communications will be different again. Digital convergence, the concept that distinctions between different forms of content - still and moving pictures, sound, conversations, internet pages of text - and the distinctions between delivery mechanisms - radio, television, the internet, mobile telephones - would become first blurred and finally disappear, is a concept itself not much more than a decade old. It was first expressed in popular terms in 1995, by Nicholas Negroponte, the director of the Media Laboratory at the Massachusetts Institute of Technology, in his book *Being Digital*. At the time, many found the concept difficult to comprehend, and some pronounced it just plain daft.

Some took it seriously. One was John Birt who applied the thinking to the BBC's early entry into digital broadcasting and exploitation of content on the internet. The BBC website is now widely admired and respected. Some of those who took the concept of convergence seriously also formed estimates of the time it might take for devices, businesses and the market to adopt it which were too optimistic. But time cures things like that, and television entertainment delivered in internet protocol to the home over broadband is now a reality.

---

[137] DVB-H mobile services can also be broadcast in DAB frequencies, where there is still spectrum available. Several trials have proved the viability of doing so, but individual channel capacity limits the number of video services that can be carried.

Indeed, the rapid rise in broadband-delivered television has led some to predict that traditional over-the-air broadcasting has had its day. Whether or not that turns out to be true, the new digital technologies now in use have rendered broadcast television fit for purpose in the twenty-first century, and placed it firmly within the family of technologies which we broadly term 'new media'.

The DVB in recent years have given much thought to the role that open standards could and should play in a future of convergent communications technologies. It has now produced no fewer than 100 specifications, and the idea of pre-competitive collaboration within and between industries to form agreed international standards is now well established. That has proved its worth in facilitating the rapid deployment of new technologies across large markets. The process will no doubt continue into the coming decades, but it will face a challenge.

The speed of technological innovation continues to increase exponentially. The time taken to develop a new technology concept from theory, through prototype, to product is diminishing. In contrast, as the technology and the markets become more complex and more diversified, the time taken for large assemblies of experts representing widely different interests to agree on a common approach is, if anything, on the increase. The risk is that more proprietary systems will be on offer - and becoming de facto standards - well before any equivalent open standard solution can be agreed upon.

Or perhaps the reality is that the remarkable story of the development of digital television - the success of the international collaborative research programmes, the outstanding achievements of the DVB (which continues to flourish), and the unprecedented co-operative approach of broadcasters, manufacturers and regulators seen in the planning and launch of the growing number of digital terrestrial platforms across the world - proves the opposite, and these collaborative processes will steer technology's future more towards open systems.

So tomorrow will be another place, and time will tell what it will look like. One way or another, there will be a good story in that, too.

Chronology
List of Acronyms and Abbreviations
Bibliography
Index

Chronology

1936 BBC Television Service launched using 405-line system. Service is closed down at outbreak of the Second World War. Resumes in 1946.

1937 Englishman Alec Reeves invents the concept of Pulse Code Modulation, the basis for the digitisation of electronic signals

1945 March: Television Advisory Committee Report published: foresees desirability of a future 1000-line television.

1947 Invention of the transistor.

1950 CCIR decides on a 625-line system for Europe-wide use.

1953 NTSC 525-line colour television system approved for use in US.

1964 April: BBC-2 launches, using the CCIR 625-line standard.

1965 Gordon Moore, founder of chip-maker Intel, first states Moore's Law.

1966 CCIR fails to settle on a single colour TV standard for Europe. As a result, the two European systems, PAL and SECAM, will both be used.

BBC introduces digital sound in syncs for inter-studio circuits.

1967 1 July: BBC-2 begins colour broadcasts using PAL system.

1972 October: IBA demonstrates digital television picture converter- DICE.

1974 BBC Research demonstrates digital television recorder.

1975 Successful transmission of digital PAL television signals by BBC over 120 Mbit/s Post Office link between Guildford and Portsmouth.

American cable service provider Home Box Office establishes the first operational satellite broadcast system. The service feeds cable affiliates.

BBC Research constructs a digital device to store one TV picture frame.

1977 WARC 77 draws up assignment plans for 12 GHz satellite broadcasting, giving the UK five DBS high-power satellite channels.

IBA demonstrates all-digital studio.

1978 BBC Research Department demonstrates first broadcast quality 34 Mbit/s PAL digital television pictures

Economical analogue to digital converters become available.

1979 Digital field-store standards converter designed by BBC put into service.

1981 NHK demonstrates HDTV using MUSE.

CCIR Recommendation 601 sets the standard for a universal digital television studio system.

1982   Part Panel recommends that UK DBS services should use the MAC analogue TV system first proposed by IBA Engineering.

1984   Government proposes DBS Club of 21 venture.

YUV component-coded signals successfully transmitted by BBC over 140 Mbit/s London to Birmingham link.

BBC's first all digital terrestrial transmission of television stereo sound using the system later known as NICAM 728.

1985   405-line television transmissions come to an end in the UK.

Collapse of DBS Club of 21 consortium. Home Secretary asks IBA to review prospects for commercial DBS.

1986   CCIR Plenary Assembly meets in Dubrovnik, to discuss a worldwide HDTV studio standard; EC sets up Eureka Project 95 to develop a European HDTV standard based on D-MAC.

BSB wins DBS contract.

1987   European Community's RACE Main Phase five-year programme begins.

Spectrum found for 5th UK analogue UHF TV channel.

July: BSB signs IBA contract.

1988   Major Eureka 95 HDTV demonstrations at IBC.

Astra 1A satellite launched; Rupert Murdoch announces Sky.DTH service.

1989   Feb 1989 Sky TV launched via Astra with four channels - sports, movies, news, entertainment. It uses analogue PAL system.

EC Directive of 3 October mandates HD-MAC.

HDTV digital recordings made with the BBC's Quadriga multiplex of Sony D1 recorders at Wimbledon, the Cup Final and the Proms.

In America, FCC call for proposals for digital HTDV system produces 20 candidate systems.

1990   April: BSB launch.

First trials of DAB using the Eureka147 COFDM system.

September: At IBC the IBA presents paper on digital television broadcasting at IBC; General Instruments demonstrates Digicipher.

November: Sky and BSB merge to form BSkyB.

November: Broadcasting Act. IBA and Cable Authority abolished and replaced by ITC and Radio Authority. NTL acquires IBA's transmission and research businesses.

Completion of Phase 1 of the Eureka Project 95.

PALplus development begins as a complementary approach to HD-MAC.

1991 March: At a meeting in a German hotel, seven European industry representatives agree to start a project to define a future digital television broadcasting system. Formed European Launching Group (ELG) (predecessor of DVB).

CCETT begins development of STERNE COFDM system.

The Eureka Project 625 VADIS set up to develop world standard digital compression algorithms, later to appear as MPEG-1 and MPEG-2.

1992 IBA field trials of SPECTRE.

HD-Divine demonstrated at IBC.

Extensive HD-MAC coverage of Barcelona Olympics

FCC whittles down 20 candidate digital HDTV systems to five.

November: MPEG releases MPEG-1

November: Reimers group writes to European Launching Group setting out alternative (digital) strategy - 'Reimers Report'.

December: ELG invites satellite interests to join.

1993 September: ELG renamed DVB; MoU signing in Bonn by 83 members.

November: MPEG-2 video compression standard approved.

November: DVB agrees commercial requirements for DVB-S.

December: DVB approves DVB-S satellite specification.

The proponents of the five FCC candidate HDTV systems agree to collaborate and form the Grand Alliance.

1994 March: DVB approves DVB-C cable specification.

July: BBC writes to Secretary of State promising BBC will develop DTT.

July: DNH announces a plan for "as many as 12 digital terrestrial television services" with perhaps analogue switch-off in 15 years.

August: BBC sets up Digital Broadcasting Project.

US digital satellite platform DirecTV launches.

MPEG approves MPEG-2.

1995 March & July: BBC Digital Broadcasting Project demonstrates DTT using CCETT STERNE COFDM equipment.

March: Discussions begin about creating a Digital TV Group.

April: Montreux demonstrations of dTTb (terrestrial/cable) and HD-SAT (satellite) by BBC with RACE partners.

263

August: BBC abandons 8k FFT (at IBC95) thereby allowing UK to adopt 2k standard proposed by NTL/Motorola.

DVB adopts 2k and 8k for DVB-T.

September: BBC Digital Radio (DAB) service starts.

BBC, ITC and NTL begin preparing a joint frequency plan for UK DTT.

Autumn: EC Directive 95/47/EC requires CA and EPG access to be on 'fair, reasonable and non-discriminatory terms'.

November: VALIDATE begins work.

December: Broadcasting Bill published.

DVB-CI specification released.

1996 January: DTG meets for the first time.

January: DVB-T DTT Specification finalised.

9 April: BBC demonstrates the first implementation of the final DVB-T specification.

12 April: BBC opens discussions with Astra.

13 June: First meeting of the Digital Television Initiation Group, Geneva (the group which would become DigiTAG).

15 June: BBC's digital pilot service launched with digital widescreen simulcast of *Trooping the Colour* live outside broadcast.

24 July: Broadcasting Act provides framework for launch of UK DTT.

30 July: BBC initials contract with Astra for two transponders on Astra 2a.

12 September: DigiTAG formed.

late September: BBC initiates negotiations with Sky.

DVB-S and DVB-C specifications released.

15 October: all UK terrestrial broadcasters agree to take up their guaranteed digital spectrum.

12 November: as part of VALIDATE programme, interoperability between BBC modem and DMV modem is successfully demonstrated.

December: DTG D-Book v1 released.

C5 awarded licence for fifth analogue TV channel.

Astra 1E launched - commercial digital satellite broadcasting (Canal Plus and Kirch) begins in Europe.

1997 January: BBC begins digital TV implementation project.

17 January: DVB-T spec signed off by ETSI.

end January: ITC deadline for multiplex licence bids.

28 February: BBC Transmission sold to Castle Transmission Services.

31 March: Digital Broadcasting Project wound up.

April: DVB agrees to incorporate HDTV into the DVB-T specification.

24 June: multiplex licences awarded to British Digital Broadcasting.

June: DTG D-Book v2 released.

C5 start broadcasts on channels 35 and 37.

14-25 July: CEPT frequency planning conference in Chester.

September: At the International Broadcasting Convention, BBC's Research & Development Department receives IBC's 1997 Editor's Award for Technological Achievement for the BBC's digital pilot.

1998   March: DMux Group renamed The Digital Network.

17th March: BBC tests digital services on Astra.

29 May: BBC completes deal with Sky for CA and EPG.

June: VALIDATE final interworking demonstration.

June: DTG D-Book v3 released: much expanded following BDB's involvement.

28 July: BDB brands itself ONdigital.

18 August: Crystal Palace digital transmitters begin power testing.

28 September: BBC Digital TV launched via DSat.

1 Oct: BSkyB DSat service launched.

15 November: Launch of UK DTT.

1999   April: Carlton joins Spanish consortium led by Retevision to bid for licences to three and a half national SFNs.

1 April: DTT launch in Sweden, over three multiplexes.

end March: The BSkyB/BIB Interactive service Open... begins roll-out.

May: BBC launches Digital Text pilot service on DTT using MHEG-5.

Culture Secretary Chris Smith tells RTS Cambridge that "switchover could start to happen as early as 2006."

DCable launches: C&W in Manchester 1 July; NTL 1 September.

November: ONdigital launches pre-paid box scheme.

2000   1 January: DTT launches in Australia. Transmissions are in HDTV.

Government White Paper *A New Future for Communications* reaffirms 2006-10 as analogue switch-off dates, and sets coverage, uptake and affordability conditions.

3 April: BBC launches MHEG services; Carlton Active follows on 8 May.

5 May: Quiero launches in Spain with 14 pay services.

May: DVB approves Multimedia Home Platform (MHP).

October: DTI and DCMS set up Digital TV Action Plan.

2001 ONdigital rebrands as ITV Digital; launches ITV Sport.

27 Sept: midnight. Sky switches off last three Sky analogue channels.

November: ITV Digital announces 1.22 million subscribers.

November: Finland launches DTT.

2002 25 April: Spain's Quiero folds.

30 April: ITV Digital folds.

1 May: ITC announces plan to re-advertise DTT multiplex licences relinquished by ITV Digital.

13 June: ITC invites applications for licences.

4 July: ITC announces short-list.

19 August: Multiplex licences granted to BBC and Crown Castle.

30 September: ITC decision on transmission mode.

October: Power doubling complete at 29 transmitter sites.

30 October: Freeview launches.

1 November: first digital channels launch in Berlin.

2003 5 May: DTG Testing takes over management of the Engineering Channel.

August: last Berlin analogue services come off air.

18 December: Ofcom takes over from ITC.

2004 1 January: European satellite broadcaster Euro 1080 begins High Definition broadcasts.

July. Tessa Jowell puts back UK switchover target to 2008-12.

November: DVB approves DVB-H standard for television broadcasting to hand-held portable devices.

December: Government Action Plan wound up.

2005 UK homes watching DTT near 8 million.

List of Acronyms and Abbreviations

ACTS   Advanced Communications Technologies and Services: a European Community research and development programme.

API   Applications Program Interface.

ATSC   Advanced Television Systems Committee (US).

BDB   British Digital Broadcasting.

BREMA   British Radio Equipment Manufacturers' Association.

BSB   British Satellite Broadcasting.

CCETT   Centre Commune d'Etudes de Télédiffusion et Télécommunication: French research laboratory run jointly by France Telecom and TDF.

CCIR   Comité Consultatif International des Radiocommunications (International Radio Consultative Committee).

CEPT   Conférence Européenne des administrations des postes et télécommunications (European Conference of Postal and Telecommunications Administrations).

C-MAC   A variant of MAC (q.v.).

COFDM   Coded Orthogonal Frequency Division Multiplexing: a multi-carrier modulation system now commonly used for DAB and DVB-based digital terrestrial television.

DAB   Digital Audio Broadcasting.

DAVIC   The Digital Audio-Visual Council.

D-Book   Popular title for the publication *Digital Terrestrial Television: Requirements for Interoperability*, the UK implementation guidelines for DVB-T compiled and published by the DTG.

dB   Decibel: a measure of power ratio. It uses a logarithmic scale, hence 3 dB is twice as much, 10 dB is 10 times, and 20 dB is one hundred times.

DBS   Direct Broadcasting by Satellite: originally referred to high-power satellites as envisaged in the WARC77 plan.

DCable   Digital Cable Television.

DCT   Discrete Cosine Transform - a mathematical process used in compression algorithms.

DigiTAG   Digital Terrestrial Television Action Group.

D-MAC   a variant of MAC (q.v.).

DMux Group Original name for the 'club' of UK multiplex operators. (see TDN).

DTG Digital Television Group, UK industry association.

DTH Direct-to-Home (of satellite broadcasting).

DTI Department of Trade and Industry.

DPCM Differential Pulse Code Modulation - an advance on straightforward PCM (q.v.) in which only differences between the absolute and predicted values of a sample are coded.

DTT Digital Terrestrial Television.

dTTb A collaborative project set up under the RACE II programme to develop DTT.

DSat Digital Satellite Television

DVB Digital Video Broadcasting (project).

DVB-C The DVB specification for digital cable broadcasting.

DVB-CI The DVB specification for the common interface, the PCMCIA socket for TV receivers.

DVB-S The DVB specification for digital satellite broadcasting.

DVB-T The DVB specification for digital terrestrial television broadcasting.

EACEM European Association of Consumer Electronics Manufacturers.

EBU European Broadcasting Union.

ELG European Launching Group, forerunner of the DVB.

ETSI European Technical Standards Institute.

EUREKA A pan-European programme for the promotion of market-driven R&D.

FCC Federal Communications Commission (USA).

FFT Fast Fourier Transform - a mathematical tool which translates from the frequency to the time domain.

FM Frequency Modulation, a modulation system commonly used for analogue radio broadcasting.

GHz gigahertz - one billion hertz: a measure of frequency.

HD-DIVINE A Scandinavian terrestrial HDTV project.

HD-MAC The high definition variant of MAC (q.v).

HD-SAT An international collaborative programme set up under RACE II to develop studio quality HDTV satellite broadcasting.

HDTV High Definition Television.

HDTV-T	A German national project to investigate HDTV broadcasting over several platforms.
Hz	Hertz: The unit of frequency.
IBA	Independent Broadcasting Authority.
IBC	International Broadcasting Convention - a major international exhibition and conference.
IEE	Institution of Electrical Engineers (now the IET).
IEEE	Institute of Electrical and Electronics Engineers (US).
iDTV	integrated digital television, meaning a TV set with built-in digital terrestrial tuner.
INTELSAT	An international communications satellite operator.
IRT	Institut fur Rundfunktechnik: the central research and development establishment for public broadcasting organisations in Germany, Austria and Switzerland.
ISO	International Organisation for Standardisation.
ITA	Independent Television Authority (to July 1972).
ITCA	Independent Television Companies Association.
ITVA	Independent Television Association.
ITU	International Telecommunications Union.
JPEG	Joint Picture Experts Group.
kHz	a measure of frequency, a thousand Hertz (q.v.).
MAC	Multiplexed Analogue Component: the unsuccessful hybrid analogue/digital television system introduced in Europe in the late 1980s: intended for primarily for satellite broadcasting, it was developed in a number of variants, including one for high definition.
MPEG	Moving Pictures Experts Group. Also the compression standards, e.g. MPEG-1 and MPEG-2.
MHEG	Multimedia and Hypermedia information coding Expert Group. Also the MHEG-5 API.
MHP	Multimedia Home Platform: the powerful API developed by the DVB.
MHz	Megahertz. One million Hertz - a measure of frequency.
MUSE	Multiple sub-Nyquist Sampling Encoding: the early Japanese analogue high definition system developed by NHK.
NHK	The Japanese public service broadcaster.

NTL   National Transcommunications Limited, subsidiary of an American parent company which bought the transmission and research assets of the IBA on privatisation.

NTSC   National Television System Committee (USA).

OFDM   Orthogonal Frequency Division Multiplexing: a multi-carrier modulation system without error correction.

PAL   Phase Alternation Line. An improved analogue colour television system based on NTSC; developed in Germany; used in the UK.

PALplus   A technology for improving the fidelity of letterboxed pictures when expanded to fill analogue widescreen TV displays. Used digital coding to carry 'helper' signals in the black bars of the 4:3 picture.

PCM   Pulse Code Modulation.

QAM   Quadrature Amplitude Modulation.

QPSK   Quadrature Phase Shift Keying.

RACE   A European programme set up by the EC to foster pre-competitive collaboration in the development of various broadcasting, telecommunications and computing technologies.

RAI   RAdiotelevisione Italiana. The Italian public service broadcaster.

RETRA   Radio, Electrical and Television Retailers' Association. The UK association of independent consumer electronics retailers.

SECAM   Séquentiel Couleur à Mémoire. An improved analogue colour television system based on NTSC; developed in France.

SCART   Syndicat des Constructeurs d'Appareils Radiorecepteurs et Televiseurs. Used commonly to refer to the multi-way connector commonly used to interconnect TV sets and set-top boxes, etc.

SD   Standard Definition (of television pictures: commonly 625 or 525 lines).

SDTV   see SD.

SMPTE   Society of Motion Picture and Television Engineers (USA).

SPECTRE   Special Purpose Extra Channels for Terrestrial Radiocommunications Enhancement - the experimental DTT system put together by the IBA engineering arm.

STERNE   experimental digital terrestrial system developed in France by CCETT.

TDN   The Digital Network: the 'club' of UK DTT multiplex operators. Originally the DMux Group.

UHF   Ultra High Frequency: the part of the radio spectrum between 470 and 854 MHz (Bands IV and V) used for television broadcasting.

VALIDATE Verification and Launch of Integrated Digital Advanced Television in Europe; a project within the ACTS programme.

VADIS Video/Audio Digital Interactive Systems.

VHF Very High Frequency: the part of the radio spectrum between 41 and 216 MHz (Bands I, II and III) originally used for 405-line television (Bands I and III), and now occupied principally by FM radio (in Band II) and DAB services (in Band III).

WARC World Administrative Radio Conference.

Bibliography

General Works

John Birt, *The Harder Path,* Time Warner Books UK, London, 2002
Peter Chippendale & Suzanne Franks, *Dished! - The Rise and Fall of British Satellite Broadcasting,* Simon & Schuster, London, 1991
Charles Curran, *A Seamless Robe: Broadcasting Philosophy and Practice*, Collins, London, 1979
Greg Dyke, *Inside Story*, HarperCollins, London, 2005
Matthew Horsman, *Sky High: The Inside Story of BSkyB*, Orion, London, 1997
Marmaduke Hussey, *Chance Governs All: A Memoir,* Macmillan, London, 2001
Alasdair Milne, *DG: The Memoirs of a British Broadcaster*, Hodder & Stoughton, London, 1988
Nicholas Negroponte, *Being Digital*, Hodder & Stoughton, London, 1995
Will Wyatt, *The Fun Factory: A Life in the BBC*, Arum Press, London, 2003

Technical Works

Richard Brice, *Newnes Guide to Digital TV (second edition)*, Newnes, Oxford, 2003
Gordon Drury, Garik Markarian & Keith Pickavance, *Coding and Modulation for Digital Television*, Kluwer Academic Publishers, Norwell, Massachusetts, 2001
Edward Pawley, *BBC Engineering 1922-1972*, British Broadcasting Corporation, London, 1972
Professor Dr.-Ing Ulrich Reimers, *DVB: The Family of International Standards for Digital Video Broadcasting,* second edition (in English), Springer, Berlin Heidelberg, 2005
C.P. Sandbank (ed), *Digital Television*, John Wiley & Sons, Chichester, 1990

Periodicals and Papers:
Listed chronologically by publication date

EBU Technical Review (EBU-TR)
NOTE: All the papers listed below are available to download in PDF from the EBU website: www.ebu.ch

Horses for Courses, George Waters, Director, EBU Technical Department EBU-TR (editorial) Autumn 1992
Analogue HDTV in Europe: What are the key issues in analogue HDTV/ETV systems? B. Pauchon, Deputy Director for International and Industrial Affairs, GRF-TDF. EBU-TR Autumn 1992
Analogue HDTV in Europe: PALplus today, Ulrich Reimers, Director of Engineering, Norddeutscher Rundfunk EBU-TR Autumn 1992

Digital HDTV in Europe: Key issues in HDTV/ATV systems, John Forrest, Chief Executive, National Transcommunications Limited (NTL). EBU-TR Autumn 1992

Digital HDTV in Europe: A rugged and flexible digital modulation scheme for terrestrial high definition television, N.K. (Nick) Lodge, Head of Standards and Technology, Independent Television Commission, and A.G. (Arthur) Mason, group Leader of the Raidio Frequency Laboratory R&D group and manager of the SPECTRE Digital Television project, NTL. EBU-TR Autumn 1992

HD-DIVINE, a Scandinavian terrestrial HDTV project, Per Applequist, Head of Research, SVT. EBU-TR April 1993

European perspectives on digital television broadcasting: Conclusions of the Working Group on Digital Television Broadcasting (WGTB), Dr. Ulrich Reimers, Director of the Institute for Telecommunications at the University of Braunschweig. EBU-TR Summer 1993

European perspectives on digital television broadcasting: Quality objectives and prospects for commonality, David Wood, EBU. EBU-TR Summer 1993

European activities on digital television broadcasting: From company to cooperative projects, B.Marti (CCETT), P. Bernard (CCETT), N. Lodge, (ITC), R. Schäfer (Heinrich-Hertz-Institut). EBU-TR Summer 1993

On the eve of the revolution: Digital television broadcasting in April 1994, David Wood, EBU. EBU-TR Summer 1994

Digital broadcasting demonstrations by HD-SAT and dTTb at Montreux '95, Andrew Oliphant (BBC) and L. Combarel (Alcatel Espace). EBU-TR Summer 1995

Ten years of EBU participation in European collaborative projects. Jean-Pierre Evian, EBU. EBU-TR Summer 1995

Digital Audio Broadcasting - radio now and for the future, P. Kozamernik, EBU. EBU-TR Autumn 1995

Digital terrestrial television. The 8k system. Lis Grete Møller, Tele Danmark. EBU-TR Winter 1995

Satellites, science and success: The DVB story, David Wood, EBU. EBU-TR Winter 1995

MPEG video coding: A simple introduction. Dr S.R. (Bob) Ely, R&D manager, BBC Research & Development. EBU-TR Winter 1995

RAI: Combining European collaborative projects with vital in-house R&D, Dr. Mario Cominetti, Head of Transmission & Broadcasting Division, RAI. EBU-TR Autumn 1997

SVT: Understanding the repercussions of technology development, Per Applequist, Assistant Director of Corporate Development, SVT. EBU-TR Autumn 1997

The BBC: R&D in the 90s, Dr Ian Childs, Head of Research & Development, BBC. EBU-TR Autumn 1997

Predicting the future of broadcasting, P.A. (Phil) Laven, EBU Technical Director. EBU-TR Summer 1998

A milestone in the history of the DVB Project, Peter Marshall, Technical Director, Digital Television Group. EBU-TR Winter 1998

The how and why of COFDM, J.H. Stott, BBC Research & Development. EBU-TR Winter 1998

Safe Areas for Widescreen Transmission, Ian Baker (BBC). EBU-TR Summer 1999

Numerology: 525 + 625 = 601? Phil Laven EBU (editorial). EBU-TR October 2005

The dawn of Rec. 601 (interview with Peter Rainger), David Wood (EBU). EBU-TR October 2005

Rec. 601: the origins of the 4:2:2 DTV standard. Stanley Baron and David Wood. EBU-TR October 2005

The worldwide ITU dimension to DTV standards - the impossible took a little longer! Stanley Baron and David Wood (EBU). EBU-TR July 2006

Proceedings of the International Broadcasting Convention
(published in the IEE Conference Proceedings series)

Digital Television to the Home - When will it come? A.G. Mason, G.M. Drury, N.K. Lodge, Independent Broadcasting Authority, IBC 1990

Digital Terrestrial Television Development in the SPECTRE Project, A.G.Mason, (NTL) and N.K. Lodge (ITC). IBC 1992

The Plan for Digital Terrestrial Television in the UK. M.C.D. Maddocks (BBC), B. Tait (NTL), N.J. Lafflin (BBC), G. Doel (NTL). IBC 1996

The Simultaneous Transmission of Widescreen and 4:3 Programmes, M.L. Bell and H.M. Price (BBC). IBC 1996

The DVB Terrestrial (DVB-T) Specification and its Implementation in a Practical Modem, J.H.Stott (BBC). IBC 1996

The Design of a Practical Network for Digital Terrestrial TV Trials, A. Oliphant, R.P. Marsden, R.H.M. Poole and N.E. Tanton, (BBC). IBC 1996

Evaluation of a DVB-T compliant terrestrial television system. C.R. Nokes, I.R. Pullen, J.E. Salter, BBC R&D. IBC 1997

Validate and Motivate: Collaborative R&D to Speed up the Launch of Digital Terrestrial TV. Andrew Oliphant, BBC R&D and P. Christ, Deutsche Telekom Berkom. IBC 1998

Practical Experience of System Integration for Digital Terrestrial TV. M. Brooks, K.D. McCann, M.J. Sansom, NTL. IBC 1998

A Centrally Based Service Information (SI) System for UK Digital Terrestrial Television, Chris Hibbert (BDB) and Mike Tooms (Michael Tooms & Associates). IBC 1998

RF Engineering for Digital Terrestrial TV, Clive Morton and Gordon Verity, NTL. IBC 1998

Delivering Digital Television to Multiple Platforms, P.A.O. Gardiner and P.G. Layton, BBC IBC 1999

Other Papers and Reports

Digital Methods in Television, G.D. Monteath and V.G. Devereux. BBC Research Report No T-127 (1967/55). 1967

Television Motion Measurement for DATV and Other Applications, G.A.Thomas, BBC Research Department Report (BBC RD 1987/11). 1987

Advisory Committee Final Report and Recommendation. Federal Communications Commission Advisory Committee on Advanced Television Service, 1995

A Case Study - UK Digital Terrestrial, consisting of eleven short papers by various
 authors covering various aspects of the UK DTT service implementation,
 presented at an IBC Miniconference by the Digital TV Group, and
 published by the DTG. 1999

International co-ordination of DVB-T frequencies in Europe, Jan Doeven, Nozema.
 ITU-D Seminar, Kiev, November 2000

Technical Impediments to Analogue Switchover: Final Report. Digital TV Group,
 2000

DVB - Worldwide Technology for Digital Broadcasting. State of the Project
 Address to the DVB World 2001 Conference by Theo Peek, Chairman of
 the DVB. 2001

Final Report of DTT (DVB-T) Transmission Mode Trials, DTG 2002

*Berlin Goes Digital: The switchover of terrestrial television from analogue to
 digital transmission in Berlin-Brandenburg - Experiences and
 Perspectives.* Published by DasÜberallFernsehen (www.mabb.de). 2003

Final Report of the Digital TV Project, Michael Starks, published by the Digital
 Action Plan. 2003. Available from the DTI website:
 http://www.digitaltelevision.gov.uk/pub_actionplan.html

Report of A Digital Switchover Technical Trial at Ferryside and Llansteffan, July
 2005. Available from the DTI website:
 http://www.digitaltelevision.gov.uk/publications/pub_digitalswitchover_trial.html

Periodicals

BBC R&D Annual Review
BBC Year Books and Annual Reports
Broadcast Engineering
Digital News
DigiTAG newsletter
DVB Scene
ITC and IBA Annual Reports

Index

Page numbers in italics refer to references in footnotes

www.ingramcontent.com/pod-product-compliance
Lightning Source LLC
LaVergne TN
LVHW012328060326
832902LV00011B/1769